THE INTEGRATION OF EUROPEAN FINANCIAL MARKETS

The last decade has seen the increasing integration of European financial markets due to a number of factors including the creation of a common regulatory framework, the liberalisation of international capital movements, financial deregulation, advances in technology, and the introduction of the euro. However, the process of integration has proceeded largely in the absence of any comprehensive legal regulation, and has rather been constructed on the basis of sectorial provisions dictated by the needs of cross-border transactions. This has meant that many legal barriers still remain as obstacles to complete integration.

This book considers the discipline of monetary obligations within the wider context of financial markets. It provides a comparative and transnational examination of the legal rules which form the basis of transactions on financial markets. Analysing the integration of the markets from a legal point of view provides an opportunity to highlight the role of globalisation as the key element favouring the circulation of rules, models, and especially the development of new regulatory sources.

The Integration of European Financial Markets examines market transactions and the institutes at the root of these transactions, including the type of legislative sources in force and the subjects acting as legislators. The first part of the book concentrates on the micro-discipline of money, debts, payments, and financial instruments. The second part goes on to analyse the macro-context of integration of the markets, looking at the persistence of legal barriers and options for their removal, as well as the development of new legal sources as a consequence of the transfer of monetary and political sovereignty. The final section of the book draws on the results of the previous parts and assesses the consequences of changes on the macro-level (regulation) and the micro-level (monetary obligations) with a particular focus on the emergence and growing importance of soft law.

Noah Vardi is Assistant Professor of Private Comparative Law at the University of Roma Tre, Italy.

The University of Texas at Austin Studies in Foreign and Transnational Law

General Editors: Sir Basil Markesinis and Professor Dr Jörg Fedtke

This Series aims to publish books both in the area of transnational law and foreign private, criminal and public law. This broad ambition reflects the General Editors' belief that in a shrinking world there is a growing need to expand our knowledge of other legal orders – national and supranational – and to publish books that help develop more refined approaches to comparative methodology.

THE INTEGRATION OF EUROPEAN FINANCIAL MARKETS

The regulation of monetary obligations

Noah Vardi

Routledge·Cavendish
Taylor & Francis Group
LONDON AND NEW YORK

First published 2011
by Routledge-Cavendish
2 Park Square, Milton Park, Abingdon, Oxon, OX14 4RN

Simultaneously published in the USA and Canada
by Routledge-Cavendish
270 Madison Avenue, New York, NY 10016

*Routledge-Cavendish is an imprint of the
Taylor & Francis Group, an informa business*

© 2011 Noah Vardi

Typeset in Sabon by Glyph International Ltd
Printed and bound in Great Britain by CPI Antony Rowe,
Chippenham, Wiltshire

British Library Cataloguing in Publication Data
A catalogue record for this book is available
from the British Library

Library of Congress Cataloging in Publication Data
Vardi, Noah.
The integration of European financial markets : the regulation of
monetary obligations / Noah Vardi.
p. cm.
ISBN 978-0-415-60263-1 — ISBN 978-0-203-83408-4 1. Capital
market—Law and legislation—Europe. 2. Money—Law and
legislation—Europe. I. Title.
KJC2245.V37 2011
343.24'032–dc22   2010027084

ISBN 13: 978-0-415-60263-1 (hbk)
ISBN 13: 978-0-203-83408-4 (ebk)

To my mother and father.
And to Dany

Contents |

Acknowledgements

I am deeply indebted to many people for their help during the preparation of this book.

Special thanks go, first of all, to Professor Vincenzo Zeno-Zencovich for his unfailing guidance and support over several years. To Professors Micheal Joachim Bonell and Giorgio Resta I am thankful for taking the time to read earlier drafts of this work and for their valuable advice. Thanks also go to Professor Jörg Fedtke not only for the useful discussions on the topic but also for having decided to host my study in this Series.

I would also like to thank those institutions which, through their generous hospitality, have allowed me to conduct parts of my research: the Max Planck Institute for Comparative and International Private Law in Hamburg, the Institute of Advanced Legal Studies in London, and Yale Law School.

Finally, I am grateful to all those who have found the time and interest in discussing different aspects of this study and for all the helpful advice and suggestions that were made. All mistakes, errors and views expressed remain, of course, my own.

Noah Vardi
University of Roma Tre, Italy

Table of Statutes and Cases I

Austria

Belgium

France

Germany

Italy

The Netherlands

Portugal

Spain

Switzerland

United States

United Kingdom

Cases

Italy (in chronological order)

United Kingdom (in alphabetical order)

United States (in alphabetical order)

Arbitration (in alphabetical order)

Introduction 1

The process of integration of financial markets offers one of the most interesting examples of the effects of globalisation. The case of European financial markets is particularly significant in this regard. To a large extent, the process of integration has proceeded in the absence of comprehensive legal regulation, and has rather been constructed on the basis of sectorial provisions dictated by the needs of cross-border transactions. This development explains why one of the remaining obstacles to the completion of the integration process is represented by the so-called 'legal barriers'.

The removal of these legal barriers entails not only a series of regulatory choices, but also important consequences on the possible harmonisation of laws regulating the discipline of the markets and of the transactions taking place on those markets. Furthermore, the implementation of this integration process is carried out by new subjects embodying legal sovereignty over the markets and their regulation.

An analysis of this process of integration of the markets from a legal point of view provides an opportunity to highlight the role of globalisation as the key element favouring the circulation of rules, models, and especially the development of new regulatory sources. The methodological approach is that of identifying the sources which regulate the different legal institutes involved in market transactions and providing a cross-section of the forms of regulation, competences and policy issues that characterise these sources – an imaginary journey through the different floors of a multi-storey building representing financial markets.

A critical approach to financial markets cannot ignore the very serious disruptions which have taken place across world markets starting from the so-called 'subprime crash' in 2007 and which have led to a wider, global financial crisis. Many of the central issues involved in the financial crisis are beyond the scope of this study. The problems of regulation and supervision of the markets, for example, require more detailed *ad hoc* studies that will not form the main focus of this analysis (although regulatory issues cannot be ignored, as they constitute a necessary compass to frame the wider picture of the evolutionary trends of the markets, and the wide discrepancy between the existing regulatory tools and the reality of financial transactions across global markets is a problem of great topicality). Rather, what will be examined in more detail is the problem of the legal foundation of many of the financial instruments involved in the recent crisis (and which are often accused of causing this crisis). This is especially true for those complex instruments of structured finance which are the outcome of securitisation processes that are not always transparent. Furthermore, the problems related with the default of many of these securities, especially asset-backed securities (such as collateralised-debt obligations known as CDOs), which in turn have led to a more general fall in the confidence of the market in securitised titles and an ensuing contraction of access to credit, have highlighted that the legal differences in the rights lying at the basis of the securitised titles are often the key to understanding the weak link in the system.

A few examples of the weight of legal disparities in the overall reasons which can be identified as the causes of the recent financial crisis can be found in the first place in the fact that securitisation involves the commercialisation of debt (through mechanisms which convert, for example, mortgage securities or corporate bonds from illiquid assets to liquid financial instruments, which in turn transfer credit risk from intermediaries to consumer-investors), and the way in which the underlying debt is structured necessarily affects the probabilities of realisation of the credit; that in the case of asset-backed securities (and more specifically in the example of mortgage-backed securities) there are disparities in the conditions for the granting of mortgages (as has been the case, precisely, in the 'subprime' titles) and these differences are often also due to implementation of political directives; that there are disparities in the composition of the portfolios which make up collateralised-debt obligations and other structured titles; there are differences in the criteria with which securities are rated (differences which are also due to the multi-layered structure of many of these titles, each representing different assets carrying their own conditions and documentation and often made up of unique combination of underlying assets, with the consequence that each title can be sold and rated on the basis of disparate evaluations on future interest rates and defaults); often the ways in which securities are recorded and traded, for example, through indirect holding systems, create problems in identifying to whom the underlying securities belong. All of these problems involve the legal discipline of the securities, and more specifically their trading, their recording and their realisation. This study aims precisely at identifying these legal sources, which are not always vested in the form of national laws.

As will emerge further from the conclusions of this research, which aims at providing a cross-sector analysis of the legal sources regulating financial instruments and markets, a pre-eminent role in the determination of the content of many of these instruments is indeed played by rules developed by market operators. Discipline and content of important financial instruments are left to the contracts setting the conditions for their sale and trade. This source will be referred to as *financial lex mercatoria*.

The study proceeds from an examination of the discipline of market transactions and of the institutes at the root of these transactions, of the type of legislative sources in force, and of the subjects acting as legislators.

The institute which can serve as a paradigmatic point of reference for the observation of the changes taking place in the legal regulation of financial markets is represented by the notion of monetary obligation. An examination under different perspectives of the regulation of monetary obligations allows the tracing of trends emerging from the legal integration process of financial markets. By starting from the root of financial regulation (that is to say money) and by proceeding with an analysis first of one of the legal institutes that is most closely affected by money (debt and payment obligations), and then, at a further level of complexity, with an analysis of transactions in financial instruments (representing a complex form of exchange of monetary obligations), the legal integration process can be assessed at different levels.

The analysis of these single institutes clearly cannot be carried out without considering the macro-economic and regulatory context in which transactions take place. Indeed, the study of the legal discipline of monetary obligations in their broadest construction has to be conducted against the background of the political process of implementation of the European Economic and Monetary Union and has to take into consideration the regulatory debates ensuing from the economic integration of the markets.

The study can therefore be roughly divided into two areas of focus: the first part concentrating on the micro-discipline of money, debts, payments and financial instruments; and the second part analysing the macro-context of integration of the markets, the persistence of legal barriers and options for their removal, and the development of new legal sources as a consequence of the transfer of monetary and political sovereignty.

Finally, the link between the two areas consists in trying to assess the consequences of the changes at the macro-level of regulation on the micro-level of legal discipline of monetary obligations, with special focus on the emergence and growing importance of soft law.

Chapter 1:
The Root of Transactions
in Financial Markets:
Monetary Obligations

1. Introduction

If an inquiry into legal sources of financial markets can be imagined as trying to provide a cross-section of a multi-storey building, each floor of which represents different legal institutes and different legal sources, a logical starting point is the ground floor of the building. One of the legal institutes at the basis of transactions taking place in financial markets is the monetary obligation, an institute which broadly defined also comprises rules on payments and financial instruments. An examination of the changes in the regulation of this institute is paradigmatic of the development of new sources disciplining financial market transactions. Before assessing the consequences of this evolution and the role of new and old forms of regulation, it is necessary to briefly recall the main legal problems and developments surrounding the notion of monetary obligations.

2. Money

Monetary obligations are functionally associated with the object that renders them typical: money. The traditional approach to the study of these obligations begins with tentative definitions of money from a legal standpoint.[1] This methodological approach appears to be justified

---

[1] Over decades, scholars have tried to approach this problem in different ways. It is impossible to recall even briefly the numerous theories that have been developed. Only a few of the fundamental studies will be mentioned in the following notes as an indication of the variety of doctrines. Among the most significant contributions, some (F.A. Mann, *The Legal Aspect of Money: With Special Reference to Comparative Private and Public International Law,* 5th edn, Oxford, 1992, p. 5), albeit recognising that a legal definition of money reflects certain economic considerations, nonetheless warn that the legal point of view focuses on different aspects when compared with the functional economic definition. Others define the economic notion of money and then to try and translate it into a legal notion (B. Inzitari, 'La moneta', in *Trattato di diritto commerciale e di diritto pubblico dell'economia* dir. da Galgano, vol. VI, Padova, 1983, p. 4; J. Carbonnier, *Droit civil, 3, Les biens,* 19th edn, Paris, 2000, p. 48), or further single out the functional identity underlying the 'economic' and 'legal'

in view of the particular rules to which money is subject and which consequently reflect on the obligations involving the payment of a sum.

While some of the definitions and theoretical approaches that have been developed over the course of centuries may appear today as purely academic and to a certain extent have been outdated by practice,[2] a very brief account of the central notions of what may be qualified as 'money' from a legal point of view may however be useful as a guideline when it is necessary to assess the characteristics of new payment and financial instruments.

This assessment consequently allows, following the corollary that transactions involving the payment of a sum of money are referred to as 'monetary obligations', a series of operations that are carried out in financial markets worldwide (and that will be the object of analysis of this study, with special focus on the European Union (EU) markets after the introduction of the euro) to be considered as monetary obligations.

In most legal systems, the notion of money is nowhere explicitly defined by the legislator.[3] However, the law invariably refers to money as an acquired notion in disciplining payments, interests and so forth.[4] The

---

definitions (E. Quadri, 'Le obbligazioni pecuniarie', in *Trattato di diritto privato* dir. da Rescigno, vol. IX, 2nd edn, Torino, 1999, p. 525). There are purely legal approaches to the definition of money (i.e. R. Libchaber, *Recherches sur la monnaie en droit privé*, Paris, 1992, p. 7) or, by way of contrast, a practical approach that highlights the sterility of the debate on what constitutes money, in favour of focus on the notion of payment, which is central in commercial transactions (R. Goode, *Commercial Law*, 3rd edn, Trowbridge, UK, 2004, p. 452). The latter distinction between money and payment reinforces the idea that economists and lawyers conceive money in a different way: what may be money from the functional point of view for an economist (i.e. a bank deposit) may not be considered as such by a lawyer who tends to focus on private rights and the problem of legal discharge of monetary obligations (and therefore with 'payment'); (see C. Proctor, *Mann on the Legal Aspect of Money*, 6th edn, Oxford, 2005, p. 11; for this distinction the pioneering work is L. von Mises, *Theorie des Geldes und der Umlaufsmittel*, München and Leipzig, 1924, pp. 44–45).

[2] The debate on metallism, for example, has lost its centrality with the (relatively very recent) abandonment of gold parity or other intrinsic standards in coinage.

[3] An interesting exception can be found in the Uniform Commercial Code §1-201(2.4) which defines money as 'a medium of exchange currently authorised or adopted by a domestic or foreign government. The term includes a monetary unit of account established by an intergovernmental organisation or by agreement between two or more countries'. The relevance of this legal definition also lies in the clear nexus of the notion of money with that of monetary sovereignty. The point is examined *infra*.

[4] See A. Nussbaum, *Das Geld in Theorie und Praxis des Deutschen und Ausländischen Rechts*, Tübingen, 1925, pp. 1–2; T. Ascarelli, *Obbligazioni pecuniarie*, in *Comm. cod. civ.* a cura di Scialoja e Branca, *Libro IV, Delle obbligazioni, artt. 1277–1284*, Bologna–Roma, 1959, p. 8.

main difficulty lies therefore in the appraisal of a purely legal notion of money. From the economic point of view money is considered as a medium of exchange, a measure of value, and a store of wealth (that serves as a reserve of liquidity).[5] One of the most authoritative legal transpositions of these concepts identifies money as 'chattels, which are issued under the authority of the law in force within the State of issue, are denominated with reference to a unit of account, and are to serve as the universal means of exchange in the State of issue'.[6]

When money serves as a means of payment, it not only allows the reduction of two chattels that may have profoundly different characteristics to a homogeneous equation in terms of value;[7] it also comes into consideration in its physical quality as a chattel that is given or promised. It is under the latter notion, however, that the particular nature of money affects the obligation based on it. Indeed, in those legal systems where money under the law of property should be disciplined by the general rules on circulation of chattels (and a monetary obligation would be classified as belonging to the general category of 'delivery obligations'), a series of exceptions arise.[8] The fact that money, with the end of metallism, is an abstract 'ideal unit', completely dematerialised and unconvertible, entails that it is not a commodity but rather a 'function', which serves as a medium of exchange and as a measure of value. Hence the difficulties in applying possessory rules or rules on performance of a delivery obligation to a 'function'.[9]

A transfer of money will be disciplined differently depending on whether money is being transferred as a commodity (i.e. a sale or exchange of foreign currency, or of specific coins) or as a medium of exchange (money paid in discharge of a debt). For example, the rules on specific performance are only available in the case of money being transferred as a commodity; damages in the case of non-performance or delay can be awarded only in the case of money as a commodity

---

[5] With special emphasis on the notion of medium of exchange, see G. Crowther, *An Outline of Money*, London, Edinburgh, Paris, Melbourne, Toronto, New York, rev. edn, 1955, p. 20, defining money as '*anything* that is *generally acceptable* as a means of exchange (i.e. as a means of settling debts)' (italics in original).

[6] See F.A. Mann's definition in *The Legal Aspect of* Money, 5th edn, Oxford, 1992, p. 8.

[7] Inzitari, *La moneta*, p. 5.

[8] For example, the difficulty in applying the rule of having to tender chattels of a quality not below the average: Article 1246 French *code civil*; §243 I, *BGB;* Article 1178 Italian *codice civile*; or the rules on the ways in which fungible goods are to be singled out from the mass for delivery (Article 1378 Italian *codice civile*).

[9] Inzitari, *La moneta*, p. 11.

(a transfer of money as such only provides entitlement to the nominal value of the debt and in the case of delay the remedy is interest).[10]

As for the difficulties in applying possessory actions to recover money, the problems are due to the fact that, while an action for recovery cannot involve specific coins because money is inherently fungible, there can be no proprietary claim to a mere 'debt' either. In the Common Law there is a possibility of applying the personal 'action for money had and received' to follow money into the hands of an accounting party even when the subject matter is not money itself but some form of security or equivalent, provided that 'the parties have treated it as money or a sufficient time has elapsed so as to raise an inference that it had been converted into money by the defendant'.[11] In equity too, the doctrine of equitable tracing extends beyond the expression 'money' to all assets capable of being identified from a mixed fund.[12]

German scholarship has developed the special notion of a 'debt of a sum of money' (the *Betragsschuld*), to which special recovery actions could be applied (i.e. the *Surrogationstheorie* or the *Wertvindication*).[13]

The modern relevance of these distinctions lies in the correct assessment of certain monetary transactions (i.e. especially banking transactions). For example, a transfer of foreign currency can be either a repayment obligation (a loan of foreign currency) or an exchange/sale obligation (a purchase of foreign currency); the distinguishing feature between the two being that usually a repayment transaction implies that the recipient has to return the sum in the same currency or in a different currency whose *quantum* is determined with reference to the currency received. The same parameters enable a distinction to be made between a currency swap with a commitment to re-exchange (in which two currencies are exchanged in a sale followed by a later reverse counter-sale) from a back to back loan (in which the currencies are exchanged as two concurrent loans, the repayment of which will be measured by the currency of the initial transfer).[14] The notion of money as a means of exchange (or means of payment) relates to the further important distinction between money and

---

[10] See R. Goode, *Payment Obligations in Commercial and Financial Transactions*, London, 1983, pp. 5–8.

[11] *MacLachlan v. Evans* (1827), 1Y&J 380, 385; *Pickard v. Bankes* (1810), 13 East 20; *Spratt v. Hobhouse* (1827), 4 Bing. 173) (Mann, *The Legal Aspect of Money*, pp. 3–4).

[12] *Re Diplock* (1948), Ch 465, 517 et seq., Ibid.

[13] See M. Kaser, 'Das Geld im Sachenrecht', *Archiv für die civilistische Praxis*, vol.143, 1937, p. 10; S. Simitis, 'Bemerkungen zur rechtlichen Sonderstellung des Geldes', *Archiv für die civilistische Praxis*, vol. 159, 1960, p. 443 and p. 460; J. Esser-E. Schmidt, *Schuldrecht*, Bd.I, 5th edn, Karlsruhe, 1975, p. 133; B. von Maydell, *Geldschuld und Geldwert*, München, 1974, p. 12; Inzitari, *La moneta*, p. 25.

[14] See Goode, *Payment Obligations in Commercial and Financial Transactions*, p. 5.

currency. The latter indicates money that has legal tender in a State (an attribution which is possible due to monetary sovereignty).[15] In order to comply with the function of means of payment, money paid in the performance of a debt has to discharge the debtor.

The discharging effect is due to the monetary sovereignty of the State. The fundamental State Theory of Money, holds that only the State can attribute the character of 'money' to a chattel independently of an intrinsic value it may have because of the material from which it is coined (an assumption, on the contrary, at the basis of the metallistic theory).[16] This state sovereignty entails the right to control money; not only by setting its value at the moment of issue, but also by retaining the power to change the means of payment and the basic money unit, to exercise exchange controls, abrogate gold standards and so forth. According to a development of this theory, by tendering currency in discharge of an obligation, the debtor ultimately delegates the State that has issued that money to discharge the debt between himself and the creditor.[17]

A theory opposed to the State Theory of Money (the 'social' or 'societary theory of 'money') holds that it is commercial usage or social confidence that qualifies 'money'. This view corresponds to the wide notion that economists tend to have of what money is, and therefore this view is often considered insufficient by those authors in search of a strictly legal definition of money.[18] It constitutes one of the criticisms of Knapp's theory which cannot explain how historically and in practice different chattels and/or titles, not issued nor designated as money by the State, have been accepted as such.[19]

These considerations are at the root of another of the key contributions on the nature of money: the theory of the Ideal Unit developed by Arthur Nussbaum.[20] According to this theory, 'money, the concrete object, is a thing which irrespective of its composition, is by common usage given

---

[15] Monetary sovereignty can also be exercised at a supranational level, as is the case for the Member States of the European Economic and Monetary Union (EMU) that have adopted the euro. The transfer of monetary sovereignty and its consequences in the EMU will be analysed *infra*, *sub* Ch.V.

[16] The State Theory of money was developed by G.F. Knapp, *Staatliche Theorie des Geldes*, München, Leipzig, 1905.

[17] J. Carbonnier, *Droit civil*, 4 – *Les Obligations*, 22nd edn, Paris, 2000, pp. 34–36.

[18] Proctor, *Mann on the Legal Aspect of Money*, p. 23; Goode, *Commercial Law*, p. 450.

[19] See A. Nussbaum, *Money in the Law National and International: a comparative study in the borderline of law and economics: a completely revised edition of 'Money in the law'*, Brooklyn, 1950, pp. 8–9.

[20] *Das Geld in Theorie und Praxis des Deutschen und Ausländischen Rechts*, Tübingen, 1925.

and received as a fraction, integer or multiple of an ideal unit'.[21] The importance of this theory lies in the fact that it too serves as a basis for nominalism, emancipating the notion of money from metallistic theories, but by providing an alternative to the State Theory of Money (and thus overcoming the criticisms of the excessive rigidity of the latter because of its failure to explain certain concrete historical experiences). Nominalism ensues from the social 'acceptance' of money that follows once money is given or taken in pure reliance on the 'name' of the weight, without a concrete measurement of the monetary units exchanged.[22]

The notion of monetary sovereignty and legal tender, which attribute to money one of the characteristics that distinguish it from the general category of chattels, are at the base of the universal default principle applied to monetary obligations: a debt is extinguished at its nominal value.

The nominalistic principle finds its first theoretical basis in the State Theory of Money. If the State formally designates a chattel as money, and if it does so independently of any intrinsic value (such as a gold or metallic standard), the 'value' of the currency derives simply from the nominal value that the state 'declares' that it shall have. Therefore if a debtor extinguishes his debt through payment of money issued by the State for a quantity that nominally corresponds to the sum for which the debt was contracted, he pays good money and must accordingly be discharged.

Nominalism has developed as a principle opposed to the metallistic or intrinsic value of money theories (according to which money derives its value from the substance in which it is coined or from the parity in terms of gold or another substance). Among the historical achievements of the nominalistic principle is the provision of a foundation for circumventing the effects of the widespread ancient practice of debasement of coins. The affirmation of nominalism (today universally accepted as a legal principle for monetary obligations) was also strongly favoured by the diffusion of banknotes (which though at first convertible into metallic money, have been progressively detached from the underlying gold or metallic standard and have been imposed as unconvertible legal tender). The value of banknotes as legal tender at their nominal value has been sustained not only by constitutional and legal provisions, but also by jurisprudence of the courts.[23] As a consequence, private parties have developed ways to avoid devaluation of debts that ensues where

---

[21] Nussbaum, *Money in the Law*, p.13.

[22] Ibid.

[23] See, for example, in England, where the affirmation of the principle dates back to the *Case de mixt moneys* (*Gilbert* v. *Brett*) (1604) Davies 18; 2 State Trials 114; or in

nominalism is applied to obligations which have in the meantime been subject to the effects of devaluation or depreciation of currency, or of inflation. This has been done through the recourse to monetary clauses and different forms of indexation, and has given rise to voluminous case law in most legal systems during approximately the same historical periods: the extraordinary inflationary conjunctures following the two World Wars.[24] The application of the principle of nominalism and the possible exceptions to it, the development of the related theory of valorism (and of so-called value debts or adaptable debts), have been at the centre of reflections on monetary obligations in legal scholarship throughout legal systems worldwide.

3. Means of payment

Given a variety of features that characterise the notion of money, one of the central issues, beyond theoretical qualifications, for a reflection on monetary obligations in modern trade revolves around the concept of payment: what are the chattels that tendered in payment lawfully discharge the debtor?[25]

This issue necessarily requires some of the notions examined above, such as the state of origin of money (public theory), to be set aside in favour of a focus on the 'societary' meaning of money:[26] not so much because a social acceptance qualifies a means of payment as money (other parameters have to be met), but rather, because social acceptance serves as an indicator of those new or widely diffused means of payment for which the question can be posed and on which analysis should concentrate.

The common feature of widely used means of payment that bear similarities with money is that they are issued by private entities, usually banks. Indeed, the form of payment whose qualification as 'money' has been most discussed is that of bank transfers.

---

the US: see the so-called Legal Tender Cases: *Knox* v. *Lee* and *Parker* v. *Davies* (1871) 12 Wall (79 US) 457.

[24] See also *infra* par. 3.

[25] From a strictly logical point of view, money should not be confused with a means of payment: indeed, payment presupposes a debt, and a debt presupposes the knowledge of what money is, 'debt' being the monetary obligation (Nussbaum, *Money in the Law*, p. 12). However, for practical reasons, the centrality of means of payment requires this type of translation. That payment is of central importance in dealing with monetary obligations is demonstrated by the fact that the discipline of pecuniary debts is widely concerned with the issues of modes, time, place, refusal and delay of payment.

[26] See Proctor, *Mann on the Legal Aspect*, p. 37.

The legal nature of most of the new mediums of payment remains a debated issue. Some recent theories tend to regard a bank transfer as an equivalent to a cash transfer and therefore as 'money' for legal purposes.[27] Under the same line of reasoning, a similar conclusion can be extended to other forms of payment (existing or to be developed in the future) that maintain the monetary characteristic of the obligation they discharge.[28] For example, the failure to exhibit some of these features suggests that payment by credit card does not constitute an equivalent to payment in tender;[29] whilst payment by electronic money does.[30]

Some of these theories are controversial;[31] however, since the scope of this study is not to examine the legal nature of mediums of payment, but rather to identify those that have the widest diffusion and whose use can affect the conduct of monetary policy in the EU, the concrete functional approach, which proposes to qualify the nature of new means of payment on a case-by-case basis and focuses on whether the new instruments

---

[27] This conclusion derives from the observation that, as long as some of the fundamental characteristics of payment in legal tender can be found in a bank transfer, then it can qualify as a transfer of money, namely the irrevocability of the credit to the transferee's account and the transferee's immediate possession and entitlement to the funds; the transferee's right, upon receipt of the funds in good faith and for value, to retain the funds without the need to inquire as to the transferor's original source of funds; the immediate full availability of the entire amount received; the acquisition by a transferee in good faith of good title to funds free of any prior equities; the neutrality of the transferee as to the credit-standing of his debtor, or to any mistake, error or want of authority on the part of the transferring bank (see Proctor, *Mann on the Legal Aspect*, pp. 42–43). Where these features should be encountered in a new form of payment, that new means should consequently also qualify as an equivalent to a cash transfer (Ibid.). According to a similar theory, in order to qualify for legal recognition as money, any new medium of payment has to satisfy the following technical requirements: it must be commonly accepted as a medium of exchange and as final payment, requiring no link with the credit of the transferor; it should pass freely and be fully transferred by delivery and should not require collection, clearing or settlement, nor leave any record (see B. Crawford and B. Sookman, *Electronic Money: A North American Perspective*, in M. Giovanoli (ed.), *International Monetary Law*, Oxford, 2000, p. 347).

[28] The means of payment must not alter the principle of nominalism, and must not therefore serve for the transfer of a sum incremented by interest (as is the case, for example, for the transfer of interest-bearing securities) (Proctor, *Mann on the Legal Aspect of Money*, pp. 42–43).

[29] Rather it is a hypothesis of a novation of the debt, since there is no immediate transfer of funds but merely the acquisition by the creditor of the right to payment from the card issuer at a later date (Proctor, *Mann on the Legal Aspect of Money*, p. 43).

[30] The use of a card in e-money entails an immediate and irrevocable transfer of funds to the bank account of a creditor in good faith, regardless of the identity or credit-standing of the card holder (Proctor, *Mann on the Legal Aspect*, p. 44).

[31] See, for example, Goode, *Commercial Law*, p. 452, according to whom both bank transfers and e-money lack most of the characteristics of physical money: they are

maintain the monetary nature of the transfer of a sum, seems to be the most appropriate one.

An indication of the possible monetary implications of certain new forms of payment can also be inferred from the type of regulation that these means of payment have received. Indeed, Directive 2000/46/EC on the taking up, pursuit and prudential supervision of electronic money institutions has introduced a supervisory discipline on the entities that can issue e-money.[32] It should be noted that this type of regulation is partly due to concerns that the increased use of private forms of money could affect the implementation and conduct of monetary policy.[33]

Similar considerations between the nature of the means of payment and type of regulation enacted can apply with reference to bank transfers and bank money. Although it is not formally recognised as 'money', the banking system creates its own 'private' means of payment. According to economic theory, this is done (thanks to the accumulation of current deposits against which only a percentage of currency has to be held). The banking system can thus create means of payment proportionately to the ratio between the currency on hand and the effective or legal reserve kept; this book money implies that the bank contracts a debt against a promise to pay a sum of money, and the transfer of this debt constitutes a means of payment. A reduction of the legal reserve rate entails the possibility of creating proportionately more means of payment without any additional deposit of currency.[34]

'not issued under the authority of the state, are not legal tender, do not serve as a universal medium of exchange, and are not negotiable'. See also the conclusions of the American Bar Association Task Force 'A Commercial Lawyer's Take on the Electronic Purse: An Analysis of Commercial Law Issues Associated With Stored-Value Cards and Electronic Money', *Business Lawyer*, 1997, vol. 52, pp. 20–21, denying that e-money is legal tender. The same conclusion is drawn by J. Braithwaite and P. Drahos, *Global Business Regulation*, Cambridge, 2000, p. 112, who highlight that, whilst digital cash does not constitute legal tender, its acceptance by banks, merchants and their customers renders it a 'global medium of exchange'.

[32] Directive 2000/46/EC of 18 September 2000, *OJ* L275, 27 October 2000, p. 3.

[33] Proctor, *Mann on the Legal Aspect of Money*, p. 43; see also Committee on Payment and Settlement Systems (CPSS) 'Survey of Electronic Money Developments, 2001', which deals with possible concerns of Central Banks on policy issues such as, *inter alia*, the impact of e-money on monetary policy and seigniorage revenues. In the same survey, the US Authorities p. 90 affirm that 'electronic money liabilities issued by depository institutions are likely to be regarded as transaction balances, subject to reserve requirements, and included in M1'.

[34] See R.G. Hawtrey, *The Gold Standard in Theory and Practice*, London, 1927, p. 6; E. Hirschberg, *The Nominalistic Principle: A Legal Approach to Inflation, Deflation, Devaluation and Revaluation*, Ramat-Gan, 1971, p. 18; K. Olivercrona, *The Problem of the Monetary Unit*, Stockholm, 1957, p. 145.

Accordingly, a significant proportion of banking regulation at EU level (in part as an implementation of international standards set by the Basel Committee on Banking Supervision Capital Accord of 1988) carried out by the Banking Directives deals with capital adequacy requirements, which are concerned mainly with credit risk, even though separate requirements have been developed in respect of market risk as well as interest rate and currency risk.[35] However, the implications for the banks' capability of creating private means of payment, in relation to the ratio of minimum reserves, should not be underestimated either, and the existence of this type of regulation suggests, *inter alia*, the importance of these means of payment.

The consequence of these considerations is that, if the notion that "'bank money" is "money"' is accepted, the law of bank (and cross-border bank) insolvency and the problems of minimum deposit requirements for banks also affect the notion of monetary obligations, as they may ultimately constitute mandatory rules affecting the capacity of the debtor (bank) to pay in case of insolvency.

Most of the criticisms denying the monetary nature of certain new forms of payment have highlighted the absence of two distinctive legal features of money: (a) issue by the State and (b) the obligation by the creditor to accept these new forms of payment. A tentative modern analysis of the phenomenon should however note that, given that new forms of payment are issued by private entities and creditors are free to refuse means of payment other than legal tender, and given what occurs in practice, the central point is that a relevant new source disciplining payment is private, both in the potential for creating new mediums of exchange (which will be 'privately issued money') and in the potential for deciding whether to accept them. From the legal point of view, the creditor is free to refuse tender made in a means of payment different from cash. If he does accept a different means, however, that is considered as an equivalent of cash, then payment (which requires a bilateral consensus) will be considered as performed at different moments, according to the means of payment that is being used.[36]

---

[35] The Banking Directives are now consolidated in the single Directive 2000/12/EC of 20 March 2000 relating to the taking up and pursuit of the business of credit institutions, *OJ* L126, 26 May 2000, p. 1, that comprises the Own Funds Directive (89/299/EEC) of 17 April 1989, *OJ* L124, 5 May 1989, p. 16, the Solvency Ratio Directive (89/647/EEC) of 18 December 1989, *OJ* L386, 30 December 1989, p. 14, and the First Banking Directive (77/780/EEC), of 12 December 1977, *OJ* L322, 17 December 1977, p. 30; see also the Capital Adequacy Directive (93/6/EEC) of 15 March 1993, *OJ* L141, 11 June 1993, p. 1.

[36] In the case of a cheque, letter of credit or similar instrument, English, American and French courts, for example, are oriented to considering the payment made at the date

Even in the absence of a legal obligation in this sense, the observer cannot ignore the concrete *usus* that takes place in the market, and that is central both in defining what constitutes an equivalent to cash and when it is commercially reasonable to accept these means of payment.[37] In very broad terms, it can be said that the role of a form of *lex mercatoria* is central to this issue. It is this new source which will be examined further in parallel to the denationalisation of the discipline of monetary obligations. Furthermore, since control over means of payment implies a virtual control over all economic activities,[38] and has in the past been a governmental prerogative, special focus should be given to the subjects who are *de facto* in a position to issue new means of payment and to influence their regulation (either directly, as can be the case for technical supranational institutions such as the European Central Bank, or indirectly, as can be the case for market operators through the proposal and adoption of standards and different forms of soft law).[39]

---

in which the instrument is given, subject to clearance (see for the UK: *Re Hone* (1951) Ch 85; *ED & F. Man Ltd v. Nigerian Sweets and Confectionary* (1977) 2 Lloyds Rep 50; *WJ Alan & Co. Ltd v. El Nasr Export & Import Co.* (1972), 2 All ER 127 (CA); *Day v. Coltrane* (2003) EWCA Civ 342, (2003) 2 EGLR 21; for USA and France, see respectively i.e. *Ornstein v. Hickerson*, (1941), 40 F Supp 305; *Cour de Cassation*, Ch. Soc. 17 May 1972, D 1973, 129); German courts are oriented towards the date of dispatch of the instrument (not the receipt) (see *Bundesgerichtshof*, 7 October 1965, *NJW* 1966, 47; and *Bundesgerichtshof*, 29 January 1969, *NJW*, 1969, 875).

In the case of payment by credit card, the acceptance of the means of payment implies the immediate discharge of the debtor, since the creditor accepts a novation of the debt towards the credit card issuer.

In the case of payment by bank transfers, controversies may arise regarding the precise time and date at which payment has been received when the actual time of payment differs from the time agreed to by contract. Some decisions are oriented towards recognition of payment at the moment in which the funds are received by the creditor's bank (but before the bank further allocates these funds to the creditor's account) (see for the UK *The Afovos* (1980) 2 Lloyd's Rep 479) or once the electronic transfer to the creditor's bank has become inalterable or irrevocable (see, for the United States, *Delbreuck & Co. V. Manufacturers Hanover Trust Co.* (1979) 609 F 2d 1047), while others require that the credit be effectively allocated to the creditor's account and that he obtain full availability of the funds for there to be 'good payment' (see, for the UK, *The Brimnes,* (1975), QB 929; for Germany the *Bundesgerichtshof*, 25 January 1988, *BGHZ* 103. The International Law Association is also of the same opinion: see the Report of 63rd Conference, Warsaw, 1988). See Protcor, *Mann on the Legal Aspect of Money*, pp. 167–172.

[37] Payment in cash constitutes a small percentage of all payment transactions; hence the importance of examining the ways in which alternative payment instruments are issued, settled and cleared. This will be done in the following chapters.

[38] See Hirschberg, *The Nominalistic Principle*, p. 28.

[39] The role of regulators is evident when considering that if money is to carry out its functions of means of payment and standard of value, it must be accepted by the

Finally, as an introductory methodological premise, given the above definitions of money and of means of payment, the next step is to extend and to consider as 'monetary obligations' those transactions that involve a sale or exchange of financial instruments. This is due to the fact that financial instruments can be ultimately analysed as sophisticated forms of exchange of debts (either under the form of debt instruments or under the form of equity instruments) or as an 'exchange of present monetary payments against future monetary payments'.[40]

4. Financial instruments

Financial instruments comprise different types of securities. Securities may be defined more or less broadly, usually with the scope of identifying those instruments which fall within the sphere of statutory regulation of securities. According, for example, to one of the most elaborate statutory definitions of a security, the one contained in §2(1) of the US Securities Act of 1933 and in §3(10) of the US Securities Exchange Act of 1934, 'the term "security" means any note, stock, treasury stock, bond, debenture, evidence of indebtedness, certificate of interest or participation in any profit-sharing agreement, collateral-trust certificate, preorganisation certificate or subscription, transferable share, investment contract, voting-trust certificate, certificate of deposit for a security, fractional undivided interest in oil, gas or other mineral rights, any put, call, straddle, option, or privilege on any security, certificate of deposit, or group or index of securities (including any interest therein or based on the value thereof), or any put, call, straddle, option or privilege entered into on a national securities exchange relating to a foreign currency, or, in general, any interest or instrument commonly known as a "security", or any certificate of interest or of participation in, temporary or interim certificate for, receipt for, guarantee of, or warrant or right to subscribe to or purchase, any of the foregoing'.[41]

---

parties to the transaction; this acceptance necessarily depends on a stabilisation of the functions of money and has always been carried out by some third party through regulatory devices. (J. Braithwaite, P. Drahos, *Global Business Regulation*, Cambridge, 2000, p. 88).

[40] A. Ferrari, E. Gualandri, A. Landi, P. Vezzani, *Strumenti, mercati, intermediari finanziari*, 3rd edn, Torino, 2001, p. 264.

[41] Such comprehensive definitions of 'securities' are not found in all legal systems; this is due to different historical developments in the need to regulate securities and securities markets. Significantly however, the British Financial Services and Markets Act of 2000 (Schedule 2, part II) contains another example of a broad definition of 'investment' (activities which fall within the scope of regulation of the Act) which comprises 'securities, instruments creating or acknowledging indebtedness,

The first distinction that ought to be made, the one between debt and equity instruments, depends on the type of claim that the holder of the instrument has towards the issuer. Debt instruments are those in which the claim is for a fixed amount, whereas equity instruments entitle the holder to obtain an amount based on earnings (if any) after the debt instruments have been paid.[42]

Debt instruments comprise loans, money market instruments, bonds, mortgage-backed securities and asset-backed securities. According to whether their term to maturity is shorter or longer, debt instruments characterise the markets in which they are traded as 'money markets' (instruments with one year or less to maturity) or 'capital markets' (instruments with a maturity greater than one year and equity instruments). Debt instruments can be further classified as 'open market' instruments or 'directly negotiated' instruments, according to their technical form; open market instruments, which are issued for the first time are traded on 'primary markets', whereas instruments that are already in circulation are traded on 'secondary markets'.[43]

A central notion that highlights the tie between debt instruments and monetary obligations is that of the par value (or 'principal', 'face value', 'redemption value' or 'maturity value'). The par value indicates the amount that the issuer agrees to repay the holder at the date of maturity. Debt instruments may also have an interest payment, obtained by multiplying the par value by the coupon rate (or 'nominal rate' or 'contract rate'), which is the interest rate that the issuer agrees to pay each year.[44]

The analogy with the notion of payment of a debt at its nominal value is counter-intuitive. It is precisely on the basis of such a fixed 'nominal' value that debt instruments can be traded on the markets above or below their par value. The market will allow the bargaining power of issuers

---

government and public securities, instruments giving entitlement to investments, certificates representing securities, units in collective investment schemes, options, futures, contracts for differences, contracts of insurance, participation in Lloyd's syndicates, deposits, loans secured on land, rights in investments'.

[42]Some securities, such as preferred stock or convertible bonds belong to both categories, as they respectively entitle to a fixed sum (even if only after debt instruments have been paid) or they allow conversion of debt into equity (See F.J. Fabozzi, *The Handbook of Financial Instruments*, Hoboken, New Jersey, 2002, at pp. 2–3).

[43]See G.N. Mazzocco, *Gli strumenti finanziari di mercato aperto*, 2nd edn, Torino, 2005, p. 28 et seq.

[44]Debt instruments that do not entitle holders to periodic coupon payments are known as 'zero-coupon instruments'. Other forms of interest payments are reset periodically according to a reference rate (usually either an interest rate or an interest rate index) and give rise to 'floating-rate securities' or 'variable-rate securities'. (Fabozzi, *The Handbook of Financial Instruments*, pp. 4–5).

and investors to find expression in the conditions of repayment of the loan and of its interest (coupon rate) and in its trading price.

For example, with reference to floating-rate securities, a 'cap' (restriction on the maximum coupon rate that will be paid) is a clause advantaging issuers, whereas a 'floor' clause (a minimum coupon rate to be paid at maturity) advantages investors.[45] Another example of an option requiring a balance between opposing interests is the call provision. The insertion of a 'call option' (allowing the issuer/borrower to retire a debt instrument prior to the maturity stated) gives the issuer the possibility of replacing his loan through a new issue with a lower coupon rate (assuming that in the period between the first issue and the call of the instrument the general level of interest rates has fallen below the original coupon rate); at the same time it obliges the investor to reinvest at a lower interest rate.[46] The balance is struck by the call price, and/or the existence of a provision protecting against early calling or refunding of the bonds.

In the case of a rise of market interest rates after the issue of a debt instrument, the same considerations are true for the investor with the 'put' option (granting the right to sell back the debt instrument to the issuer at a specified 'put price' on specified dates), and with the conversion option (allowing the investor to convert or exchange the debt instrument for a specified number of shares of common stock).[47]

The tie with the law of monetary obligations is also present when considering derivative instruments, which can be ultimately analysed as exchanges of payments. Derivative instruments are those financial instruments that give the choice (option contract) or oblige (future/forward contract) the contract holder either to buy (call option) or sell (put option) a financial instrument at some future time, at a contract price that will be determined by the price of the underlying financial instrument or financial index or interest rate.[48]

The general categories of derivative instruments comprise future contracts, swaps and options. Future contracts, which include forward rate agreements and different types of financial futures (on obligations, on indexes, on stocks, on commodities, on currencies), are all contracts by which parties are obliged to exchange, at a specified date, the sums which are respectively the positive difference and the negative difference in the value of a chattel or financial instrument between the date on

---

[45] Ibid.

[46] Fabozzi, *The Handbook of Financial Instruments*, p. 6.

[47] Fabozzi, *The Handbook of Financial Instruments*, p. 7.

[48] Fabozzi, *The Handbook of Financial Instruments*, pp. 12–13; F. Caputo Nassetti, *I contratti derivati finanziari*, Milano, 2007, p. 2.

which the contract was concluded and the value of that same chattel at the specified due date.[49]

Swaps (interest rate swaps, interest rate and currency swaps, and further types of swaps belonging to these two categories) can be very generally defined as those contracts according to which two parties are obliged to reciprocally exchange payments, the amount of which will be determined on the basis of different parameters.[50]

Options include both contracts by which one party is obliged, in exchange for a premium, to pay the counterparty a sum of money within the limit of certain variations in a determined parameter of reference (i.e. interest rate options; commodity call, put and collar; weather call, put and collar; credit default swaps; economic call or put options) and contracts by which one party is obliged, while the other has the option, to conclude a second contract belonging to one of the categories of derivatives (swap options, currency options, index options, equity options, fund options, commodity options, credit spread options and so forth).[51]

Different parameters according to which derivatives can be classified include the scope for which the instruments are created (hedging, trading, arbitraging); the nature of the underlying risk (market risk, credit risk, etc.); the market of negotiation (regulated markets or over-the-counter markets); the basic contractual structure (option-based or forward-based derivatives); the type and nature of the underlying instrument (derivatives on currency, on interest rates, on equity, etc.).[52]

As a very brief overview suggests, for the scope of this study the inclusion of financial instruments within the wider notion of monetary obligations is necessary if the changes in the law regulating debts is to be analysed on a more comprehensive scale.

5. Problems of legal integration of European financial markets: a need for general rules?

The focus of the following chapters will be to provide a brief overview of the trends of capital markets and financial services in the euro area after the introduction of the single currency. As will be noted, the process of financial integration is mostly ahead of legal integration; furthermore, often the process of integration of the markets is hampered

---

[49]See Caputo Nassetti, *I contratti derivati finanziari*, p. 263 et seq. and p. 586 et seq.
[50]Caputo Nassetti, *I contratti derivati finanziari*, p. 28 et seq. and p. 55 et seq.
[51]Caputo Nassetti, *I contratti derivati finanziari*, pp. 586–587; see also B. Libonati, *Titoli di credito e strumenti finanziari*, Milano, 1999, pp. 119 et seq.; G.N. Mazzocco, *Gli strumenti finanziari di mercato aperto*, 2nd edn, Torino, 2005, pp. 117 et seq.
[52]Mazzocco, *Gli strumenti finanziari di mercato aperto*, p. 118.

precisely by the existence of a series of legal barriers. This confirms the impression that legal integration is bound to follow financial integration. Indeed, it is the very market that requires a uniform set of rules as the pre-condition for removing the existing obstacles to complete financial integration.

Whilst some provisions have already been adopted or are under way (e.g. the many measures that have been adopted under the framework of the Financial Services Action Plan (FSAP) and that concern the specific sectors of Accounting and Auditing, Banking and Financial Conglomerates, Company Law and Corporate Governance, Financial Markets Infrastructure, Insurance and Occupational Pensions, Insurance, Securities Markets, Retail Financial Services and Payments, Securities and Investment Funds, and Taxation[53]), what is still missing is a set of binding common general rules (whereas soft law rules, as will be illustrated below, have been drafted under different forms).

Such common general rules could be applied (according to the typical civil law systematic method) to all institutes that lack a specialised discipline. An equivalent of the general discipline for the regulation of monetary obligations contained in many national civil codes. These general rules would, for example, include, to name those institutes that have been the most problematic in national historical experiences, a common discipline – not only in the banking sector – for the maturity of interests; or a common discipline for the moment in which a debtor is considered in delay; common principles on the admissibility of derogations to nominalism; and common principles on the techniques of revalorisation.

What this study purports to demonstrate is that these general rules could be (and to a certain extent already have been) replaced by rules elaborated by non-institutional actors: a form of soft law that because of its origin can be referred to as financial *lex mercatoria*.

5.1. Recent historical developments in the law of monetary obligations

Whilst integration of financial markets is a relatively recent process, strongly accelerated and triggered by the Economic and Monetary Union and the single currency, the trend towards convergence of general rules or, where rules are different, to jurisprudential orientations, is a phenomenon that can be observed historically. In recent times, this trend has emerged preponderantly for certain aspects of the discipline

---

[53] For further details, see the report by the European Commission Internal Market and Services DG 'FSAP Evaluation', p. 32 et seq.

of monetary obligations in those periods of global monetary crisis in which legislators and courts had to face identical problems of regulation.

A significant example is that of the widespread experience in numerous legal systems during the extreme inflationary crisis following the First and the Second World Wars.[54] The troubles at the macro-economic level were necessarily reflected at the micro-economic level, especially as far as the legal regulation of monetary obligations was concerned. This is exemplified by a convergence in jurisprudential patterns across legal systems as a reaction to similar monetary policy choices. More specifically, courts where called to face the problems arising in private law from the currency depreciation measures adopted by the national systems and from the ensuing devaluation of the debts formed during this period.

A first example of this convergence in dealing with the consequences of monetary policy decisions at the level of private law is found where courts recognised the validity of different types of monetary clauses in order to permit the revaluation of debts, notwithstanding the strict rule of nominalism in force everywhere.

---

[54] From the macro-economic point of view, during this period international monetary regulation was left to national (and nationalist) politics. Foreign exchange regulation until the First World War was administered through a *laissez-faire* approach, in which government interventions, under the form of changes in bank rates, were an exception. The few attempts at promoting international monetary cooperation (i.e. the Brussels Conference of 1920 and the Genoa Conference of 1922) did not produce tangible results and, as a consequence, after the 1929 Wall Street crash, monetary policy of the leading powers in the 1930s was characterised by unilateral currency depreciations in the hope of reviving their national economies. This currency depreciation race initiated a vicious circle of retaliatory devaluations among the states; even the ultimate effort made in 1936 by the three currency powers (US, UK and France) with the Tripartite Monetary Agreement arrived too late and with insufficient binding force to avoid the drastic consequences that would follow from the Second World War. An exchange rate stabilisation would only be achieved a decade later, with the creation of the Bretton Woods System in 1944. This represented the first multi-lateral attempt (until then monetary relations had mostly been bilateral in nature) to impose, through rules and principles and not through gentlemen's agreements, certain obligations on states in the conduct of their monetary policy (with a view to achieving economic coordination between states). However, eventually this system broke down in 1971 when, under the pressures for the convertibility into gold of the dollar (the major international reserve currency after the world conflict) accompanied by growing trade deficits in the US balance of payments, the US announced the abandonment of the gold standard. This announcement put an end to the exchange rate regime negotiated at Bretton Woods thirty years earlier (see Braithwaite, Drahos, *Global Business Regulation*, pp. 95–99).

Whether through a broad interpretation of good faith (*ex* §242 *BGB*) and of the *rebus sic stantibus* clause, as occurred in Germany;[55] through a construction of nominalism as not implying a mandatory principle of public order, as occurred in France;[56] through the application of the institute of supervening excessive burden of obligation, as occurred in Italy,[57] the judiciary in most of the legal systems found a way to allow the revaluation of debts through the use of monetary clauses in periods of extreme inflation and monetary devaluation, and this notwithstanding the codified principle imposing the payments of monetary debts for their nominal value and the compulsory tender legislation existing at the time.

In the Common Law systems, on the other hand, the admissibility, in the name of the parties' freedom of contract, of debt indexing through the use of monetary clauses (index clauses and gold clauses mainly), has a longstanding tradition. In England, a legislative provision dating as far back as 1575 ('Act for the maintenance of the Colleges in the Universities, and of Winchester and Eaton') provided a scheme for indexing leases to market values (the corn market specifically).

In the United States (US), the admissibility of gold clauses was affirmed by the Supreme Court in the leading cases *Bronson* v. *Rhodes*[58] and *Butler* v. *Horwitz*,[59] affirming the validity of gold clauses and rejecting the interpretation of the Legal Tender Acts as prohibiting the payment of debts in money other than legal tender notes. In *Willard* v. *Tayloe*[60] the Supreme Court recognised the admissibility, in the event of inflation, of payment in gold and silver coins instead of in legal tender notes, as specific performance in order to maintain the value of consideration in the contract. It was only later that in the US the Joint Resolution of Congress of 1933 put a legislative prohibition on the use of these clauses.

When monetary conjunctures returned to normal fluctuation values, in many systems the legislator intervened to limit the possibility of indexing debts, in order to avoid private parties producing indirect inflationary effects through the use of these monetary clauses.[61]

---

[55] See the famous judgment of the *Reichsgericht*, 28 November 1923, *RGZ*, pp. 107–78.

[56] This construction refers to Article 1895 *code civil*.

[57] *Ex* Article 1467 *codice civile*; however, the Italian legislator also enacted specific legal provisions for the defence of certain socially protected categories of creditors such as employees, pensioners and beneficiaries of life annuities.

[58] (1869), 7 Wall. (74 U.S.) 229.

[59] (1869), 7 Wall. (74 U.S.) 258.

[60] (1869), 8 Wall. (75 U.S.) 557.

[61] (1869), A few of the provisions limiting the use of monetary clauses include the *Währungsgesetz* of 1948 in Germany; the French *Ordonnance no. 58–1374* of 30 December 1958, and the *Ordonnance no. 59–246* of 4 February 1959, restoring

A first converging pattern between legal systems thus emerges in the most ancient problem concerning monetary debts: the mandatory character of nominalism and the techniques to circumvent this principle under pressure of endemically inflationary monetary conjunctures.

Another common trend can be found in the identification of a special category of debts (the so-called 'value' debts or 'adaptable' debts) that are excepted from the nominalistic principle because of their particular nature. The original object of these debts is not a sum, but an abstract value (such as a payment of damages for tort or breach of contract, or compensation, or of sums anticipated for reparation), that has to be liquidated into monetary terms.[62] Not only has the identification of this category of debts been widespread (even if nowhere formally codified[63]), basically for reasons of fairness; but a common trend emerges also, after a range of sometimes disparate solutions, in identifying, as the relevant moment for the 'liquidation' of these debts, the moment of payment.[64]

---

as a condition of admissibility of index clauses the existence of a direct and logical relationship (so-called *indexation interne*) between the nature of the debt and the type of index chosen; the US Joint Resolution of Congress of 1933. On the relation between a diffuse use of indexing debts and indirect inflationary effects see Mann, *The Legal Aspect of Money*, p. 180, summarising the results of different studies on this issue carried out in different legal systems.

[62] For a definition of 'value debts', see, *ex multis*, for the different legal systems: A. Nussbaum, *Money in the Law*, Chicago, 1939, p. 255 et seq.; T. Ascarelli, *Obbligazioni pecuniarie (Art. 1277–1284)*, in A. Scialoja, G. Branca (eds.), *Commentario al codice civile*, Bologna, Roma, 1959, p. 170 et seq. and p. 441 et seq.; Mann, *The Legal Aspect of Money*, p. 123 et seq.; G.L. Pierre-François, *La notion de dette de valeur en droit civil. Essai d'une théorie*, Paris, 1975.

[63] In certain countries, specific legislative provisions indirectly identified certain debts as 'value debts'. In Germany, the *Umstellungsgesetz* of 1948, in fixing the conversion rate between the old *Reichsmark-forderungen* and the new *Deutsche Mark* excluded 'value debts' from its sphere of application; in Italy, the special nature of wages emerges from Article 429, 3rd par., of the *codice di procedura civile*, prescribing the inclusion of possible damages for loss of value in the calculation of sums due as salary.

[64] See the historical judgments in Germany (*Reichsgericht,* 12 March 1921, *RGZ*, pp. 101–418, *Reichsgericht* 13 June 1921, *RGZ*, pp. 102–383, *Reichsgericht*, 6 October 1933, *RGZ*, 142, p. 8, and *Bundesgerichtshof*, 12 January 1951, *BGHZ*, 1, 52); in France, (*Cour de Cassation* 24 March 1942, Cass. Req., *D.A.* 1942, 118); in Italy, (*Corte di Cassazione* 8 April 1952, n. 950, *Foro it.*, 1953, I, 39, *Corte di Cassazione* 4 September 1982, *Rep. Foro it.*, 1982, entry 'danni civili', n. 51, *Corte di Cassazione* 23 November 1985, n. 5814, *Rep. Foro it.*, 1985, entry 'danni civili', n. 119; and *Corte di Cassaz ione S.U.*, 9 January 1978, n. 57, *Giust. civ.*, 1978, I, p. 7); in Austria, (*Oberster Gerichtshof*, 4 April 1923, *SZ*, v., no.72 and *Oberster Gerichtshof*, 11 September 1975, *Juristische Blätter*, 1976, 315); in England, (in case of personal damages, *Wright* v. *British Railways Board*, (1983), 2.A.C. 773, and *Mallet* v. *McMonagle*, (1970), A.C. 166; for damages to property where repairs are possible, *Dodd Properties (Kent) Ltd.* v.

In other aspects of the discipline of monetary obligations, convergence is not quite as marked, and it is probably for these institutes that a common general set of rules would be the most desirable.

A recurring problem, for example, is that of compensation in case of delay, with reference to the possibility of including, in addition to the legal interest due, further damages suffered as a consequence of monetary devaluation. The problem occurs where the computation of legal interest rate on the overdue sums does not take into account monetary depreciation.

On the one hand, several legislatures have agreed in recognising a possible further 'loss from monetary depreciation' in case of late payment (provisions to this effect are found for example in the French, German, and Italian civil codes).[65] In other systems this type of legislative provision is missing and courts have refused to admit damages for monetary depreciation in case of delay or breach, holding, as is the case in England and in the US that only (legal) interest is the measure of damages for withholding payment.[66]

On the other hand, even where the possible damage has been recognised, differences lie in the methods used by the judiciary for the assessment of damage and in the calculation of the interest due as compensation.[67]

Canterbury City Council, (1980), 1. W.L.R. 433); and in Belgium (*Cour de Cassation*, 26 February 1931, *Pasicrisie*, 1931, i.94, and *Cour de Cassation*, 24 January 1966, *Pasicrisie*, 1966, i.658).

[65] See Article 1153 *code civil*; §288 abs.4. *BGB*; Article 1224 2°c., *codice civile*.

[66] See e.g. for the United States *Meinrath* v. *Singer Co.* (1980) 87 F.R.D. 422; and on this rule A.L. Corbin, *Law of Contracts*, V, St. Paul, Minnesota, 1964, s.1005, p. 52; S. Williston, *Law of Contracts*, 3rd. edn, New York, 1968, vol. ii, p. 605. See for a dissenting analysis of English practice, Mann, *The Legal Aspect of Money*, pp. 116–7.

[67] For example, in Germany the assessment refers to presumptions on the typical use of money made by different categories of subjects (e.g. 'private citizens' as opposed to professional investors such as banks), and consequently the calculation of the rate of interest due as damage caused by devaluation refers to the cost of money on the bank market (see e.g. *Bundesgerichtshof*, 29 October 1952, *NJW*, 1953, p. 337; *Bundesgerichtshof*, 1 February 1974, *Ent. Bund. Ziv.*, 1974, Bd. 62, p. 103; *Bundesgerichtshof*, 8 November 1973, *Wert. Mitt.*, 1974, p. 128). In Italy, the assessment of damages is also based on a series of legal presumptions on the use of money made by different 'standardised' categories of creditors; see *Corte di Cassazione*, *S.U.*, 4 July 1979, n. 3776, *Giur.it.*, 1979, I, 1, c.1410; later confirmed by *Corte di Cassazione*, *S.U.*, 5 April 1986, n. 2368, *Foro it.*, 1986, I, 1265. In France interest for delay is determined (after the Law of 11 July 1975 n. 619) with reference to the discount rate applied by the Central *Banque de France* in the preceding year (with the legal rate increased by 5 per cent in case of further delay in payment after a judicial order to pay).

The problems of admissibility of revalorisation and the different treatment in case of delay or breach (to quote the most diffuse issues) oblige legal systems to confront a particularly problematic institute of monetary obligations: foreign-money debts. A similarity can be noted in the type of issues raised for these debts, but the proposed solutions often diverge.

The conflict between different rules derives from the multiplicity of laws involved in foreign-money debts: the *lex obligationis* (or *lex causae*), the *lex monetae* and the *lex fori* (or *lex loci solutionis*). These laws may or may not coincide, with a fundamental role thus being played by private international law. The problems that have emerged in the past concerned the determination of which of these laws governs the different aspects of the obligation. The main issues, once the admissibility of payment in foreign money is recognised, concern the option for the debtor of choosing in which currency to discharge the debt; the risk of monetary depreciation of the currency chosen for the determination of the sum (the money of account), particularly in case of delay; and the choice of the moment for the conversion of the debt from the money of the obligation to the money of payment.

The analysis of historical data, however, permits a further important observation: the pattern of converging solutions, from a comparative perspective, can be drawn in most cases beyond the civil law/common law distinction of legal traditions. This is especially interesting in view of the fact that certain legal systems do not have a systematic discipline for monetary obligations. This has significantly occurred in the law of the US, where although a general set of rules for 'monetary debts' (such as those codified, for example, in the German, Italian or French civil codes) is missing, long-standing and consolidated case law has recognised the same principles of nominalism, of admissibility of revaluation mainly through the use of gold clauses, and of recognition of foreign value debts, as are found in the abovementioned civil codes.[68]

---

[68] The fundamental element which has permitted the development of a consistent body of case law on monetary obligations in the US legal system lies in the existence of key provisions in the Constitution (such as Article I, section 8 and section 10; Article I section 10, clause 1 (contracts clause)) and in the construction of these Articles carried out by the judiciary. Indeed, the role of the US Supreme Court has been pivotal in affirming the right of Government to define legal tender (attributing it to banknotes or paper money) as an exercise of monetary sovereignty (see the controversial affirmation through the so-called 'Legal Tender cases': *Hepburn* v. *Griswold* (1870), 75 U.S. (8 Wall.) 603; *Knox* v. *Lee, Parker* v. *Davis*, (1871), 79 U.S. (12 Wall.) 457; *Julliard* v. *Greenman* (1884), 110 U.S. 421, the related principle of nominalism (much later indirectly confirmed by the Gold clause jurisprudence) but also the principles of party autonomy in defining the conditions for performance of monetary debts (see *Bronson*

5.2. Harmonisation of general rules: Directives, Unidroit Principles and Principles of European Contract Law

The examined historical and comparative data seem to indicate converging trends in the rules disciplining monetary obligations, which it may be logical to assume will strengthen even more with progress in the integration of the market in the euro area and with the existence of a single currency. However, there is no codification of these rules, since they are mostly due to consolidated jurisprudential orientations. Whilst this may be reassuring for Common Law countries, it is somewhat less of a rule in those civil law legal systems that do not acknowledge the formal binding value of precedent. The opportunity of adopting a common set of rules arises from the need to solve some of the problems emerging from a not yet unified law of monetary obligations notwithstanding a single monetary policy.[69]

A significant example of predisposition of a common set of general rules on monetary obligations is Directive 2000/35/EC on combating late payments in commercial transactions.[70] Although limited in its sphere of application to commercial transactions, this Directive faced the problem of discouraging late payments by increasing interest rates in case of delay, thus making late payment a practice that can no longer be considered convenient from an economic point of view. The adoption of a common general rule refers to the determination of the moment from which *mora debitoris* can be calculated, even without the need of a formal notice or reminder;[71]

---

v. *Rhodes* (7 Wall. (74 U.S.) 229, (1868); *Willard* v. *Tayloe* (8 Wall. (75 U.S.) 557, (1869)), especially where these principles were the result of a wide construction of clauses (such as the Contracts clause) which may not have been immediately identifiable as related to monetary issues.

Another significant aspect for the European observer which can be found in the American legal system is the development throughout the twentieth century of a series of uniform laws (such as the Uniform Negotiable Instruments Law approved by all the States in 1924; the Uniform Sales Act of 1906, the Uniform Commercial Code, the 1989 Uniform Foreign Money Claims Act) which have codified in statute form the discipline of several aspects concerning payments, debts and obligations.

[69] Problems which can be synthesised in the fact that a single *lex monetae* and different (national) *leges obligationis* do not assure that a debt, for the same nominal value expressed in euros, will be discharged in the same way throughout the different member states who have adopted the single currency.

[70] Directive 2000/35/EC of 29 June 2000, *O.J.*L200, 8 August 2000, p. 35.

[71] Article 3, par.1.(a) and (b), Directive 2000/35/EC provides that 'Member states shall ensure that: (a) interest [...] shall become payable from the day following the date or the end of the period for payment fixed in the contract; (b) if the date or period for payment is not fixed in the contract, interest shall become payable automatically without the necessity of a reminder'.

to the measure of legal interest rates,[72] to the recognition of the right to compensation from the debtor for all relevant recovery costs incurred because of late payment.[73]

However, a limit in the harmonisatory reach of this legislative measure resides in its form. As a directive requiring transposition, and allowing member states, through a final safeguard clause, to maintain or bring into force provisions which are more favourable to the creditor than those set down by the directive itself,[74] this Community provision does not ensure the uniformity of solutions that would be required. For example, in stating the right of the creditor to compensation for the costs incurred because of late payment, the Directive does not specify whether 'devaluation damages' may also be included; thus leaving it to the different national rules to allow or deny this further compensation.

Another example of predisposition (though not legislative in nature) of general rules regarding some of the most common aspects of cross-border commercial transactions can be found in the Unidroit Principles for International Commercial Contracts[75] and in the Principles of European Contract Law.[76] Both sets of rules have disciplined some of the most diffuse institutes regulating payment of debts, and in so doing have often offered a uniform solution to certain rules characterised by problematic diversity between national regulations.

For example, unless otherwise fixed or determinable by the contract, the place of performance of a monetary obligation shall be the creditor's place of business.[77] By leaving the risk of transmission of the payment with the debtor, this provision implies freedom of choice for the debtor

---

[72] Article 3, par.1., (d), Directive 2000/35/EC: 'The level of interest for late payment ("the statutory rate"), which the debtor is obliged to pay, shall be the sum of the interest rate applied by the European Central Bank to its most recent main refinancing operation carried out before the first calendar day of the half-year in question ("the reference rate"), plus at least seven percentage points ("the margin"), unless otherwise specified in the contract […]. '

[73] Article 3, par.1., (e), Directive 2000/35/EC states that 'unless the debtor is not responsible for the delay, the creditor shall be entitled to claim reasonable compensation from the debtor for all relevant recovery costs incurred through the latter's late payment.'

[74] Article 6, par.2, Directive 2000/35/EC.

[75] See the latest version edited by M.J. Bonell, *An International Restatement of Contract Law. The UNIDROIT Principles of International Commercial Contracts*, 3rd ed., Ardsley (NY), 2005.

[76] See O. Lando and H. Beale (eds.), *Principles of European Contract Law. Parts: I and II combined and revised*, The Hague, London, Boston, 2000.

[77] Article 6.1.6 Unidroit Principles and Article 7:101 Principles of European Contract Law.

on how to send or transfer the money to the creditor.[78] Indeed, both sets of principles provide for the admissibility of payment in any form used in the ordinary course of business at the place for payment,[79] including payment by funds transfer.[80] Usages can thus prevail over many national laws providing that payment be made by transfer of legal tender.[81] While the admissibility of alternative forms of payment favours a debtor who prefers to discharge his obligation in a form different from legal tender, the creditor is protected from burdensome or unusual methods of payment by two provisions. The first requires the alternative method of payment to be 'usual' in the ordinary course of business (and thus depends on the nature of the transaction); the second, specific to payment by cheque or other order to pay or promise to pay, provides that acceptance of this alternative form of payment is conditional to performance and that if the cheque or promise to pay is not honoured, the original claim of the creditor remains.[82]

---

[78] The choice made by these principles in favour of the rule according to which default payment shall be made at the creditor's place of business is common for example to the United Kingdom (see *Chitty on Contracts* §21–043), the Netherlands (Articles 6:115–6:118 *Burgerlijk Wetboek*), Italy (Article 1182(3) *codice civile*), Austria (§905 (2) *ABGB*), Portugal (Article 774 *código civil*), and to the Nordic Instruments of Debts Act of 1938 §3(1), but not to French (Article 1247(3) *code civil*), Belgian (Article 1247 *code civil*), and Spanish (Article 1171(3) *código civil*) laws. According to German law (§§269 and 270(4) *BGB*) the place of performance is the debtor's place of business, however the debtor is responsible for transferring the money to the creditor and bears both the expense and the risk of loss in transfer. See the official comment and notes to Article 7:101 Principles of European Contract Law in O. Lando and H. Beale (eds), *Principles of European Contract Law. Parts: I and II combined and revised.*

[79] Article 6.1.7. Unidroit Principles and Article 7:107 Principles of European Contract Law.

[80] Article 6.1.8. Unidroit Principles.

[81] Express provisions in this sense are found in Italy (Article 1277(1) *codice civile*), Portugal (Article 550 *código civil*), Spain (Article 1170 *código civil*); however, in many other legal systems it is also accepted practice (France, Belgium, Luxembourg, Greece, England and Scotland).

[82] The conditionality of performance of a monetary obligation through a form of substituted payment is the rule in most legal systems (expressly stated, for example, in Germany (§364 *BGB*), the Netherlands (Article 6:46 *Burgerlijk Wetboek*) and the United States (Uniform Commercial Code §2-511(3) and Restatement of Contracts 2d, §249). It is sometimes accompanied by provisions that allow creditors to refuse payment other than by legal tender (such is the case in the US under Uniform Commercial Code §2-511(2)).

As for payment through transfer of funds, Article 6.1.8 Unidroit Principles allows payment to be made by a transfer 'to any of the financial institutions in which the obligee has made it known that it has an account' (unless the obligee has indicated a particular account). The provision also solves the widely controversial issue of when payment by a funds transfer is considered as completed (and the debtor is discharged)

Both the Unidroit Principles and the Principles of European Contract Law discipline the hypothesis of a monetary obligation that is expressed in a currency other than that of the place of payment and provide that, unless the parties have agreed on a currency clause, the debtor has a right of conversion, allowing him to pay in the currency of the place of payment rather than in the currency in which the obligation is expressed.[83] Furthermore, the exchange rate for the conversion will be, according to both rules, the rate of exchange prevailing at the place of payment when payment in due. In case of delay, the creditor may require payment in the currency of the place of due payment according to the rate of exchange prevailing there either at the time when payment is due or at the time of actual payment, thus transferring the risk of currency depreciation on the defaulting party by allowing the creditor the choice of the better exchange rate.[84]

In general, in case of delay in payment, both the Unidroit Principles and the Principles of European Contract Law affirm the right of the aggrieved party to obtain interest (according to a specified rate) on the sum due from the day of the maturity to the day of payment, and further include the possibility of recovering additional damages if the non-payment caused greater harm.[85] The Principles of European Contract Law further provide

---

by adopting the rule according to which payment will be considered effective when the transfer to the creditor's financial institution becomes effective (thus considering the institution as the creditor's agent). (See the official comment to Article 6.1.8 Unidroit Principles.)

[83] Article 6.1.9 Unidroit Principles and Article 7:108 Principles of European Contract Law.

[84] The problem of the exchange rate for conversion in case of late payment is controversial and opposite approaches are found in different legal systems based either on the rate of exchange on the day of payment (as in England, Austria, Germany, Greece, the Netherlands, and in the Nordic Instrument of Debts Act) or on the rate of exchange on the date of maturity (France, Italy, Belgium, Luxembourg, Portugal). The unsatisfactory result in case of depreciation during delay has led many legal systems to adopt supplemental rules in order to avoid damage to the creditor (i.e. requiring that the debtor pay the difference between the exchange rates at the day of payment and the higher rate at the day of default or maturity, or granting the creditor damages for late payment). The Unidroit Principles and the Principles of European Contract Law have adopted the alternative remedy of allowing the creditor to choose the better exchange rate (a solution adopted in the French and Spanish legal systems). (See official comments to the Unidroit Principles and to the Principles of European Contract Law).

[85] See Article 7.4.9. Unidroit Principles and Article 9:508 Principles of European Contract Law. The conferral of a general right to interest on obligations to pay exists in all continental European countries, and has also been affirmed in English law for commercial debts and in the US. The ways in which the rate of interest is calculated, however, as well as the option between a fixed and flexible rate, differ considerably between legal systems. The Unidroit Principles and the Principles of European Contract

for a capitalisation every 12 months of interest due on the outstanding capital in case of delay in payment.[86]

It is interesting to note that the examples of harmonisation mentioned above (Directive 2000/35/EC and Unidroit and European Contract Law Principles), derive from different sources: the former institutional (a legislative act of the EU); the latter voluntary soft law prepared by private subjects. This introduces one of the further perspectives under which the law of monetary obligations in European private law should be examined: the perspective focusing on the new subjects who embody legal sovereignty and on the new sources of regulation.

5.3. Harmonisation of rules as a result of financial instruments governed by transnational commercial law

Finally, the emergence of a pattern of legal convergence in relation to monetary obligations is also visible in the development of financial instruments governed by transnational commercial law, which as such necessarily implies common rules for the legal institutes concerned.

One of the first evident cases of financial instruments disciplined by a transnational commercial law in practice is the case of euro-issuances giving rise to euro-obligations. The process leading to an issuance of euro-obligations involves the conclusion of different sets of contracts (namely a loan agreement, an underwriting agreement, an agreement among underwriters, a selling agreement, a paying agency agreement, a contract – usually a trust – between the borrower and the entity representing the lenders subscribing the obligations, a warranty agreement made by holding companies which formally issue the obligations, etc.).

The development of this sector of the international financial market took place without any reference to precise national rules, but rather through the practical contribution of market operators who elaborated transnational common rules for these sets of contracts and gave rise to a primary and secondary market without the intervention of any national legislature.[87]

Law fix the measure of the interest rate at the 'average commercial bank short-term lending rate to prime borrowers prevailing for the contractual currency of payment at the place of payment'. Both Principles also admit the recoverability of additional loss (beyond interest) caused by the delay; a possibility which is not recognised in all legal systems (especially when the loss at issue is loss caused by inflation).

[86] Article 17.101 Principles of European Contract Law (Part III).

[87] See P. Kahn, 'Lex mercatoria' et contrats internationaux, in Le contrat économique international, Bruxelles-Paris, 1975, p. 174.

However, the role of market operators as producers of rules was concentrated in the banking sector. Whilst the euro-issuance operation involves bankers, borrowers and lenders, only the bankers were sufficiently organised in professional associations (such as the Association of International Bond Dealers) and were thus able to elaborate the applicable rules under the form of standard contracts and recommendations concerning euro-markets. Furthermore, the banking associations were able to organise arbitral institutions for the resolution of controversies between its members arising within the euro-issuance procedure or in the euro-obligations market. The borrowers, on the other hand, constitute a less homogenous group (composed mainly of multi-national companies and public borrowers) and were thus not able to impose their own common rules. The legal relations between the borrowers and the banks therefore remained strictly bilateral (and often under state control as far as authorisation for the loan and its conditions were concerned). The same can be said for the category of the lenders subscribing the euro-obligations.[88] The possible implications as to the corporative and unilateral characteristic of the norms thus produced and adopted is not a secondary issue.

One of the most significant examples of conflicts between the interests of the different parties involved in an issue and collocation of euro-obligations (also representing an instance of the possible problematic derogation to national rules on monetary obligations) concerns the insertion of monetary clauses in the obligations. The type and content of these clauses reflect the distribution of risks between the parties and the balance that is struck between the opposed interests of borrowers and lenders.

Indeed, the lenders of an obligation loan are interested in receiving timely payments, which have not lost their value, and in obtaining an interest rate which is at least as high as what they would gain from a comparable investment. Therefore lenders are concerned with the risk of non-performance of the borrowers, with the risk of market fluctuations which lead to an increased interest rate for new investments, and with the risks of devaluation of the currency of payment of the loan. The two latter risks correspond inversely to possible advantages for the borrowers.[89]

---

[88]Kahn, *Lex mercatoria et pratique des contrats internationaux*, pp.174–175. The author also recalls the example of large oil companies, which though constituting one of the most significant groups of issuers of euro-obligations, did not contribute to the creation of general international rules for borrowers in this financial sector (whereas their contribution to *lex mercatoria* in other domains, such as concession contracts, has been relevant).

[89]The existence of a monetary clause which favours the lender can be counterbalanced by a high price for its subscription or by a lower interest rate (T. Treves, 'Les clauses

There are different types of clauses which tend to favour the interests of either one of the parties. Most of them concern the determination of the amount of the payment (given that clauses concerning the currency of payment do not necessarily reflect opposed interests of lenders and borrowers and usually converge on the 'option of place' clause, which allows the creditor to choose the currency of payment according to the place of payment).

Among the clauses concerning the methods of determination of the amount of the obligation of payment, the vast majority are represented by clauses which link the obligation to a certain currency (known as 'currency of account'), chosen because of its presumed stability. Whereas so-called 'floating' interest rates on this type of obligation represent a clause favouring the interests of the lenders (whose investment will be repaid according to the interest rate on the London market for six-month deposits in euro-dollars and in any case not below a certain ceiling), this type of clause is rarely used in practice; on the contrary clauses on conversion of obligations into securities are more numerous since they are convenient in different respects to both parties.[90] Similarly, so-called 'option of change' clauses, which link the amount of the payment obligation to a plurality of currencies linked with one another according to fixed exchange rates depending on their parity at the moment of the issue of the loan, are once again very advantageous for the lenders and rarely used in practice.[91] However, the generally stronger contractual power of the borrowers is signalled by the rare adoption in practice of clauses which safeguard the value of the debt against the most common devaluation processes.

The operativity of these clauses also interacts with certain national provisions enacted by the State of the borrowers or lenders, or the State where the loan is issued, or where it has to be paid, and that reflect public interests such as control over the balance of payments.[92]

---

monetaires dans les emissions d'euro-obligations', *Rivista di diritto internazionale privato e processuale*, 1971, p. 779).

[90] Treves, 'Les clauses monetaires', pp. 782–3.

[91] Treves, 'Les clauses monetaires', pp. 784–5.

[92] The State of the lenders is interested in a timely and non-discriminatory repayment of the loan, but at the same time it may be interested in controlling the reserves in foreign currency of its citizens and may thus introduce special rules for the control of these payments. The State of the borrowers is interested in favouring the access to international capital markets of its undertakings and public subjects; however, it may impose limitations on the outflow of national currency (i.e. by allowing payments only through special controllable and blocked accounts) or may defend the national monetary system by prohibiting any clause which derogates from the principle of nominalism. Finally, the State where the loan has to be repaid may be interested in

The effectiveness of the clauses, inserted in the obligations as a result of an agreed balance between opposing interests of lenders and borrowers, will ultimately depend on the possibility of these clauses derogating to mandatory public principles that will be applicable to the debts according to the rules of private international law.

More specifically, according to whether the national provisions belong to what is traditionally known as *lex monetae* or *lex contractus*, they will or will not be possibly derogated by privately negotiated clauses. Where the currency chosen for the obligation (either as currency of payment or as currency according to which the amount of the obligation has to be determined) is affected by measures such as devaluation or revaluation, alteration of an existing gold standard or parity with other foreign currencies, or provisions affirming the nominalistic principle, these measures concerning the *lex monetae* and expressing the monetary sovereignty of the state of the currency will have to be accepted by the private parties carrying out transactions in that currency.[93]

National provisions concerning the validity or prohibition of gold or index clauses or of other revalorisation techniques will on the other hand affect the operativity of the clauses inserted by the parties in the obligation only if these national rules are part of the law applicable to the obligation according to the criterion of the *lex contractus*.[94] As a consequence, and with the scope of ensuring that the law that will govern the obligation will be the one most favourable to the interests of the parties, most obligations have explicit clauses on the applicable law.[95]

Given this theoretical basis and given the historical application of these monetary clauses in important euro-issuances during the 1970s, a few further considerations can be added with reference to possible current

---

controlling all payments in foreign currency; whereas the State of the currency in which the loan has to be repaid may try to oppose an excessive flow of its own currency to foreign residents, and the State of the currency according to which the amount of the obligation has to be determined may oppose an excessive use of monetary clauses such as may alter the international 'status' and value of its currency. (see Treves, 'Les clauses monetaires', pp. 792–3; see also C. Segré, *Emissioni obbligazionarie estere sui mercati europei*, in *Moneta e Credito*, vol. XVII, n.65, 1964, pp. 22–3).

[93] See Nussbaum, *Money in the Law*, p. 349 et seq.; Mann, *The Legal Aspect of Money*, p. 229 et seq.; Ascarelli, *Le obbligazioni pecuniarie*, pp. 132 and 194 et seq.

[94] The *lex contractus* criterion also applies, according to the generality of conflict of law rules, to measures referring to currency exchange controls. The application of the latter type of regulation can to a certain extent be avoided through the 'option of place' clause. See Treves, 'Les clauses monetaires', pp. 795–802.

[95] It should be noted, as has been observed (Treves, 'Les clauses monetaires', p. 813), that often the applicable law is that of the managing underwriting bank that organises the issue of the obligations; a fact that can readily be explained in view of the central role of the underwriters in this type of operation.

applications to other financial instruments. More specifically, in order to avoid the applicability of mandatory national rules, it suffices that modern financial instruments tailor their clauses so as to place them, according to private international law rules, in the sphere of the *lex contractus* (and not of the *lex monetae*). It will then be possible, if the idea of the existence of a transnational financial *lex mercatoria* is accepted,[96] to refer to this transnational law as the law governing the transactions.

Furthermore, by submitting any controversy that may arise from these operations to alternative dispute resolution methods or to arbitral tribunals, the derogation from national rules and the application of privately created law will be removed from any form of state control.

It is under this last aspect that questions may arise with reference to the wide notion of monetary obligations which is at the basis of this study. To what extent can privately originated rules derogate from mandatory principles governing monetary debts? The incidence of rules attributed to *lex mercatoria* on national discipline of monetary obligations is not new in commercial practice. Arbitral judges have often construed the relevant national rules applicable in an international contract concerning performance or meaning of monetary obligations, according to the content of 'general commercial practice' or 'common commercial law' or 'common principles of international commerce'.

A famous amiable composition arbitral award of 1956 recognised, in an international contract that had been concluded with no speculative intention, a warranty against devaluation of the currency as an implicit principle of *lex mercatoria* (without any express stipulation in this sense on behalf of the contracting parties).[97]

The reference to the non-speculative nature of the contract reflected the conviction of many arbitrators according to which every far-sighted merchant has to guarantee his position against the risks of devaluation, and consequently a contract in which this type of warranty is missing would normally be characterised as a speculative contract.[98] However,

---

[96] See *contra*, Treves, 'Les clauses monetaires', pp. 802–809, excluding the existence of a new law merchant in the domain of euro-obligations.

[97] Amiable composition, Case of 2 July 1956, *Société européenne d'études et d'entreprises* c. *R.P.F. de Yougoslavie*, in *Journal du Droit International*, 1959, p. 1074. See also International Chamber of Commerce Case 2291/75, in *Journal du Droit International*, 1976, p. 989.

[98] See Y. Derains, in note on Case 1717/72 of the International Chamber of Commerce, in *Journal du Droit International*, 1974, p. 892, quoting Case n.519/32. Another interpretation for this solution is that given the empirical observation that in commercial practice most long-term contracts of sale or production contain different types of price-revision clauses, and that the scope of these clauses is to maintain the economic value of the prestations, the general rule deriving from *lex mercatoria* is that

this case did not express a unanimous position on the content of *lex mercatoria*. Indeed, the recognition of an implicit value clause against devaluation seems to be quite exceptional. *Lex mercatoria* notoriously struggles between the principle of *rebus sic stantibus* (which would allow for an implied revision of the contract under change of circumstances) and the principle of *pacta sunt servanda* (which defends the security of legal transactions by excluding any interference in the contract justified by a supposedly implied will of the parties).[99]

The refusal on the part of arbitrators to adjust penalty clauses for example, in such a way as to take account of a devaluation of the currency in which the penalty must be paid, is not so much justified by a defence of the nominalistic principle as it is rather an expression of respect for the (declared) will of the parties.[100] On the other hand, under the same principle, the will of the parties will be considered to prevail over any conflicting provision of national law prohibiting the use of monetary (gold or index) clauses. Indeed, arbitral awards have recognised the validity of gold clauses without referring to the relevant national law that was otherwise considered as the law applicable to the contract.[101]

---

the performance obligations in long-term contracts should remain financially balanced. Thus, if in the absence of an express price-revision provision a controversy has to be decided according to 'general commercial practice', then the applicable rule would be in favour of a revaluation of unbalanced performance. See Kahn, *'Lex mercatoria' et pratique des contrats internationaux*, pp. 194–9.

[99] See B. Goldman, 'La lex mercatoria dans les contrats et l'arbitrage internationaux: réalité et perspectives', *Journal du Droit International*, 1979, p. 494.

[100] See Y. Derains, in note to International Chamber of Commerce Case n. 1990/1972, *Journal du Droit international*, 1974, p. 901. The principle according to which the parties have to protect their own interests is confirmed in several arbitral judgments: see International Chamber of Commerce Case n. 1512/71 in *Journal du Droit International*, 1974, p. 905; International Chamber of Commerce Case n. 2216/74, in *Journal du Droit International*, 1975, p. 917; International Chamber of Commerce Case n. 2404/75 in *Journal du Droit International*, 1976, p. 995.

[101] See International Chamber of Commerce Case n. 1717/72, *Journal du Droit international*, 1974, p. 890; International Chamber of Commerce Case n. 1990/72, *Journal du Droit international*, 1974, p. 897; however, see International Chamber of Commerce Case 2520/75, *Journal du Droit International*, 1976, p. 993 refusing to recognise the validity of a gold clause not expressly stipulated in the contract.

In a large number of arbitral awards or settlements concerning claims against national Governments for damages caused to individuals by depreciation of currencies as a result of introduction of new currencies or of legislative provisions setting new par values of national currencies against gold or against foreign currencies, arbitral tribunals have affirmed that 'it is a generally accepted principle that a state is entitled to regulate its own currency' (*Serbian and Brazilian Loan Cases*, 1929, Permanent Court of International Justice, Ser. A Nos. 20–21 p. 44) and that states do not

Another important principle was affirmed in the same 1956 judgment quoted above (*Société européenne d'études et d'entreprises* c. *R.P.F. de Yougoslavie*). The arbitrators considered *inter alia* that 'according to common law' (general usages), where the losses resulting from devaluation arise for a notable part from the fact of the delaying debtor, the latter is obliged, 'in addition to the moratory interest, to pay damages for the prejudice caused by its delay'.[102] The statement is significative given the strong contrast in domestic case law between different legal systems on so-called devaluation damages. Furthermore, here again taking position in conflicting case law, dated arbitral awards have found that liquidation of monetary sums has to be carried out on the day in which the obligation is due, rather than on the day of effective payment, in case of delay. This would be in conformity to 'general principles of commercial law', according to which, in case of delay, the creditor should not bear the consequences of devaluation, even if no such express clause has been included in the contract.[103] In case of devaluation during delay, the simple payment of moratory interest would not be sufficient to repair the prejudice caused to the creditor.

On the contrary, in case of timely performance, liquidation or conversion of sums (either from foreign currency to the currency of payment or from a 'value' to a sum) takes place, according to 'international legislative, conventional and jurisprudential practice' on the day of

---

incur international responsibility by reason of their currency policy (except when there is an abuse of rights or breach of treaty obligations) and as long as there is no discrimination between nationals and aliens. See, for example, Foreign Claims Settlement Commission, *Alois Szpunar* v. *Poland*, 8 May 1963, *F.C.S.C. Rep.*, p. 471; Foreign Claims Settlement Commission of the United States, *Herbert S. Hale* v. *Poland*, 20 December 1961, *F.C.S.C. Rep.*, p. 32; Foreign Claims Settlement Commission of the United States, *Karolin Furst* v. *Czechoslovakia*, 16 May 1960, *F.C.S.C. Rep.*, p. 116; Foreign Claims Settlement Commission of the United States, *Gordon T. Malan* v. *Italy*, 18 December 1957, *F.C.S.C. Ann.*, p. 292; Foreign Claims Settlement Commission of the United States, *Walter J. Zuk* v. *U.S.S.R*, 5 November 1956, *F.S.C.A. Rep.*, p. 172; Foreign Claims Settlement Commission of the United States, *Joseph Winkler* v. *Yugoslavia*, 13 August 1954; Foreign Claims Settlement Commission of the United States, *Hans H. Kohler* v. *Yugoslavia*, 2 September 1954; American-Mexican Claims Commission, *Scott and Bowne, Inc.* v. *Mexico*, 4 April 1947, *Report*, p. 142; American-Mexican Claims Commission, *Bordon Covel, Administrator, Estate of Leo Sigmund Kuhn, Deceased* v. *Mexico*, 4 April 1947, *Report*, p. 168; American-Mexican Claims Commission, *Singer Sewing Machine Company* v. *Mexico*, 4 April 1947, Report, p. 330.

[102] Case cit. in *Journal du Droit International*, 1959, p. 1081.

[103] See International Chamber of Commerce Case n. 369/1932; see also Court of Appeal, *The Teh Hu* (1969), 3 All E.R. 1200.

payment and with reference to the conversion rate of that day.[104] Arbitration has also dealt with some of the basic notions of performance of monetary obligations, such as the determination of the 'place of payment',[105] or the admissibility of determining the amount payable in discharge of a bond other than by its 'face value'.[106]

Given empirical evidence of the way in which *lex mercatoria* has been construed by arbitrators, and of the impact that it has had on the efficacity of certain principles governing monetary obligations that are often stipulated as mandatory by national legislators (i.e. the nominalistic principle), the following question arises: if the soft law that will here be identified as financial *lex mercatoria* should also be applied by arbitral courts as representing 'general principles of commercial law', would there be a further erosion of the normative primacy of national legislation governing monetary obligations?

When considering that mandatory principles such as the nominalistic principle, which have governed monetary obligations in most legal systems, have been laid down for specific policy reasons such as legal certainty (*mark gleich mark* principle) or to impede privately created indexation mechanisms from somehow encouraging inflation in a vicious circle,[107] the possibility that these principles might be disapplied in favour of rules that are the product of privatised law-making should not be underestimated.[108]

The justification of course could lie in the principle of private autonomy (parties choose the rules and choose who shall enforce them); however, it should be recalled that private autonomy can be invoked only because it finds an operative space according to the mechanisms of private international law that are construed under the needs (and pressures) of international commercial transactions (in globalised markets).

Here, it may not only be contractual relations which are at issue: the very nature of transactions involving money affect the global economy in

---

[104] See the 'Diverted cargoes' (Greece/United Kingdom) case of 10 June 1955, *R.S.A.XII*, p. 65, and the famous *Serbian and Brazilian Loan Cases*.

[105] Arbitral Tribunal for the Agreement on German External Debts, *Swiss Confederation* v. *Federal Republic of Germany*, 3 August 1958, *I.L.R.*. XXV, 1958, p. 33.

[106] U.S.-Japanese Property Commission, *Continental Insurance Company*, 20 August 1960, *R.S.A.* XIV, p. 475.

[107] See E. Quadri, *Le obbligazioni pecuniarie*, in P. Rescigno (ed.) *Trattato di diritto privato*, vol. 9, I, Torino, 1999, p. 589.

[108] Furthermore, these policy reasons are common to all legislators (or have been enforced by courts where the principle was not enshrined in a legal provision) and certainly professional associations, market operators and industry representatives lack the democratic legitimation of national legislators.

a much more direct and incisive way than even mass contractualisation does. This last element has to be taken into consideration when examining the possible effects of this transfer of legislative competence to non-institutional actors.

Indeed, if it may be true that in the past, certain derogations to mandatory national principles governing monetary debts that have been supported by arbitral jurisprudence have not entailed significant consequences on the general legal framework disciplining monetary obligations and have not excessively affected legal certainty, this is likely to be due to the relatively low number of disputes decided by occasional arbitral awards and of the scant impact that these decisions may have had on the overall volume of case law decided by national judges applying domestic rules.

However, if the same phenomenon is transferred from the occasional arbitral award concerning single contracts to a systematic dispute resolution method on a massive scale, such as the typical case for many controversies concerning financial instruments, the incidence of these derogative norms and the possible ensuing legitimation of this privately created law may become much more significant.

Whether or not the time has come to introduce new operative principles on performance of debts that may be functionally assimilated to monetary debts, what must be borne in mind is that the rules are formulated by actors representing different policy needs compared to those embodied by national legislators.

Chapter 2:
The Process of Integration of European Financial Markets

1. The European Economic and Monetary Union and integration of markets

The analysis of the changes in the discipline and sources of legal institutes at the basis of financial market transactions cannot be conducted without considering the macro-economic context in which these transactions take place. Indeed, the legal discipline of the institute of monetary obligations is emphatically conditioned by its object of regulation: that is, payment of sums of money. Events affecting money directly affect the regulation, existence, modification and extinction of debts. These events are external to the legal sphere within which debts have arisen (usually private autonomy), and thus monetary obligations are subject to hetero-elements.[1] It is clear that an event such as the largest monetary takeover in history, implemented as the final stage of creation of the European Economic and Monetary Union, requires special attention whenever monetary obligations are taken into consideration. The effects of the adoption of the euro and the creation of the Economic and Monetary Union are relevant not only as a change of currency, but especially in view of the wider integration of financial markets which is taking place in the European Union.

The creation of the Economic and Monetary Union was considered as the natural consequence of an integrated common market, or to use the expression adopted by the 1995 Green Paper on the Introduction of the Single Currency, as 'the logical and essential complement' to the common market.[2]

Whilst the birth of the Economic and Monetary Union is usually set in the 1970s, an embryonic idea of economic and monetary coordination can actually be traced back to the European Economic Community

---

[1]Devaluation, depreciation, change of currency, restriction of exchange of foreign currency, changes in legal interest rates, changes in market interest rates, are but a few of the most common 'hetero-elements' affecting monetary obligations.

[2]European Commission, Green Paper on the Practical Arrangements for the Introduction of the Single Currency, COM (95) 333 final, 31 May 1995.

Rome Treaty.[3] However, apart from the creation of the Committee of Governors of the Central Banks in 1964,[4] it was only after the fall, in 1971, of the Bretton Woods system (when under the pressure on currency markets the US dollar abandoned the gold standard), that the process for the creation of the Economic and Monetary Union gained momentum.[5]

It was the Werner Report, issued in that period (1970), that set a stage by stage plan for the achievement of an economic and monetary union over a ten-year period. However, the original plan for the Economic and Monetary Union by 1980 suffered a series of setbacks.[6] By the end of the 1970s, the Economic and Monetary Union had not been achieved yet; a significant event, however, was the institution of the European Monetary System in 1979.

The European Monetary System established an artificial monetary unit (the ECU),[7] an Exchange Rate Mechanism (ERM)[8] and a system of mutual support between national central banks in the form of loans and

---

[3] The Title II on Economic Policy of the Rome Treaty contains several articles on economic and monetary coordination. These include Article 104, requiring each Member State to 'pursue the economic policy needed to ensure the equilibrium of its overall balance of payments and to maintain confidence in its currency, while taking care to ensure a high level of employment and a stable level of prices'; Article 105 requiring states to 'coordinate their economic policies', as well as policies 'in the monetary field'; Article 106 which liberalises current transborder payments for goods and services; Articles 108 and 109 which permit safeguard measures for states encountering serious balance of payments difficulties. For further observations, see R.J. Goebel, 'Legal framework: European Economic and Monetary Union: will EMU ever fly?', *Columbia Journal of European Law*, 1998, vol. 4, p. 256.

[4] The Committee of Governors of the Central Banks were empowered to encourage cooperation between the National Central Banks of the Member States of the European Economic Community. See Council Decision 64/300/EEC of 8 May 1964 on cooperation between central banks, 1964, *O.J.* L 1206, 21 May 1964, p. 1. Article 105(2) of the European Economic Community Treaty also created the Monetary Committee, with the role of reviewing the monetary and financial situation of the Member States of the European Economic Community.

[5] Ever since its creation in 1947, the Bretton Woods system had guaranteed the global system of fixed exchange rates, in which the dollar was anchored to the gold standard (thus providing monetary stability), and the other currencies fixed their value in terms of the dollar. The abandoning of the gold standard allowed the US dollar to float against other currencies and gave rise to a system of floating exchange rates.

[6] The setbacks were due to the global energy crisis of the mid-1970s and to subsequent monetary crises in certain member states.

[7] The value of the ECU was fixed as a composite basket of national currencies of the member states weighted against one another.

[8] In the Exchange Rate Mechanism exchange rates between national currencies were fixed and allowed to float only within a band of 2.25 per cent above or below the established exchange rates; in exceptional cases of monetary pressure some currencies were allowed to float within a broader measure.

credits in case of currency crises. Further progress was marked by the Delors Report of 1989,[9] containing proposals for Monetary unification, to be realised through a three-stage process, and which were then inserted into part of the 'Economic and Monetary Union' provisions of the Maastricht Treaty in 1992.[10]

The important preconditions set by the Delors Report for the achievement of the Economic and Monetary Union consisted in the total and irreversible convertibility of currencies, complete liberalisation of capital transactions and integration of the financial sector, and irreversible locking of exchange rates. The Report also proposed the creation of the European System of Central Banks (ESCB) and the ultimate adoption of a single currency, as a prospective conclusion of the different stages laid out for the attainment of the Economic and Monetary Union.

The commencement of the First Stage towards the Economic and Monetary Union was set in 1990, with the entrance into force of the 1988 Directive on freedom of capital movement[11] and the requirement (in principle) that member states adhere to the European Monetary System and increase the level of their monetary coordination. The further stages outlined by the Delors Report were then inserted in the Treaty on the European Union, which amended the European Economic Community Treaty in 1992, and introduced provisions on the Economic and Monetary Union.

Thus Stage Two, whose starting date was fixed by Treaty Article 109(e) in 1994, provided for the creation of the European Monetary Institute (EMI) having the institutional goals of, *inter alia*, strengthening cooperation between national central banks (whose process towards independence was required as a political criterion by Article 109(e) of the Treaty on the European Union), coordinating the monetary policies of the member states, and preparing the instruments and procedures necessary for carrying out a single monetary policy in the Third Stage and for the functioning of the European System of Central Banks and the European Central Bank.[12]

---

[9]Report on Economic and Monetary Union in the European Community, *O.J.* 1989, C 329, p. 44.

[10]See Title VI, 'Economic and Monetary Policy', Treaty on the European Union. The process was also largely stimulated by the success of the internal market programme, which had been set by the 1985 Commission White Paper on Completing the Internal Market (COM (85) 310 final, 1985). See Goebel, 'Legal framework: European Economic and Monetary Union: will EMU ever fly?', p. 262.

[11]Directive 88/361, EEC of 24 June 1988, *O.J.* L178, 8 July 1988, p. 5.

[12]Article 109(f), Treaty on the European Union. The European Monetary Institute was an intermediary body that substituted the Committee of Governors of the Central Banks (dissolved at the start of the second stage of the Economic and Monetary Union)

It was also during Stage Two that the important four 'convergence criteria' for joining the third and final stage of the Economic and Monetary Union were established, consisting namely of: (a) the achievement of a high degree of price stability; (b) the sustainability of the government financial position (budgetary discipline); (c) currency stability (within the fluctuation margins provided for by the Exchange Rate Mechanism of the European Monetary System); and (d) interest rate convergence.[13]

After the establishment of the European Central Bank and the European System of Central Banks in 1998, the transition to the third and final stage of the Economic and Monetary Union, with the objective of the adoption of a single currency, the euro, as legal tender, was ready in 1999. The entry into the Third Stage of the Economic and Monetary Union for the member states was conditional on a decision of the European Council of Ministers on the attainment of the goals set by the convergence criteria. As a result, eleven member states (Austria, Belgium, Germany, Finland, France, Ireland, Italy, Luxembourg, Spain, Portugal, and the Netherlands[14]) entered the Third Stage in 1999 (Greece joined later in 2001).[15] The Third Stage consisted of a two-year transitional process (1999–2001), which served to prepare for the monetary takeover which finally took place on 1 January 2002, when the euro coins and banknotes became the sole legal tender in the above mentioned member states (also known as 'the euro-zone'). The euro was adopted by Slovenia in 2007, by Cyprus and Malta in 2008 and by Slovakia in 2009.

This very brief historical overview is justified by two factors. The first is that the process towards the Economic and Monetary Union, characterised by leaps forward and setbacks over an almost 30-year period, received special impetus in those periods in which the positive results of other forms of integration were achieved. This is particularly evident as far as the completion of the common market is concerned, and is demonstrated more specifically in the field of monetary obligations, by the measures adopted to ensure the freedom of capital movement.

The second lies in the conclusion that can be drawn from this historical data. Just as a common currency was considered the natural conclusion of an integrated market, thus a common 'law of money' has to be considered an inevitable and desirable consequence of the single currency.

---

and was then later to be substituted by the European System of Central Banks and the European Central Bank.

[13] Article 109(j), Treaty on the European Union.

[14] The United Kingdom and Denmark, according to Protocols to the Maastricht Treaty, had the option to withdraw from the Third stage of the Economic and Monetary Union with the right to join later.

[15] This confirms the so-called 'two- speed' approach towards Economic and Monetary Union.

Both as precondition and as preparation, the integration of the market preceded the Economic and Monetary Union. At the same time, however, after the Economic and Monetary Union, the integration of those areas of the market still in search of common regulation received a strong impulse. The creation of a common regulatory framework for the European financial market has been considered as part of the effort towards the completion of the internal market of financial services.[16]

These efforts towards the creation of a common regulatory framework, together with the globalisation fostered by the liberalisation of international capital movements, financial deregulation and advances in technology, and the changeover to the euro, have been identified as the three main factors behind the acceleration in the process of integration of European Union (EU) financial markets that has occurred in the last few years.[17]

A significant early attempt to create a legislative framework for a fully harmonised European market was the adoption, in 1993, of the Investment Services Directive which aimed at implementing 'mutual recognition' of regulations across the EU.[18] The Investment Services Directive set high level principles for national securities regulations and adopted the concept of a single 'passport' for investment firms, authorised and supervised according to the principle of home country control. However, technological innovations and the development of alternative trading systems revealed the necessity of revising the system laid down by the Investment Services Directive.[19] The process of revision, which eventually led to the adoption of the Market in Financial Instruments Directive (repealing the Investment Services Directive) was inserted within a wider process of reform of legislative action, initiated at institutional level.

Indeed, two important Community initiatives, one deriving from the other, need to be briefly accounted for before examining the capital markets. The first concerns the 'Financial Services Action Plan'[20] (FSAP),

---

[16] See Communication from the Commission of the European Communities, 'The euro area in the world economy – developments in the first three years', 19 June 2002, COM(2002) 332 final, p. 6 (hereinafter, Commission Report 'The euro area in the world economy').

[17] See Commission Report, 'The euro area in the world economy', p. 28.

[18] Directive 93/22/EEC of 10 May 1993 on Investment services in the securities field, O.J.L141, 11 June 93, p. 27.

[19] See R. Davies, A. Dufour, B. Scott-Quinn, 'The MiFID: competition in a new European equity market regulatory structure', in G. Ferrarini, E. Wymeersch (eds), *Investor Protection in Europe. Corporate Law Making, The MiFID and Beyond*, Oxford, 2006, p. 187.

[20] Commission Communication of 11 May 1999, 'Implementing the framework for financial markets: Action Plan', COM (1999)232, available at http://europa.eu.int/comm/internal_market/finances/docs/actionplan/index/action_en.pdf.

prepared by the Commission under mandate of the Cardiff European Council in 1998 and endorsed by the Cologne European Council in 1999.

The Financial Services Action Plan (with a deadline fixed by 2005) contained a legislative programme for the elimination of the existing regulatory barriers in European financial markets. The FSAP set out strategic objectives to promote the integration for the wholesale market, for open and secure retail markets, for improvement of prudential rules and supervision, and outlined the measures (building in part on existing EU legislation) to be approved for the implementation of these objectives. The general objectives of the FSAP for promoting wider conditions for an optimal single financial market included addressing disparities in tax treatment and ensuring an efficient legal system for corporate governance.[21]

In confirming the FSAP, the Lisbon ECOFIN Council in 2000 decided upon the second of the initiatives mentioned above: the establishment of a Committee of Wise Men on the Regulation of European Securities Market (also known as the 'Lamfalussy Committee' after the name of its chairman, Alexandre Lamfalussy), with the remit of evaluating the priorities of the measures in the FSAP and assessing further needs to ensure greater convergence of the markets. The Final Report of the Lamfalussy

---

[21] In pursuance of these objectives, the FSAP elaborated a programme comprising 42 measures (not all legislative in nature), most of which have been implemented by the fixed deadline. These measures will be examined *infra* when analysing the different market areas. An account of the measures can be found not only in the 10 Progress Reports of the FSAP (available at http://europa.eu.int/comm/internal_market/finances/actionplan/index_en.htm#action%20plans), but also in several reports of different committees,including: the Reports of the Four Independent Groups of Experts on European Financial Integration (available at http://europa.eu.int/comm/internal_market/finances/actionplan/stocktaking_en.htm); the European Parliament's Economic and Monetary Affairs Committee's report on the Current State of Integration of EU Financial Markets (report A6-0087/2005) ('van den Burg report') (available at http://www.europarl.eu.int/omk/sipade3?PUBREF=-//EP//NONSGML+REPORT+A6-2005-0087+0+DOC+PDF+V0//EN&L=EN&LEVEL=0&NAV=S&LSTDOC=Y); and the European Commission Internal Market and Services DG 'FSAP Evaluation', available at http://europa.eu.int/comm/internal_market/finances/docs/actionplan/index/051028_fsap_evaluation_part_i_en.pdf).

The Commission presented a new Green Paper on Financial Services Policy (2005-2010) (COM (2005)177) in May 2005, aiming at consolidation of existing legislation with few new initiatives; ensuring the effective transposition of European rules into national regulation, and a more rigorous enforcement by supervisory authorities; and removing the remaining economically significant barriers. These objectives are confirmed, under the '*leitmotiv* of Dynamic Consolidation', in the White Paper 'Financial Services Policy 2005–2010' (COM (2005)629 final), that followed in December 2005.

Committee,[22] published in 2001, proposed, as a possible solution to the existing regulatory problems of financial markets, a new approach to the drafting of legislation, known as the 'Lamfalussy Process'.

The 'Lamfalussy Process' or 'Lamfalussy Framework' consists of a four-level approach for the drafting of legislation. At Level One, framework principles to be decided by normal EU legislative procedures (i.e. co-decision) are enacted. Two new committees (the European Securities Committee and the Committee of European Securities Regulators) have been established to assist, at Level Two of the process, the European Commission in determining how to implement the details of Level One framework. Level Three consists in enhanced cooperation and networking among EU securities regulators to ensure consistent and equivalent transposition of Level One and Two legislation (through the proposition, for example, of common technical standards). Finally, Level Four concerns strengthened enforcement of Community rules.[23] This legislative process has been adopted so far in securities market regulation to four measures under the Financial Services Action Plan: the Market Abuse Directive,[24] the Prospectus Directive[25] the Markets in Financial Instruments Directive[26] and the Transparency Directive.[27]

2. The free movement of capital

The creation of an integrated financial market clearly requires and presupposes the freedom of capital movement, and not surprisingly the achievement of free movement of capital was set as the starting mark for the First Stage of the Economic and Monetary Union. It is only through capital liberalisation, with the abolition of restrictions and administrative controls on cross-border financial transactions, that the deregulation of financial markets and the abolition of rules on the participation in domestic financial markets of foreign institutions can be achieved.[28]

---

[22] Final Report of the Committee of Wise Men on the Regulation of European Securities Markets, Brussels, 15 February 2001, available at http://europa.eu.int/comm/internal market/securities/docs/lamfalussy/wisemen/final-report-wise-men en.pdf (hereinafter Lamfalussy Report).

[23] See Lamfalussy Report, cit., *passim.*

[24] Directive 2003/6/EC of 28 January 2003 on insider dealing and market manipulation (market abuse), *O.J.*L 096, 12 April 2003, p. 16.

[25] Directive 2003/71/EC of 4 November 2003, *O.J.* L 345, 31 December 2003, p. 64.

[26] Directive 2004/39/EC of 21 April 2004, *O.J.* L145, 30 April 2004, p.1.

[27] Directive 2004/109/EC of 15 December 2004, *O.J.* L390, 31 December 2004, p. 38.

[28] See M. Andenas, 'Who is going to supervise Europe's financial markets?,' in M. Andenas, Y. Avgerinos, (eds), *Financial Markets in Europe: Towards a Single Regulator*, The Hague, 2003, p. xvi.

Although inserted in the Rome Treaty (Article 67) along with the freedom of goods, persons and services to form the four fundamental freedoms of the European Economic Community, the freedom of capital movement remained at length unimplemented (even after the transitory period for the removal of barriers to the other fundamental freedoms had expired in 1969); this was also due to the interpretation of the European Court of Justice that, relying on the provision requiring abolition of restrictions to the movement of capital between member states 'to the extent necessary to ensure the proper functioning of the common market',[29] denied direct effect to Article 67 of the European Economic Community Treaty, *de facto* favouring the maintenance of existing member state legislation on exchange controls.

Exchange controls constituted an important instrument of monetary policy; and capital restrictions, as the prerequisite for the efficacy of the direct instruments of monetary and credit control, ensured that the monetary and credit policies were relatively autonomous.[30] The abolition of national regulations on exchange controls is among the most indicative signs of the loss of monetary sovereignty of the member states.

Exchange and capital control regulations existed in all the member states. Using the emergency safeguard clauses of Articles 73, 108 and 109 of the European Economic Community Treaty, exchange controls were used by member states to try and protect their monetary policies during the global recession of the 1970s.[31] Two early directives, the First and the Second Capital Directive,[32] had provided a liberalisation from exchange restrictions of most common commercial and private capital movements; however, these measures did not touch on most banking and financial transactions.

A gradual liberalisation of domestic financial markets (through a progressive substitution of direct instruments of monetary control with indirect instruments) took place in the 1980s, after assessments of the

---

[29] Ex Art.67 EEC Treaty now replaced by art.56 (ex art. 73) EC Treaty.

[30] See Andenas, 'Who is going to supervise Europe's financial markets?', p. xvii. Credit control was carried out by limiting the growth of clearing banks' and other financial institutions' assets, thus allowing for monetary objectives to be achieved at lower interest rates than would have otherwise been possible. Capital restrictions, by controlling the outflows of capital, enabled the preservation of low interest rates in the short term, and protected domestic markets and savings in the long term; whilst the control of capital inflows maintained price stability in the short term and protected domestic control of key industries in the long term. (Ibid.)

[31] See Goebel, 'Legal framework: European Economic and Monetary Union: will EMU ever fly?', p. 269.

[32] Directive 921/60 of 11 May 1960, *O.J.*43, 12 July 1960, p. 921, and Directive 63/21 of 18 December 1962, *O.J.*9, 21 January 1963, p. 62 respectively.

high costs and low effectiveness that capital control entailed in the long run.[33] It is in this context of gradual deregulation of domestic markets that first the 1988 Capital Liberalisation Directive[34] for the implementation of Article 67 of the Treaty was adopted, and later Article 67 was replaced by Article 73 with the Maastricht Treaty in 1992, providing an unconditional prohibition of all restrictions on the movement of capital between member states. By 1994, with the complete transposition of Directive 88/361/EEC in all member states, the free movement of capital was implemented, although a series of further measures was necessary to guarantee effective liberalisation of financial markets.[35]

3. Financial markets

The process of integration of financial markets has made significant progress in the period largely coinciding with Stage Three of the Economic and Monetary Union and then with the first years following

---

[33] The costs of capital control were both administrative in nature, and macroeconomic, in the form of inefficient capital allocations on the market due to distortions in asset prices and interest rates. (Andenas, 'Who is going to supervise Europe's financial markets?', p. xvii.)

[34] Directive 88/361/EEC of 24 June 1988, O.J.L178, 8 July 1988, p. 5.

[35] These measures concern mainly freedom of access of credit institutions in foreign markets and include: the 'Second Banking Directive', (Directive 89/646/EEC of 15 December 1989, on the coordination of laws, regulations and administrative provisions relating to the taking up and pursuit of the business of credit institutions and amending Directive 77/780/EEC ('First Banking Directive'), O.J. L386, 30 December 1989, p. 1); Directive 89/299/EEC of 17 April 1989, on the own funds of credit institutions, O.J. L124, 5 May 1989, p. 16; Directive 89/647/EEC of 18 December 1989, on a solvency ratio for credit institutions, O.J. L386, 30 December 1989, p. 14; Directive 92/30/EEC of 6 April 1992 on the supervision of credit institutions on a consolidated basis,O.J. L110, 28 April 1992, p. 52; Directive 92/121/EEC of 21 December 1992 on the monitoring and control of large exposures of credit institutions, O.J. L29, 5 February, 1993, p. 1; Directive 93/6/EEC of 15 March 1993 on the capital adequacy of investment firms and credit institutions, O.J. L141, 11 June 1993, p. 1; Directive 94/19/EC of 30 April 1994 on deposit-guarantee schemes, O.J. L135, 31 May 1994, p. 5.

A partial recognition of the direct effect of freedom of capital movement had been reached with a new orientation in the European Court of Justice jurisprudence. First with the case *Luisi and Carboni v. Ministero del Tesoro* (Cases 286/82 & 26/83, E.C.R., 1984, p. 377) recognising the direct effect of Article 106 of the Treaty and liberalising the movement of capital for the cross-border payment of services; then with the case *Sanz de Lera* (Cases C-163/94, 165/95 and 250/94, E.C.R., 1995, I-4821) which affirmed the direct effect of Article 73 of the Treaty and recognised as admissible only limited controls on the large capital movements for the purpose of trying to prevent illicit activities.

the changeover to the euro. This is due to the fact that, before 1999, the presence of many national currencies, and the resulting existence of exchange rate risk, constituted an obstacle to financial integration in the Union, by limiting the attractiveness of cross-border investments and discouraging the process of regulatory harmonisation.[36]

The degree of financial integration that followed the introduction of the euro and the elimination of exchange rate risk is visible both in the greater homogeneity of the markets (with a consolidation among intermediaries and exchanges and the emergence of new products and techniques), and in the fact that policy-makers (once the euro has highlighted the costs of the remaining fragmentation), have assigned a high political priority to the completion of the internal market as a means of preserving the competitivity of previously protected national financial systems.[37]

A very brief overview of the different sectors of financial markets that have undergone changes with the Economic and Monetary Union and the euro may be useful in assessing the effective degree of integration achieved and the areas where the process is still taking place.[38]

---

[36] See Commission Report 'The euro area in the world economy', p. 28.

[37] Ibid.

[38] For the scope of the analysis, it is convenient to provide a definition of the notion of 'integration' of the market. Among the various definitions which have been proposed, a broad definition that has been used for measuring precisely the degree of integration of financial markets in the euro area (and that deals mainly with the asymmetric effects of existing frictions or barriers to the intermediation process, where the smaller the asymmetric friction is, the greater the degree of integration), affirms that a market for a given set of financial instruments and/or services is integrated when all potential market participants: (a) face the same set of rules when dealing with those financial instruments or services; (b) have equal access to the instruments or services; and (c) are treated equally when they are active in the market. See L. Baele, A. Ferrando, P. Hördahl, E. Krylova, C. Monnet, 'Measuring financial integration in the euro area', European Central Bank Occasional Papers, n. 14, April 2004, p. 6.

This definition of integration also encompasses, as its most significant implication, the law of one price, which states that, if assets have identical risks and returns, then they should be priced identically regardless of where they are transacted; therefore, where the law of one price is not in equilibrium, there is room for arbitrage opportunities. (Baele, Ferrando, Hördahl, Krylova, Monnet, 'Measuring financial integration in the euro area', p. 7.)

The studies on the effective degree of integration take into consideration different factors (market structure, qualitative and quantitative integration, convergence) and most of them analyse the data from an economic point of view. The scope of this brief overview, instead, is that of accounting for the areas where the adoption of common financial instruments and regulations has been the key to promoting integration, thus highlighting those areas where operators and study groups have identified the need for further legal harmonisation.

3.1. The money market

The first sector of the market that can be analysed is the money and derivatives market. The money market segment (which refers to short-term debt) generally comprises unsecured debt derivatives of short-term debt and secured debt. This market is central in the transmission mechanism of monetary policy (as it is used by the Eurosystem to distribute liquidity to the market), and therefore the integration of this market is essential to allow a smooth and equal distribution of liquidity between markets and across country borders.[39]

In the unsecured market segment, the introduction of the euro has eliminated exchange rate risk in cross-border transactions; this has allowed better management of liquidity between banks (which can occur through a single pool), also owing to systems such as Real Time Gross Settlement (RTGS), which are used to transfer liquidity in the Gross Capital Market.[40] Cross-border transactions account for a large part of the total inter-bank activity of the largest market participants.[41] The efficient distribution of liquidity in cross-border transactions also encourages interest rate convergence; and the convergence of short-term interest rates constitutes another index of the integration of the short-term money market, together with the availability of large volumes on the money market (even for a limited maturity spectrum) and an increase in the average deal size.[42]

---

[39] Baele et al., 'Measuring financial integration in the euro area', p. 23. As noted by some of the more recent reports on financial integration in Europe which take account of the effects of the 2007-2008 financial crisis on market integration, the money markets, which by its nature is most vulnerable and sensitive to counterparty risk, while on the one hand was strongly affected by the crisis, on the other hand seems to have been the market where recovery was more prompt and evident (see the European Central Bank's 'Financial Integration in Europe 2010', p. 13).

[40] See European Central bank, 'Developments in banks' liquidity profile and management', 2002, p. 14 et seq.; see R.G. Barresi, 'The European Union: the impact of monetary union and the euro on European capital markets: what may be achieved in capital market integration', *Fordham International Law Journal*, 2005, vol. 28, p. 1291.

[41] The inter-bank market has developed a two-tier structure for the distribution of liquidity, with large banks dominating cross-border transactions and smaller banks operating transactions at local level using the larger banks for their funding. The explanation of this apportionment lies in the fact that only large banks can access the cross-border capital market, while smaller banks, taking advantage of market segmentation, can be more selective in their operations. See Commission Report 'The euro area in the world economy', p. 29. European Central Bank, 'Developments in banks' liquidity profile and management', p. 12; Barresi, 'The European Union: the impact of monetary union and the euro', p. 1295.

[42] European Central Bank, 'Developments in banks' liquidity profile and management', p. 16.

The convergence of interest rates is also confirmed by the full acceptance by market operators of EONIA (Euro Overnight Index Average)[43] and EURIBOR (Euro-Inter-Bank Offered Rate)[44] as uniform price references. While the interest rate in the money market is leveraged on reserves regulations by the European Central Bank on a weekly basis (through weekly auctions carried out by the European Central Bank), for shorter periods in between auctions, banks which wish to improve their monthly deposit average have to borrow liquidity either from the European Central Bank or from their National central banks. This is when the EONIA and EURIBOR indexes are used.

For longer periods, 'repo' transactions are carried out. Repos are liquidity-providing reverse transactions based on repurchase agreements, whereby an asset is sold while the seller simultaneously retains the right to reverse the transaction at a specific price on a future date or on demand.[45] However, the creation of an integrated repo market in the euro area is still a challenge – in part hampered by lack of legal harmonisation.[46]

It is also through these open market operations based on reverse transactions that the European Central Bank controls the monetary aggregate, steers interest rates and manages the liquidity situation in the market. The five instruments that the Eurosystem disposes of for the conduct of open market operations are: reverse transactions (operations

---

[43] EONIA is the reference rate at which liquidity is offered between Euro-prime banks for very short periods, and it is calculated by the European Central Bank as a weighted average of all overnight unsecured lending transactions undertaken in the interbank market by a number of contributing panel banks.

[44] The EURIBOR is the benchmark rate at which Euro-prime banks offer short-term deposits to each other.

[45] With reference to indexes, securities that are eligible as collateral for these operations by the European Central Bank (indicated by the EUREPO reference rate) have also become largely accepted by the private 'repo' market; accordingly the EUREPO market is used by the private sector banking for the management of liquidity requirements. See Barresi, 'The European Union: the impact of monetary union and the euro' pp. 1292–1293.

[46] Significant data collected by the European Central Bank money-market survey on the geographical distribution of collateral on the borrowing side shows that the share of national collateral is still predominant. The main obstacles to the full integration of the repo market lie, according to the same survey, in the diversity of types of securities in the euro area, the fragmentation of the settlement infrastructure, and the differences of legal frameworks. See European Central Bank, 'Euro money market study 2004', May 2005 (hereinafter 'Euro money market study 2004'), (available at http://www.ecb.int/pub/pdf/other/euromoneymarketstudy200505en.pdf), at p. 21. The same conclusions are confirmed by Baele et al., 'Measuring Financial Integration in the Euro Area', p. 33.

whereby national central banks buy or sell assets under a repurchase agreement or conduct credit operations against collateral); outright transactions; issuance of debt certificates; foreign exchange swap; and collection of fixed-term deposits.[47]

As for the market for unsecured inter-bank deposits, integration is virtually complete.[48] The euro-area derivatives market is also highly integrated. The cross-border market for euro interest rate swaps (one of the most important segments of the derivatives of short-term debt market), has expanded sharply since the introduction of the euro and the EONIA swap market has developed rapidly, leading to an increasingly homogenous and integrated swap market in the euro area.[49] Evidence of the high degree of market integration lies, *inter alia*, in narrow bid-ask spreads. In other derivatives markets, where activity has also expanded, the EURIBOR-based future contracts have substituted all

---

[47] These operations can be further classified, with regard to their aims and procedures, into: (a) main refinancing operations (regular liquidity-providing reverse transactions with a weekly frequency and a maturity of normally one week); (b) longer-term refinancing operations (with a monthly frequency and a maturity of normally three months); (c) fine-tuning operations (*ad hoc* operations, having the aim of managing the liquidity situation of the market and of steering interest rates, particularly in the case of unexpected liquidity fluctuations in the market); (d) structural operations (which can be carried out through issuance of debt certificates, reverse transactions or outright transactions, whenever the European Central Bank wishes to adjust the structural position of the Eurosystem with reference to the financial sector). See European Central Bank, 'The implementation of monetary policy in the euro area', February 2005, pp. 9–10, available at: http://www.ecb.int/pub/pdf/other/gendoc2005en.pdf.

[48] Commission Report 'The euro area in the world economy', cit. at p. 29; L. Baele et al., 'Measuring financial integration in the euro area', pp. 25–8, also reporting the results of various studies (adopting different measurement methods) on money market integration. See also for a detailed account of the characteristics and development of the money market over the very recent past years, the survey conducted by the European Central Bank and the National Central Banks part of the European System of Central Banks before 1 May 2004: European Central Bank, 'Euro money market study 2004'.

This segment of the market is also the least concentrated from a structural point of view, as opposed to the forward rate agreement, other interest rate swap and cross-currency swap segments of the market that are highly concentrated, with the ten largest institutions holding more than 70 per cent of the market share in each case. See European Central Bank, 'Euro money market study 2004', p. 5.

[49] Euro interest rate swap operations involve an exchange of periodic payments of interest rates according to some pre-specified formula, based on an underlying principal, which itself is not exchanged. When, as often occurs, there is an exchange of a fixed amount per payment period for a payment that is not fixed, the floating side of the swap is usually linked to another interest rate, such as the EURIBOR reference rate or the EONIA. See Baele et al., 'Measuring financial integration in the euro area', p. 24.

futures contracts in legacy currencies that existed before the Economic and Monetary Union.[50]

The secured market segment (comprising operations involving the exchange of liquidity for collateral) remains very fragmented, although robust growth has been registered in the last few years.[51] The establishment of the Economic and Monetary Union has accelerated the integration process of the securities trading, clearing and settlement industry within the euro area, as demonstrated by the growth in the volume of traded securities; however, the costs of cross-border transactions have remained high when compared with those of domestic transactions. One of the developing trends to overcome the increased costs of cross-system trading, clearing and settling (due to differences in trading systems) has been the international consolidation of the securities market infrastructures (especially of stock exchanges, central securities depositories and central counterparties).[52]

Studies and surveys seem to agree in identifying obstacles to integration in the persisting differences in practices, laws and regulations, the diversity of types of securities in the euro area, the different tax/legal treatments applied to securities as collateral and the fragmentation of the settlement infrastructure. The results of an *ad hoc* study group[53]

---

[50] See Commission Report 'The euro area in the world economy', at p. 30. Price-based measures of integration in the euro area interest rate swap market also confirm a high degree of integration shortly after the euro's introduction, as demonstrated by the convergence of swap rates in the Euro area. See Baele et al., 'Measuring financial integration in the euro area', p. 31.

Further development of this segment may derive from the creation (sponsored by the European Banking Federation, FBE) of a new derivative benchmark for money market derivatives: the new EONIA Swap Index, that completes the existing benchmarks for the unsecured (EURIBOR index) and secured (EUREPO) cash markets. See European Central Bank, 'Euro money market study 2004', p. 34.

[51] The possible explanations for the growth of the secured market in the last few years brought forward by the European Central Bank (See 'Euro money market study 2004', p. 17) include the ongoing securitisation/disintermediation process of the securities market; the need to limit credit risk exposures and constraints resulting from capital adequacy requirements; bank treasurers' desire to maximise return on their securities holdings; the growing integration of the securities market segment in the euro area; a wider use of tri-party repos (repo operations involving third parties, normally a custodian bank, acting as an agent to exchange cash and collateral for one or both parties) as means of reducing settlement problems.

[52] For a detailed account of the consolidation measures adopted, see H. Schmiedel, A. Schönenberger, 'Integration of securities market infrastructures in the euro area', ECB Occasional Papers, n. 33, July 2005 (available at: http://www.ecb.int/pub/pdf/scpops/ecbocp33.pdf), pp. 10–22.

[53] In 1996 the European Commission invited the Italian banker Alberto Giovannini to form a group of financial market experts to study the markets and offer advice on

assert that the securitisation of the short-term capital market failed for both legislative (differences of laws, regulations and taxes) and logistical reasons (lack of a single infrastructure platform for the market).[54]

It is partly in response to these findings that important legal provisions have been adopted, namely the Directive on Financial Collateral Arrangements[55] (concerning netting arrangements and the use of securities as collateral, and determining which national law is to apply in cross-border arrangements of collateral) and the Settlement Finality Directive.[56]

3.2. Bond markets

With the introduction of the euro, the national bond markets of the participating member states have integrated to form a more homogeneous euro-denominated bond market. This market segment has indicatively increased in its volume of issuance since 1999 as compared with the situation before the Economic and Monetary Union (and there has also been a significant surge in the share of private sector compared with

---

how to prepare for the Economic and Monetary Union. Accordingly, the Giovannini Group has produced five reports, that deal respectively with: 'The impact of the introduction of the euro on capital markets', 1997, available at http://europa. eu.int/comm/economy_finance/publications/euro papers/2001/eup03en.pdf; 'EU repo markets: opportunities for change' 1999, available at http://europa.eu.int/ comm/economy_finance/publications/euro papers/2001/eup35en.pdf; 'Co-ordinated public debt issuance in the euro area' 2000, available at http://europa.eu.int/comm/ economy_finance/publications/giovannini/giovannini081100en.pdf; 'Cross-border clearing and settlement arrangements in the European Union' 2001, available at http:// europa.eu.int/comm/economy finance/publications/giovannini/clearing1101_en.pdf; 'Second report on EU clearing and settlement arrangements', 2003, available at http://www.europa.eu.int/comm/economy finance/ publications/giovannini/clearing settlement arrangements140403.pdf .

[54] See The Giovannini Group, 'The EU repo markets: opportunities for change', 1999, p. 5. Specific recommendations to the legislators for reform, contained in the EU Repo Markets Report include: 'reforms to enable repo activity to be taken on the basis of sound and safe credit risk management, and particularly: the legal recognition of netting against counterparties in its broadest possible forms throughout the EU; ensuring the legal reliability of collateralisation techniques and practices; the extension of "finality" recognition both to bilateral repo activity and to the clearing and settlement systems supporting the repo market.' See Giovannini Group, 'The EU repo markets', p. 6. This data is confirmed by later reports notwithstanding the introduction in 2008 of the STEP initiative which fosters the integration of this market segment by prompting the convergence of market standards (European Central Bank 'Financial Integration in Europe 2010', p. 18).

[55] Directive 2002/47/EC, of 6 June 2002, O.J. L168, 27 June 2002, p. 43.

[56] Directive 98/26/EC of 19 May 1998 on settlement finality in payment and securities settlement systems, O.J. L166, 11 June 1998, p. 45.

sovereign issuance).[57] Integration is also shown by the creation of a common trading platform, the EuroMTS, for the public debt issues of the twelve euro-area member states.

A sign of the greater homogeneity of the government bond market lies in the highly convergent short-term yields across the member states (when compared with the pre-Economic and Monetary Union situation), and this convergence in the short term yields can be attributed both to the elimination of exchange rate risk and to the improvement of the budgetary conditions of several member states.[58] However, for long-term interest rates, there remains a persisting difference between the national debt issuances of the member states.[59]

There has also been a growth in the importance of the euro as an international investment currency on the international bond market, and the attractiveness of euro-denominated bonds can be attributed to increased competition between market segments and to different issuer types in the euro area.[60]

As for legal instruments which have helped to promote the integration and growth of the bond market, two directives must be mentioned: the Prospectus Directive[61] establishing a European standard for the documents that support the issuance of securities (thus simplifying the reference for market operators from different national regulations to a single set of European rules), and the Transparency Directive[62] concerning the harmonisation of transparency requirements in relation

---

[57] The sovereign issuance segment remains the most important segment of the bond market in the euro-area and this dominance can be attributed to several factors. According to the European Central Bank's 'Euro Bond Market Study 2004', these factors include: 'the size of the market, the credit-worthiness of the borrowers, the availability of a wide range of maturities, the fungibility of issues facilitating trading, the high liquidity (particularly of recently issued securities), the fact of being accepted in open market operations and lending facilities, the existence of well-developed repo- and derivatives market and, as a result of these features, the coexistence of benchmark yield curves'. See European Central Bank, 'The Euro Bond Market Study 2004', (available at http://www.ecb.int/pub/pdf/other/eurobondmarketstudy2004en.pdf), p. 10.

[58] See Commission Report 'The euro area in the world economy', p. 31.

[59] Attempts at explaining this persisting spread have alternatively indicated liquidity factors (implying an inefficient market due to differences in national issuing techniques, shares and durations, and calling for public debt issue coordination) or credit risk factors (implying on the contrary an efficient market where capital is allocated according to expectations in the performance of the national economies). See Barresi, 'The European Union: The Impact of Monetary Union and the Euro', p. 1296.

[60] See for further details, European Central Bank, 'The Euro Bond Market Study 2004', p. 8.

[61] Directive 2003/71/EC of 4 November 2003, *O.J.* L 345, 31 December 2003, p. 64.

[62] Directive 2004/109/EC of 15 Decmeber 2004, *O.J.* L390, 31 December 2004 p. 38, amending Directive 2001/34/EC.

to information about issuers whose securities are admitted to trading on a regulated market.

3.3. Equity markets

Since the introduction of the single currency, the equity market segment of the euro-area has undergone both a significant growth, with an increased demand for cross-border equity investments, and important structural changes, in the form of mergers between stock exchanges.[63] The consolidation of formal stock exchanges of some of the member states in the EU has been one of the responses to increased competition in the markets, competition which has also been enhanced by the various electronic trading networks established in recent years.

The merger of the Amsterdam, Brussels and Paris stock exchanges in 2000 to form Euronext, further enlarged in 2001 with the incorporation of Liffe, the London derivatives trading platform, and the Lisbon and Porto stock exchanges, is the most prominent example of this type of consolidation. At the same time, the failure of the merger between the London stock exchange and the Deutsche Börse (under the name of iX, International Exchange) indicates that the consolidation of equity markets is not yet complete.

The existing differences and fragmentation in regulatory and cross-country settlement and clearing systems between the member states account for the relatively slow speed of consolidation of the equity markets, with the consequence that cross-border equity transaction costs are considerably higher than the costs for domestic transactions.[64] Evidence of integration in this market segment can be found in an increase

---

[63] Although Continental Europe continues to be characterised (with reference to industry financing) as a 'bank-based' system when compared to the 'market-based' US and UK systems, the equity market in the euro area has grown substantially over the last years both in absolute value and in reference to gross domestic product. (See L. Baele et al., 'Measuring financial integration in the euro area', p. 67.)

The growth can be attributed to different factors, including a relatively high amount of new equity issues in the euro area. As for the increase in demand originating both from households and institutional investors, explanations identified by L. Baele et al. ('Measuring Financial Integration in the Euro Area', p. 69) lie in: (a) the demographic trend of an ageing population with the consequent increase in the total assets managed by euro-area pension funds, with a rise in the proportion of equity in their total portfolios; (b) the convergence of interest rates across euro area countries to historically low levels, resulting in a reallocation of investments towards equity markets; (c) the removal, achieved by EU directives, of the existing barriers to international equity investments; (d) the growth in the number of investment funds, entailing a facilitated construction of diversified portfolios for smaller investors.

[64] See L. Baele et al., 'Measuring financial integration in the euro area', p. 69.

in sectorally related movement of equity prices across the markets of the member states, indicating a shift in investor choices from country-based investments toward sector-based investments (where the differences in indices depend on the differences in composition).[65] Investors have also gradually decreased the proportion of domestic equity in their portfolios and have opted for pan-European or global asset strategies, with a resulting increase in the number of pan-European or global indices and the success of related derivative contracts.[66]

4. Payments: the Single Euro Payment Area and the Directive on Payment Services

Market-driven forces towards integration have concerned not only the capital markets, but other sectors as well, particularly the banking sector, with efforts towards single payments and single market conventions. There are different factors that may explain the delay in developing efficient cross-border retail payment systems in Europe, even though the issue has attracted the attention of EU policy-makers and has been monitored by public authorities ever since the creation of the single market. Among the infrastructural factors, there is the existence of different national payment systems, which have developed under different historical contexts, governance, access, pricing and transparency traditions, and legislative environments, and are thus responsible for a fragmented retail payment infrastructure in the EU largely based on national payment habits and characteristics. It has also been observed that payment habits are slow to change.[67]

Another factor which has hampered the development of efficient cross-border retail payment systems is standardisation. Whereas at the domestic level standards in retail payment systems have indeed been traditionally set by national authorities and banking associations (relatively small and homogenous stakeholder groups), at the cross-border level the existence of a greater number of different parties and the adherence to heterogeneous domestic standards has made standardisation more problematic.[68] What must be noted, however, is that the total volume of cross-border retail payments is very low. These data can be read in two ways, in a sort of vicious circle: it may on the one

---

[65] See Commission Report 'The euro area in the world economy', p. 33. See also European Central Bank 'Financial Integration in Europe 2010' pp. 25–26.

[66] L. Baele et al., 'Measuring financial integration in the euro area', p. 69.

[67] For these observations, see K. Kemppainen, 'Regulation of cross-border retail payment systems – a network industry problem', in D.G. Mayes, G.E. Wood, *The Structure of Financial Regulation*, London and New York, 2007, pp. 308–310.

[68] Ibid.

hand depend on the absence of efficient and low-cost cross-border retail payment systems; on the other, the low volume of overall transactions of this type may be a scant incentive for service providers to develop efficient cross-border systems.

The problem of the disparities in costs of retail payments, cash withdrawal and credit transfers between member states in the euro area after the introduction of the euro, notwithstanding the principles of 'fair dealing' contained in Directive 97/5/EC,[69] induced the Commission, after a Communication[70] calling for a 'market-led approach requiring voluntary cooperation by the banking sector' which however did not lead to any concrete results, to propose the Regulation on Cross-border payments in euros.[71]

The reaction of the banking sector to the Regulation, which aimed at bringing the costs of cross-border payments and credit transfers into line with national transaction fees, was the proposal for the creation of a Single Euro Payment Area (SEPA) by 2010[72] under the guidance of the European Payments Council.[73] The banking sector advocated a market-driven solution to the problem of the costs of cross-border retail payments and proposed that the necessary harmonisation of payment systems and instruments be implemented as much as possible by self-regulation. Given the existence of heterogeneous payment areas within the EU, especially

---

[69]Directive 97/5/EC, of 27 January 1997 on cross-border credit transfers, O.J. L043, 14 February 1997, p. 25.

[70]COM (2000)36, 30 January 2000, Communication from the Commission on Retail payments in the internal market.

[71]Regulation 2560/2001/EC of 19 December 2001, O.J. L344, 28 December 2001, p. 13. The Regulation obliges banks to reduce charges for cross-border payments (up to a certain amount) to the level of those corresponding to domestic payments. This Regulation has been repealed by Regulation 924/2009/EC of 16 September 2009, on cross-border payments in the Community, O.J. L266, 9 October 2009, p. 11, which while maintaining the parameter of domestic payments for the determination of charges for cross-border payments, also aims at solving the problems due to the disruption of the internal market in payments caused by divergent statistical reporting obligations, the absence of out-of-court redress bodies for disputes related to Regulation 2560/2001, the problems in the enforcement of Regulation 2560/2001 due to a lack of identified national competent authorities, and the fact that Regulation 2560/2001 does not cover direct debits.

[72]European Banking Federation White Paper 'Euroland: our single payments area'.

[73]The European Payments Council is the decision-making organism in payment processing for the European banking industry. It is a self-regulatory body, which consists of 65 European banks, including the three European credit sector associations and the Euro Banking Association. The European Payments Council also proposed the development of a Pan-European Automated Clearing House (PEACH) for the processing of cross-border credit transfers, as a response to the obstacle to integration constituted by the different standards used by the national Automated Clearing Houses.

as far as retail payment systems at the national level are concerned, it has been noted that the creation of the SEPA may not necessarily mean a total harmonisation of the national payments and habits, but rather, the establishment of a reliable and efficient cross-border retail payment system.[74]

The European Payments Council has proposed a gradual harmonisation of the infrastructures, starting from credit transfers, in combination with existing clearing and settlement systems, and then proceeding to the creation of a pan-European infrastructure for payments. The project of the banking industry has focused principally on the development of SEPA payment instruments, to be implemented by addressing three main fields. First of all the industry developed new payment schemes for credit transfers and direct debits and formulated a framework for card payments. Second, additional optional services, which could improve the handling of payments were investigated. Finally, the industry identified principles for the underlying processing infrastructures and addressed standardisation issues.[75]

---

[74]Kemppianen, *Regulation of Cross-border Retail Payment Systems*, p. 310.

[75]As far as credit transfers and direct debits are concerned, the European Payments Council has proposed a 'replacement' strategy, with new common schemes designed for euro payments which are recorded in a rulebook covering the rules, practices and standards applicable to such euro payments. For card payments, a different 'adaptation' strategy has been chosen, allowing the existing schemes and their operators to adjust to a new set of business and technical standards and processes. In both approaches there is a separation of schemes (rules, practices and standards) from infrastructures.

The Single Euro Payment Area credit transfer scheme is an interbank payment scheme that defines a common set of rules and processes for credit transfers denominated in euros. Its main features are that any customer can be reached; the full amount is credited to the beneficiary's account; there is no limit on the value of the payment; there is a maximum settlement time; the International Bank Account Number (IBAN) and the Bank Identifier Code (BIC) are used as account numbers; there are rules covering the case of rejected or returned payments.

The direct debit scheme (applicable to transfers initiated by the payee via the payee's bank after agreement between the payee and the payer) is characterised by full-reach to any receiver; covering of both recurrent and one-off payments in euros; a maximum settlement time; separation of scheme and processing infrastructure; the use of IBAN and BIC as account identifiers and the provision of a set of rules for rejected and returned payments.

As far as the creation of infrastructures is concerned, the SEPA project aims at creating a clearing and settlement framework providing the principles upon which infrastructure providers will support the payment instrument schemes (credit transfer and direct debit schemes). Standardisation within the project aims at developing standards to allow automated processing of all euro-denominated payments (including the identification of the business requirements that describe the data elements to be exchanged between financial instruments and their translation into logical data elements; and the further translation by the International Organisation for

Another market-driven initiative deriving from the banking sector has been the compilation, in 1998, of the so-called 'market conventions', regarding some of the techniques used by credit institutions (referring, for example, to the manner of computing interest rates, the periodicity of paying interest coupons, treatment of bank holidays, time differences, the method of making and describing rates between currencies, and the settlement periods).[76]

While the SEPA project and the development of the related payment instruments are purely market-led initiatives, an important EU legislative instrument was issued in 2007: the Directive on Payment Services,[77] aiming at the establishment at Community level of a legal framework for payment services.

The interaction between the industry-led initiative and the EU legislation is visible in the fact that the European Payments Council considers the Payment Services Directive as providing the legal basis for the SEPA project. Indeed, not only does the Directive regulate the activity of the payment services industry; it also specifies certain technical terms which were 'left open' to determination in the outline of the SEPA project.[78] Furthermore, in its Preamble, the Directive refers to the need to 'establish at Community level a modern and coherent legal framework for payment services, whether or not the services are compatible with the system resulting from the financial sector initiative for a single euro payments area [...]'.[79]

The Directive covers four areas in which coordination of national provisions is pursued. These areas concern the provisions on prudential requirements; the access of new payment service providers to the market; information requirements; the respective rights and obligations of payment service users and providers.

Standardisation of these logical data elements into universal financial industry message standards, the UNIFI (ISO 20022) XML message standards).

[76]The market conventions are available at http://www.ecb.int. See also Sáinz de Vicuña, 'The legal integration of financial markets of the euro area', p. 19, who refers to two other initiatives promoted by the banking sector: the guidelines and conventions for interbank euro payments proposed by the so-called 'Heathrow Group', a forum of leading banks from Europe, New York and Japan (available at http://www.feb.be/e_pages/heathrow.htm); and the 'Guidelines on liquidity management within the framework of TARGET' for participants of the euro inter-bank money market, published by the European Banking Federation in December 1998 (available at http://www.fbe.be).

[77]Directive 2007/64/EC of 13 November 2007, O.J. L319, 5 December 2007, p. 1.

[78]For example, the settlement term for the SEPA payment instruments depends on the settlement term defined in the Payment Services Directive.

[79]Fourth recital of the Preamble to Directive 2007/64/EC.

While the first three areas concern regulatory aspects (and it should be signalled that the Directive adopts the consolidated home-country control scheme), from the point of view of substantive law, it is Title IV on 'Rights and Obligations in Relation to the Provision and Use of Payment Services' that is particularly interesting. Indeed, as far as the private law rules on payment of debts are concerned, the provisions of the Directive significantly regulate some of the fundamental aspects of payment obligations.

For example, the Directive defines the point in time of receipt of payment orders as 'the time when the payment order transmitted directly by the payer or indirectly by or through a payee is received by the payer's payment service provider'.[80] The Directive thus implicitly harmonises the moment in which the payment service provider becomes liable for the processing of the payment. The issue concerns the relation (in terms of liability) between the payment service user and the payment service provider from the moment in which the debtor transmits the payment order to the moment in which the payee receives the payment.

When considering payments, liability can arise with reference both to non-performance and to the typical risks inherent in the performance of monetary obligations (i.e. variations in the exchange rate value between the issue of the payment order and the moment of settlement).

As far as the identification of the liable subjects is concerned, a first hypothesis regards the 'internal' relation between the payment service user (either payer or payee) and the payment service provider, and can be construed in terms of non-performance; as such it is disciplined by Article 75 of the Directive ('non-execution or defective execution'). According to this provision, the payment service provider 'shall be liable to the payer for the correct execution of the payment transaction, unless he can prove to the payer, and where relevant, to the payee's payment service provider that the payee's payment service provider received the amount of the payment transaction ... in which case the payee's payment service provider shall be liable to the payee for the correct execution of the payment transaction'.

Liability is constructed in such a way that the two service providers are each liable to their 'respective' user (the payer or the payee), according to the proof of receipt of the amount of the payment transaction. The determination of when there is transfer of liability between the two service providers thus becomes central. Article 75 provides that, in order to exclude liability, the payment service provider of the payer which received the payment order has to prove that 'the payee's payment service provider received the amount of the payment transaction in accordance

---

[80] Article 64 Directive 2007/64/EC.

with Article 69(1)'. The latter provision states that payer's payment service providers will be required to 'ensure that after the point in time of receipt, the amount of the payment transaction is credited to the payee's payment service provider's account at the latest by the end of the next business day'. This provision should also be read in relation with Article 59, which provides for the hypothesis of denial by payment service user of authorisation of an executed payment transaction and of a claim that the payment transaction was not correctly executed and affirms that in such case 'it is for his payment service provider to prove that the payment transaction was authenticated, accurately recorded, entered in the accounts and not affected by a technical breakdown or some other deficiency'. It is thus possible to assume that the burden of proof (in both cases of Articles 59 and 75) of the executed payment consists in proving the payment procedure as described above.

What is not cleared is whether, with the transmission of the payment order, debtor (when the payment order is issued by the payer) can be considered to have performed their obligation. As far as the relation (and liability) between the payer and the payee is concerned, and more specifically the issue of whether the act of transferring funds to a payment service provider discharges the debtor, it seems that the problem does not come within the scope of the Directive. Not only is there no reference to this type of liability nor consideration of the relation between the payer and the payee; this conclusion can also be drawn when considering Article 4, n. 5 of the Directive, which defines 'payment transaction' as 'an act, initiated by the payer or by the payee, of placing, transferring or withdrawing funds, irrespective of any underlying obligations between the payer and the payee'.

It should be noted that the fact that the Directive does not regulate the aspects related to the underlying obligations between the payer and the payee may also be attributed to the extensive differences between national laws and judicial practice concerning the discipline of payment instruments and their efficacy as good tender.[81] These divergences in discipline depend on domestic substantive law and it seems intuitive that a harmonisation of these rules requires incisive interventions on national rules regulating debtor/creditor relations: one of the institutions of private law that very strongly characterises legal systems (and differentiates them from each other).

---

[81] See *supra* Chapter. 1.

Chapter 3:
Legal Integration of the Markets and Harmonisation of Substantive Law: Clearing and Settlement of Securities and Payments

I. Perspectives of substantive law: options for harmonisation

European capital and financial markets are undergoing a process of rapid integration, strongly accelerated with the complete realisation of the Economic and Monetary Union. The market mechanisms integrate faster than the legislative ones; however, a harmonisation of the rules is as necessary as the harmonisation of the exchange mechanisms and financial operations. This process has been summarised in the expression 'one market, one currency, one law'.[1] As already observed, it is the last and final phase that remains to be achieved.

This chapter and the next will focus on how this could be done. It will first identify the two areas which, according to study groups and reports that have examined legal integration of European Union (EU) markets, are still hampered by legal barriers. These two areas are the securities market (and related problems of the use of collateral as securities in financial transactions), and payments.

This chapter will focus on the securities market, briefly illustrating how this type of market works and what the main problems are that it poses in cross-border transactions. It will examine the European Community (EC) legislation that has been enacted with the scope of harmonising certain aspects. Whether and how this goal has been achieved, however, will be further examined in the following chapters.

Legal integration consists first of all in a removal of existing legal barriers and secondly in a quest for some form of harmonisation of the rules. The harmonisation of the rules governing debts, market transactions and processes for the carrying out of market transactions (so-called ancillary market functions) can assume different forms, including a private-international law approach, binding substantive

---

[1] The expression is from A. Sáinz de Vicuña, 'The legal integration of financial markets of the euro area', in M. Andenas, Y. Avgerinos, (eds), *Financial Markets in Europe: Towards a Single Regulator*, The Hague, 2003, p. 3.

legislation (supranational in the case of the Economic and Monetary Union), or leaving the market operators with sufficient autonomy to develop and apply soft law. What is clear is that the development of an integrated venue for financial transactions has entailed a change in the sources regulating monetary debts and certain market operations. The open issues concern which of the above options is the most efficient for the scope and which subjects would be the most appropriate legislators.

The securities market is paradigmatic because it has gone through different phases (detailed harmonisation directives, mutual recognition, general directives, a private international law convention) but still remains one of the most problematic areas for integration. What follows is a brief description of the results of reports that have studied EU financial market integration, and then a description of how this market segment works.

2. Integration of the markets and legal barriers

As observed above, the rapid advancement and completion of the Economic and Monetary Union has given a significant input to the adoption of a series of measures for the realisation of a single financial market. Areas of focus (identified by the Financial Services Action Plan) include measures ranging from taking up, pursuit and super-vision of businesses of electronic money institutions;[2] regulating insur-ance undertakings;[3] money laundering;[4] capital markets and securities;[5]

---

[2]Directive 2000/46/EC of 18 September 2000 on the taking up, pursuit of and prudential supervision of the business of electronic money institutions, *O.J.* L275, 27 October 2000, p. 39.

[3]Directive 2001/17/EC of 19 March 2001 on the reorganisation and winding-up of insurance undertakings, *O.J.* L110, 20 April 2001, p. 28; Directives 2002/12/EC of 5 March 2002, *O.J.* L77, 20 March 2002 p. 11, and 2002/13/EC of 5 March 2002, *O.J.* L77, 20 March 2002 p. 17 amending the solvency requirements in the insurance directives; Directive 2002/92/EC, of 9 December 2002 on insurance mediation, *O.J.* L9, 15 January 2003, p. 3.

[4]Directive 2001/97/EC of 4 December 2001 amending the money laundering directive, *O.J.* L344, 28 December 2001, p. 76.

[5]Directives 2001/107/EC of 21 January 2002, *O.J.* L41, 13 February 2002, p. 20, and 2001/108/EC of 21 January 2002, *O.J.* L41, 13 February 2002, p. 35, on coordination of laws relating to undertakings for collective investment in transferable securities (UCITS); Directive 2002/47/EC of 6 June 2002 on financial collateral agreements, *O.J.* L168, 27 June 2002 p. 43; Directive 2002/65/EC of 23 September 2002 on distance marketing of Financial Services, *O.J.* L271, 9 October 2002, p. 16; Directive 2003/6/EC of 28 January 2003 on insider dealing and market manipulation, *O.J.* L96, 12 April 2003, p. 16; Directive 2003/71/EC of 4 November 2003 on prospectuses, *O.J.* L345, 31 December 2003, p. 64; Directive 2004/109/EC of 15 December 2004

accounting and company law;[6] and banking supervision.[7]

Concurrently, in the effort to complete the integration process, a series of studies have been conducted to measure the degree of integration of the EU financial market.[8] The analysis of different market segments has highlighted that, in the money market, the area that still remains the most fragmented is the secured market segment, which not incidentally is the segment in which legal barriers play a major role.[9] Indeed, one of the first causes of fragmentation of the secured market segment is that regulation of securities greatly depends on single national legislation involving such significant domestic disciplines as property law and company law. Cross-border exchange of equities becomes challenging since equities are heterogeneous instruments and are more complex to manage because of corporate actions and because of the need for continuous communication between the company that has issued the equity and its holder.[10] Furthermore, securities settlement mechanisms

---

on Transparency, *O.J.* L390, 31 December 2004, p. 38; Directive 2004/39/EC of 21 April 2004 on Markets in Financial Instruments, *O.J.* L145, 30 April 2004, p. 1.

[6] Directive 2003/51 of 18 June 2003 modernising the accounting provisions of the 4th and 7th Company Law Directives, *O.J.* L178, 17 July 2003, p. 16; Directive 2001/65/EC of 27 September 2001 amending the 4th and 7th Company Law Directives to allow fair value accounting, *O.J.* L283, 27 October 2001, p. 28; Directive 2004/25/EC of 21 April 2004 on Take Over Bids, *O.J.* L142, 30 April 2004, p. 12.

[7] Directive 2001/24/EC of 4 April 2001 on the reorganisation and winding-up of credit institutions, *O.J.* L125, 5 May 2001, p. 15, and Directive 2002/87/EC of 16 December 2002 on the supplementary supervision of credit institutions, insurance undertakings and investment firms in a financial conglomerate, *O.J.* L35, 11 February 2003, p. 1.

[8] One of the conditions for measuring financial integration is, according to a widely accepted definition, the existence for all potential market participants of the 'same set of rules' when dealing with financial services or instruments, together with 'equal access to the market' and 'equal treatment in the market' (See L. Baele, A. Ferrando, P. Hördahl, E. Krylova, C. Monnet, 'Measuring financial integration in the euro area', *European Central Bank Occasional Papers*, n. 14, April 2004, p. 6). Focus of this part will concern precisely the 'same set of rules' condition. The problem of market integration will thus here be analysed exclusively from the point of view of legal integration, without taking economic indicators into consideration. For a brief overview of the main economic indicators of integration in the money market segment, see *supra* Chapter II.

[9] See H. Schmiedel, A. Schönenberger, 'Integration of securities market infrastructures in the euro area', *European Central Bank Occasional Papers*, n. 33, July 2005, pp. 10–22.

[10] See The Giovannini Group, 'Cross-border clearing and settlement arrangements in the European Union', Brussels, 2001 [hereinafter '2001 Giovannini Report'], p. 20.

are often inconsistent with each other. All this accounts for the relatively slower development of the repurchase market.[11]

Some of the problems highlighted above recur to a minor extent in other sectors of the money market, such as unsecured debt or derivatives. Here the financial instruments that are exchanged are regulated at a centralised level, and thus ensure a greater degree of harmonisation.

The cross-border trading of bonds and derivatives is also much simpler than the transaction of equities, since bonds are settled at international central securities depositories (ICSDs), which allow a direct access to the investors and the payments can be made by any commercial bank which is a correspondent of the international central securities depositories.[12] Furthermore, bond exchanges are relatively more homogenous especially where they are fixed income instruments and where they have been commoditised.

The legal obstacles hampering the proper functioning of the European securities market have been highlighted by the Lamfalussy Report,[13] which recommended a reform of the EU regulatory structure for securities markets based, *inter alia*, on the findings of an absence of clear EU-wide regulation (preventing the implementation of a mutual recognition system); inconsistent implementation of the existing rules; differences in legal systems and in taxation procedures; political and external trade barriers; excessive rigidity, inefficiency and slowness of the existing regulatory framework (which impedes a speedy reaction to changing market conditions); and failure to distinguish essential framework principles from practical day-to-day implementing rules.[14]

---

[11] See the European Central Bank, 'Euro money market study 2004', May 2005, p. 21, identifying that the main obstacles to the full integration of the repo market lie in the diversity of types of securities in the euro area, the fragmentation of the settlement infrastructure, and the differences in legal frameworks.

[12] See C. Hirata de Carvalho, 'Cross-border securities clearing and settlement infrastructure in the European Union as a pre-requisite to financial markets integration: challenges and perspectives', HWWA Discussion Paper (Hamburgisches Welt-Wirtschafts-Archiv), n. 287, 2004, p. 23.

[13] Final Report of the Committee of Wise Men on The Regulation of European Securities Markets, Brussels, 2001 [hereinafter, 'Lamfalussy Final Report'], pp. 13–14 et seq.

[14] Since then, part of the implementation of the Financial Services Action Plan has adopted the proposed and so-called Lamfalussy legislative process, and has led to the enactment of a series of measures that had been signalled in the report (e.g. Market Abuse Directive, the Prospectus Directive, the Markets in Financial Instruments Directive and the Transparency Directive).

2.1. A paradigm: cross-border clearing and settlement of securities and payments

Markets must ensure the so-called ancillary functions for the execution of trades. These include the transfer (physical or electronic) and the payment of securities. Clearing and settlement processes are used both in transactions in securities and in payment systems. Settlement systems provide the essential infrastructure in order to ensure the performance of a contract once the terms of the trade have been agreed.[15] The focus here will be on cross-border transactions in securities, where significant legal barriers still constitute an obstacle to integration. However, the observations related to the impact on the notion of monetary obligations also extend to the hypothesis in which payment is being settled in a payments system. Transactions in securities usually involve four phases: trade, confirmation, clearing and settlement. The trade and confirmation processes enable the legal constitution of the securities transaction.[16]

The post-trade custody processes are referred to as clearing and settlement. Clearing and settlement are also carried out through four phases: (a) confirmation of the terms of the securities trade; (b) clearance of the trade by which the respective obligations of the buyer and seller are determined; (c) delivery of the securities from the seller to the buyer; and (d) reciprocal payment of funds.[17]

Clearing refers to all the activities from the time a transaction involving securities is made until it is settled (such as transmission and confirmation of transfer orders prior to settlement, the calculation of net positions and the establishment of final positions for settlement).[18] Settlement refers to the process through which titles to securities or interests in securities are transferred to fulfil contractual obligations such as those arising from securities transactions on stock exchanges, and when the securities transfer involves a simultaneous payment, the process is referred to as 'delivery versus payment' (DvP).[19]

---

[15] G. Sabatini, I. Tarola, 'Is governance an issue for plumbers? Remarks on consolidation of securities settlement systems,' in G.Ferrarini, K.J.Hopt, E. Wymeersch (eds) *Capital Markets in the Age of the Euro. Cross-border Transactions, Listed Companies and Regulation*, The Hague, London, New York, 2002, p. 217.

[16] See J. De Wolf, 'Tax barriers on the way towards an integrated European capital market: the EU savings directive as a challenge for clearing and settlement systems,' in *Legal Aspects of the European System of Central Banks. Liber Amicorum Paolo Zamboni Garavelli*, ECB, Frankfurt-am-Main, 2005, p. 342.

[17] See '2001 Giovannini Report,' p. 4.

[18] See K. M. Löber, 'The Developing EU Legal Framework for Clearing and Settlement of Financial Instruments', ECB Legal Working Paper Series, n. 1, 2006, p. 6.

[19] J. Benajmin, *Interests in Securities. A Proprietary Law Analysis of the International Securities Markets*, Oxford, 2000, pp. 20–21.

The processes of trade and confirmation are carried out by traders' front and middle offices, while settlement is a back office function.[20] The process of clearing is normally carried out by clearing houses. A central counterparty (CCP) may also be involved in the clearing process, acting as the buyer to every seller and the seller to every buyer, and reducing risks for market participants by offsetting or netting buy and sell trades and charging market participants solely with the standard credit risk of the central counterparty and not with that of the individual market participants.[21]

In the clearing phase, all mutual transactions between parties are set off through a process of compensation, in order to arrive at a single claim of securities and cash to be settled by the respective debtors. Clearance can be carried out on a gross basis, in which case the respective obligations of the parties are calculated individually and executed separately, or it can be carried out on a net basis, in which case the mutual obligations of the buyer and seller are offset in order to result in a single obligation between the two parties.

When a central counterparty is involved, there may be a legal novation of obligations, as the obligation of the two parties (the seller's obligation to deliver securities and the buyer's obligation to pay the price) are taken over by the central counterparty.[22] In the case of payments too the netting process can be carried out on a net basis (if the reciprocal obligations have been expressed and are due in the same currency), or through novation, or also through close-out (which operates in case of default of one of the parties, transforming into a single net obligation all the previous reciprocal obligations between the parties irrespective of the currency in which they were expressed or of their date of expiry).[23] Finally, the process of settlement is carried out by central securities depositaries (often providing both custody and settlement services), or, when cross-border transactions are involved, by international central securities depositories.

---

[20] Benjamin, *Interests in Securities*, p. 22.

[21] See Löber, 'The developing EU legal framework for clearing and settlement of financial instruments', p. 6, and Hirata de Carvalho, 'Cross-border securities clearing and settlement infrastructure in the European Union', p. 19.

[22] See De Wolf, *Tax Barriers on the Way Towards an Integrated European Capital Market*, p. 342.

[23] Netting procedures are usually multi-lateral in regulated markets, where they are carried out by clearing houses, and bilateral in case of over-the-counter (OTC) derivatives, where it is the two parties of a Master Agreement that carry out the procedure. However, multilateral netting also exists for OTC derivatives (e.g. The London Clearing House carries out this type of procedure). See P. De Biasi, 'Un nuovo Master Agreement per strumenti finanziari sofisticati', *Banca, borsa e titoli di credito*, 2001, I, p. 646.

As for the role of intermediaries (the more intermediaries are involved in the trading process, the higher the risks and the costs for the investor counterparties), the market structures for exchange-traded derivatives have evolved differently from those for the fixed-income and equity markets. Whilst in the cross-border trading of bonds and equities the international central securities depositories are fundamental, in the market for derivatives, trades (based on an open or closed bilateral contract between two market participants) occur with the clearing house acting as a central counterparty. In an exchange-traded derivative clearing is the core process (while it is simply a post-execution stage together with settlement in a securities transaction), and therefore central counterparties play a role that is analogous to central securities depositories in a securities market.[24]

Settlement may occur either in physical form, albeit very rarely (when the securities are traded in paper form), or as is the usual case, through book-entries, when securities are either immobilised (permanently held by the central securities depository and not circulated), or dematerialised (when securities are converted into electronic records). Immobilisation necessarily involves a depositary that holds the underlying securities, whereas with dematerialisation a depositary is optional, and where one is involved the system becomes an indirect one.[25]

The book-entries (credits and debits to securities accounts) are considered from the economical and commercial point of view as being equivalent to the physical holding of securities. However, the legal status of these book-entries is not uniform across different states. As has been highlighted *inter alia* by the Second Giovannini Report on EU Clearing and Settlement Arrangements, 'there is a lack of clarity about who has what rights and of what kind when securities are held for investors by means of an intermediary's accounting records (book-entries). Are they owners because securities have been entered in the accounts, or are they already the owners and the accounts simply record the fact?'.[26]

---

[24] See '2001 Giovannini Report', p. 21.
[25] Benjamin, *Interests in Securities*, p. 26.
[26] The Giovannini Group, 'Second Report on EU Clearing and Settlement Arrangements,' Brussels, 2003 [hereinafter '2003 Giovannini Report'], p. 13; see also Löber, 'The developing EU legal framework for clearing and settlement of financial instruments', p. 5.
Account holder's rights resulting from a credit of securities to a securities account are classified in different ways in different legal systems, notwithstanding recurring similarities in the developments which have taken place in most markets throughout the world. These differences can be grouped according to those systems which recognise the account holder's rights as: (1) functionally equivalent to those of a direct owner (either

2.2. The relevance of clearing and settlement under the perspective of monetary obligations

The relevance of settlement systems under the perspective of monetary obligations is due to the observation that the volume of transactions that are concluded through this system has grown in such a significant way as to outnumber transactions involving cash or bank money. When clearing and settlement take place, the immaterial compensation of debit and credit positions, especially where carried out through book entries, substitutes transactions in cash, and constitutes an institution that corresponds to the performance of a monetary obligation through payment. This is true both for payments settled in a payment system (money v. money) and for payments settled in a securities settlement system (securities v. money, and by analogy, securities v. securities).

Although the system of compensation between credits and debts has not on the whole substituted the use of money, the significant volume of transactions that are concluded through settlement systems has, however, a strong incidence on the monetary aggregate, and can influence the implementation of monetary policy by central banks.[27] This occurs because the clearing process is not a simple set-off between debt and credit positions; rather, it may be multi-lateral when it is carried out by a central counterparty, who usually also provides collateral and issues credit to other participants. In those systems in which the central counterparty is the central bank, the central bank ultimately becomes the lender of the last resort, and the issuance of credit to the participants in central

characterising the account holder's rights as a regular deposit, special deposit, co-property right in an identifiable pool of securities or some other form of property right traceable to individual securities) and thus including the right to enforce the securities directly against the issuer or permitting or requiring that the account holder be recorded as the registered owner on the issuer's books; (2) as a purely personal (contractual) right against the intermediary to the delivery or transfer of a given type and number of securities (characterising the account holder's rights as an irregular deposit or general deposit or some other form of personal contractual right); (3) as some other form of interest which can be enforced against the issuers only indirectly, through their intermediaries (characterising the account holder's rights as an interest of a beneficiary under a trust, a statutory fiduciary interest, a *Gutschrift in Wertpapierrechnung*, co-property rights in a fungible, notional or book-entry pool of securities, security entitlements or some other bundle of property, contractual or other rights). See R. Goode, H. Kanda, K. Kreuzer, 'Hague Securities Convention. Explanatory Report' Hague Conference on Private International Law, The Hague, 2005, p. 10.

[27] See F. Merusi, 'Profili giuridici dell'equipollenza monetaria dei sistemi di pagamento', *Banca borsa e titoli di credito*, 2006, p. 115.

payment systems constitutes an instrument of control of the monetary aggregate.[28]

In these transactions one can therefore observe problems that are very similar to the typical recurring issues in monetary obligations: what may seem a simple legal transaction may influence the ways in which monetary policy is implemented. In the case of performance of payment obligations, for example, the affirmation of a binding principle such as nominalism and the choice between a strict adherence to it or the admissibility of monetary clauses, may, in case of devaluation of money, have effects on the growth of the inflation rate.

This consideration, together with the related systemic risk lying within these systems, has as a consequence the tendency of legislators to adopt supervisory regulations, and to be somewhat reluctant to give up the legislative power in areas related to the law of currency. This also explains why the regulatory debate goes beyond an issue of which national law and what type of rules should regulate the whole system, and often involves considerations of a trade off between stability and efficiency through competition, and the related issue of private party autonomy versus public regulation as disciplining sources of the system.[29]

3. The Settlement Finality Directive[30]

Securities market regulation in the EC has gone through different phases entailing the use of different techniques, ranging from detailed harmonisation, to minimum harmonisation and mutual recognition, to regulatory competition (as noted above, harmonisation may assume different forms), to encouragement of market-led technical propositions. A brief overview may be useful for understanding the current debates.

A first attempt at harmonisation through directives dates back to the Segré Report released in 1966 (linking the development of the Community, the integration of national securities markets, and rule harmonisation).[31] Then in 1977 a Code of Conduct on Transactions in Transferable Securities was issued[32] with no legally binding force. Most of its provisions have been later adopted by harmonising directives.

---

[28] Merusi, 'Profili giuridici dell'equipollenza monetaria', p. 116; See also A. Ferrari, E. Gualandri, A. Landi, P. Vezzani, *Strumenti, mercati, intermediari finanziari*, 3rd edn, Torino, 2001, pp. 71–6.

[29] See *infra* Chapter 5.

[30] Directive 98/26/EC of 19 May 1998 on settlement finality in payment and securities settlement systems, *O.J.* L166, 11 June 1998, p. 145.

[31] N. Moloney, *EC Securities Regulation*, Oxford, 2002, pp. 62 et seq.

[32] Commission Recommendation 77/534/EEC concerning a European Code of Conduct relating to transactions in transferable securities, in *O.J.* L212, 1977, p. 37.

Over the next decade, a series of detailed harmonisation directives, concerning listing requirements, minimum standards for the admission of securities to listing, publication of listing particulars and so forth, was issued.[33] However, these directives left in place many of the legislative burdens falling on issuers and allowed member states to introduce derogations and exemptions at the moment of their transposition. Furthermore, the directives related to listed securities did not harmonise the regulatory regimes dealing with providers of services in securities transactions, and thus impeded *de facto* the cross-border movement of capital within the EU, as the costs of engaging multiple sets of securities intermediaries subject to different regulatory regimes remained high.[34] As mentioned above, the method of detailed harmonisation was abandoned in favour of minimum harmonisation and the principle of mutual recognition with the adoption of the White Paper on the Internal Market of 1985.[35]

Notwithstanding these different harmonisatory efforts, in its 1998 Communication on Financial Services[36] the Commission stressed the need for an integrated securities and payments infrastructure for the full integration of the financial market, further stating that the technical developments should be market driven and apt to contain systemic risks. When the Financial Services Action Plan was adopted in 1999, it highlighted the continuing need for an integrated infrastructure for retail and wholesale market financial transactions, especially with reference to enforceability of cross-border collateral for securities transactions; it also recognised that in the meantime a market-driven technical consolidation of securities settlement systems had occurred and the Settlement Finality Directive had been adopted though not yet implemented.[37] The correlation between settlement and payment (justifying the inclusion of both areas within the directive's sphere of regulation, while the initial proposal only covered payment systems and not securities settlement systems) is due to the delivery versus payment model.

---

[33] See, for a detailed reconstruction of these different legislative phases, Moloney, *EC Securities Regulation*, pp. 62–6.

[34] See I. H-Y Chiu, 'Three challenges ahead for the new EU securities regulation directives', *European Business Law Review* 2006, vol. 17, p. 123.

[35] And indeed a harmonization in regulatory regimes for providers of services was only achieved in 1992 with the Investment Services Directive (Directive 93/22/EEC, of 10 May 1993, *O.J.* L141, 11 June 1993, p. 27), which used the mutual recognition principle to facilitate cross-border transactions.

[36] *Financial Services: Building a Framework for Action*, COM (1998), 625.

[37] See Moloney, *EC Securities Regulation*, p. 714.

In the delivery versus payment model, principal risk that may arise on the settlement date in securities transactions is eliminated; however, in order to avoid the reintroduction of systemic risk (since principal risk is the main source of credit risk in securities settlement systems and consequently also the most probable source of systemic risk), it is necessary to ensure that not only the payment, but also the delivery of securities be final in a delivery versus payment transaction, in order to avoid a possible challenge of delivery, where the payment leg of the transaction is instead final.[38]

The Settlement Finality Directive is also related to the previous Directive on cross-border transfers[39] (Directive 97/5/EC) as part of a single legislative project on cross-border transfers and payments. The project is also greatly inspired by Article 4A of the Uniform Commercial Code which disciplines both funds transfer and funds transfer systems.[40]

The Settlement Finality Directive forms part of the EC securities regulation's prudential framework, having three principal aims: (1) reduction of systemic risk linked to payment and securities settlement systems;[41] (2) the protection of systems and their participants against the effects of insolvency proceedings against a participant in a system

---

[38] See M. Vereecken, 'Reducing systemic risk in payment and securities settlement systems', *Journal of Financial Regulation and Compliance*, 1998, vol. 6, p. 113.

[39] Directive 97/5/EC of 27 January 1997 on cross-border transfers, O.J. L043, 14 February 1997, p. 25.

[40] See F. Moliterni, 'I sistemi di pagamento dalla direttiva 98/26/CE a TARGET (Sistema Trans-europeo automatizzato di trasferimento espresso con regolamento lordo in tempo reale), Diritto del commercio internazionale, 2000, p. 703 et seq. On Article 4A of the Uniform Commercial Code see *infra* par.3.2.

The Settlement Finality Directive has been amended by Directive 2009/44/EC of 6 May 2009, amending Directive 98/26/EC and Directive 2002/47/EC, O.J., L146, 10 June 2009, p. 37, so as to take into account the increasing number of linkages between systems and the effects following Directive 2004/39/EC of 21 April 2004 on markets in financial instruments (O.J., L145, 30 April 2004), and the European Code of Conduct for clearing and settlement. This has been done by including interoperable systems (defined, according to Article 5, letter (o), Directive 2009/44/EC, as 'two or more systems whose system operators have entered into an arrangement with one another that involves cross-system execution of transfer orders') within the sphere of application of the Settlement Finality Directive.

[41] The Directive first of all aims at regulating the national laws of the Member States concerning payments and settlement systems in such a way as to guarantee: (a) validity of the netting (in the case of operation on a net basis); (b) contractual irrevocability of orders (in the case of operation on a gross basis); (c) removal of any 'zero-hour' rule in case of insolvency of a participant. See D. Devos, 'The European Directive of 19 May 1998 on settlement finality in payment and securities settlement systems,' in G. Ferrarini et al. (eds), *Capital Markets in the Age of the Euro*, p. 374.

(in particular foreign participants);[42] (3) certainty as to the law applicable to the rights and obligations relating to securities used as collateral in connection with securities settlement systems or central banks.[43] The regulation of these areas is implemented both through substantive law rules and conflict of laws rules.

With the Settlement Finality Directive the Community adopted a different legislative approach, introducing, *en lieu* of mutual recognition, a harmonisation of certain rules of substantive insolvency law, international insolvency law and private international law.[44] It also extended its field of application to domestic payment systems, aiming at achieving uniformity of both international rules and national member state legislation.[45] An interesting application of this uniformation can be found in the TARGET system (composed of single national gross payment systems, the European Central Bank payment mechanism and interlinking structures), which does not, however, constitute the sole example of a payment system relevant under the scope of application of the Directive.[46]

From the point of view of substantive law, what is particularly interesting in the Settlement Finality Directive is that, through the harmonisation of the international rules concerning payment systems, the very notion of 'payments' not only at a cross-border level, but especially at the domestic level is reconceived. This is where a strong impact on the discipline of monetary obligations can be felt. The effects on the national regulation have to be examined with an eye on the private international law rules.

First of all, at the definition level, Article 2 letter (i) defines 'transfer orders' as 'any instruction by a participant to place at the disposal of a recipient an amount of money by means of a book entry on the accounts of a credit institution, a central bank or a settlement agent, or any

---

[42] Two other important EU legal provisions which deal with protection of payment and settlement systems against the insolvency of participants should be mentioned (though adopted shortly after the Settlement Finality Directive, they were drafted before this Directive and served as a source of inspiration for it): the European Regulation on Insolvency Proceedings (Regulation 1346/2000/EC of 29 May 2000, *O.J.* L160, 30 June 2000, p. 1), and the EU Directive on the Reorganisation and Winding-up of Credit Institutions (Directive 2001/24/EC of 4 April 2001, *O.J.* L125, 5 May 2001, p. 15). For further details on both instruments and their relation to the Settlement Finality Directive see Devos, *The Settlement Finality Directive*, pp. 366–74.

[43] See Devos, *The Settlement Finality Directive*, pp. 374–5.

[44] See Löber, 'The developing EU legal framework for clearing and settlement of financial instruments', p. 16.

[45] Moliterni, 'I sistemi di pagamento dalla direttiva 98/26/CE a TARGET', p. 711.

[46] Article 2, lett a), Settlement Finality Directive.

instruction which results in the assumption or discharge of a payment obligation as defined by the rules of the system, or an instruction by a participant to transfer the title to, or interest in, a security or securities by means of a book entry on a register, or otherwise'.

The first observation that must be made is that the expression 'transfer order' is broader than the simple expression 'payment order' as it also comprises transfer of amounts of money for causes other than normal 'payments' and which can be executed in several ways (book entries, or otherwise). This wide definition, which refers to transfer of an amount of money, 'has been extended to cover all existing arrangements for processing a transfer order through a system'[47] and is very similar to the definition of funds transfer system contained in Article 4A-105(a)(5), of the Uniform Commercial Code.[48]

As far as the law applicable to the payment system is concerned, Article 2 letter (a) leaves it to the participants to choose the member state (in which, however, at least one of the participants must have its head office) whose laws will apply. Where such a choice is not expressed by the participants, the classical criteria of private international law will apply, that is, the law of the member state in which the regulation takes place.

Article 3 of the Settlement Finality Directive is a substantive law provision that stipulates the irrevocability and finality of payment orders and netting of transfer orders in the event of insolvency proceedings (derogating insolvency rules which would allow transactions performed before the bankruptcy to be revised or made void). It has been described as one of the most ambiguous provisions of the Directive: the outcome of political compromise between a provision concerning the validity of netting and one concerning the validity of transfer orders in general.[49] This provision includes bilateral netting and multi-lateral netting, both by set-off, novation or any other technique.

The principal consequence of finality of a transfer is its irrevocability, while the same is not implied in the inverse hypothesis: an irrevocable order of transfer is not necessarily also final.[50]

One of the key issues is the determination of the moment in which a transfer order becomes irrevocable (for the parties), and the moment in which it also becomes binding on third parties. Article 3.1 of the Directive states that transfer orders and netting shall be legally enforceable and,

---

[47] Common Position No. 43/97 adopted by the Council, in *OJ* C375/40, 10 December 1997, at Chapter III, B), Sec. I, Article 2, n. 5.
[48] See *infra* par. 3.2.
[49] See Devos, *The Settlement Finality Directive*, p. 378.
[50] Moliterni, 'I sistemi di pagamento dalla direttiva 98/26/CE a TARGET', p. 732.

in the event of insolvency proceedings against a participant, shall be binding on third parties at the moment in which the transfer orders were entered into the system; a moment which shall be defined by the rules (and possible conditions laid down by the national law) of that system (Article 3.3 Settlement Finality Directive).[51] Netting has to resist the test of insolvency, so that, in case of insolvency of a participant, unwinding of payments should not be possible and the insolvency laws in each member state should recognise the validity of the netting.[52]

What must be signalled, however, is that the concept of 'finality' (which indicates when payment, settlement and related obligations are discharged), though central, is not expressly defined by the Directive but is, rather, the result of the different provisions contained in Article 3 of the Settlement Finality Directive: the definition of the enforceability and binding force of transfer orders and netting entered into a system; the abolition of the retroactive effects of the opening of insolvency proceedings (so-called zero hour rules); the remand to the system's rules for the definition of irrevocability of orders.

Finality is ensured not through a direct provision, but by rendering void any purported revocation. The scope of protection against systemic risks prevails over other objectives, such as those pursued, for example, by insolvency law.[53]

The problem with revocation in cross-border transactions is that the national rules on the possibility and terms for exercising revocation may be different and furthermore these rules on revocation are often

---

[51] The possibility that conditions laid down by national laws may sacrifice the harmonisatory intents of the Community legislation are intuitive when considering, once again, the possible disruptive effects on the TARGET system, (used by the European Central Bank for the implementation of part of its monetary policy), which contains its own definition of irrevocability of the transfer order and finality of funds transfer (see Articles 4 and 5 of the TARGET convention). On the point, see Moliterni, 'I sistemi di pagamento dalla direttiva 98/26/CE a TARGET', p. 733, arguing that these considerations suggest that the provision of Article 3.3 of the Settlement Finality Directive should be construed in a sense that will not bring it into conflict with the objective of harmonisation.

[52] Vereecken, 'Reducing systemic risk in the payment and securities settlement systems', p. 118.

[53] The aims of payment systems and of insolvency law are often opposed; while payment regulation aims at ensuring that the execution of payments between banks is rapid and efficient, insolvency law on the contrary is often cautious with suspiciously rapid payments and aims at preserving as much as possible the assets of an insolvent firm (See Moliterni, 'I sistemi di pagamento dalla direttiva 98/26/CE a TARGET', p. 741).

mandatory.[54] Therefore the harmonising solution adopted by the Settlement Finality Directive (Article 5) is that of leaving it to the participants of the system, within the exercise of their contractual freedom, to determine the moment after which revocation is no longer possible.

3.1. The role of financial lex mercatoria in settlement

From the perspective of monetary obligations, what an analysis of the definition of transfer orders, irrevocability and finality shows is that the ultimate source disciplining the monetary obligation underlying a transfer order is represented by the rules governing the system, which, it may be recalled, can be chosen by the participants. The impact on the domestic rules is evident.

The necessity of reconceiving the concept of national 'civil' legislation for the discipline of monetary obligations emerges forcefully. Translated into the civil law perspective, the final determination of when a debtor is discharged, and his payment becomes irrevocable, may be left to the arrangements of participants in a settlement system. It is no longer a national rule (often embodied in a civil or commercial code) that will establish when and how a payment is good. This is particularly interesting if one recalls that key principles disciplining monetary obligations in domestic law have often been mandatory in nature. May it suffice to quote the principle of nominalism, and the voluminous case law that can be found in many legal systems on the possibility and legitimacy of circumventing nominalism through the use of monetary clauses (index clauses, etc.).

Article 2 letter (a) of the Settlement Finality Directive indeed defines 'system' as a formal arrangement between three or more participants with common rules and standardised arrangements for the execution of transfer orders between the participants. The Settlement Finality Directive does not fix a limit to the possible provisions that may be contained in these arrangements. However, as has been noted, a comprehensive construction of the different dispositions contained in the Settlement Finality Directive indicates that the formal arrangement must at least contain rules concerning the moment of entry of a transfer order into a system (Article 3.3 Settlement Finality Directive), and the moment

---

[54] Some member state legislation allows for revocation of a transfer order until the beneficiary's account has been credited, while in other member states revocation is no longer possible after the originator's account has been debited. See Vereecken, 'Reducing systemic risk in payment and securities settlement systems', p. 121.

from which a transfer order may no longer be revoked by a participant in the system.[55]

These are the rules that determine the regulation concerning the performance of monetary obligations (payment). It is evident that the relevance of payments performed through this type of funds/order transfer have an expanding role and importance as compared with the traditional payments consisting in the *brevi manu* transfer of cash.[56] While the 'classical' discipline on the performance of monetary obligations only considers a debtor and a creditor, paying in cash, modern practice and use reduce this case to comparative rarity and unimportance, whereas the main discipline should focus on the regulation of payments through banks and financial intermediaries, not only in a national, but also in a cross-border dimension (justifying the idea that the Economic and Monetary Union also requires 'one law').

The second observation is that the room for expansion of soft law, inherent in the power of the participants to refer to it in determining through arrangements the functioning of these payment systems, is quite significant. Parties may indeed choose to adopt key financial standards or suggested rules for settlement, either by incorporating these rules into their arrangements, or by referring to them as commercial practice or uses, the typical hypothesis of *lex mercatoria*.

The other central rule of the Settlement Finality Directive, together with Article 3, is Article 8, which provides that, in the event of insolvency proceedings being opened against a participant in a system, the rights and obligations arising from, or in connection with, the participation of that participant shall be determined by the law governing that system (in derogation from otherwise applicable principles of private international law, under which the effects of a participant's bankruptcy are usually governed by the laws of the country under which that participant is incorporated).[57] In order to avoid choice-of-law and conflict-of-law problems arising in a cross-border situation where a defaulting participant is established in a country other than the member state of the system, the Directive leaves it to the parties to make a contractual

---

[55] Moliterni, 'I sistemi di pagamento dalla direttiva 98/26/CE a TARGET', pp. 723–4.

[56] See also Moliterni, 'I sistemi di pagamento dalla direttiva 98/26/CE a TARGET', p. 735.

[57] The law governing the system must be a law of an EU member state (Settlement Finality Directive Article 1(a), 2 (a)): therefore, in the case of insolvency proceedings against a foreign participant located in a non-EU state, the validity of operations carried out within the system may be affected if and to the extent that the effects of the foreign insolvency procedure are recognised in the country where the system is operating. See E. Hüpkes, *The Legal Aspects of Bank Insolvency. A Comparative Analysis of Western Europe, the United States and Canada*, The Hague, London, Boston, 2000, p. 161.

choice as to which law is to govern the system (in line with Article 3 of the 1980 Rome Convention on the Law Applicable to Contractual Obligations), so that the law governing the system and the insolvency law applicable to the obligations in connection with the system are both part of the same legal system.[58]

There is, however, a special conflict-of-laws provision in the case of insolvency proceedings for collateral provided to a central bank or a bank participating in the system: Article 9(2) Settlement Finality Directive establishes that the applicable law is that of the place of the relevant account, the *lex rei sitae* or *lex conto sitae*. This is to avoid, in case of default of a participant to the system, the possible conflict of laws in cross-border arrangements between the *lex contractus*, the *lex rei sitae* and the *lex concursus* (all determining the status of collateral security) nullifying the function of collateral arrangements precisely at the moment in which collateral has to ensure settlement. Thus the Directive opts for the *lex rei sitae* rule, and in order to identify which is the relevant *lex rei sitae* (a possibly difficult task in the case of collateral security consisting in securities or rights in securities which are recorded in one member state, while the right of the collateral holder is recorded on a register, account or central deposit system in another member state), the Directive considers it to be the law of the member state in which the securities provided as collateral are recorded on a register, account or central deposit system[59] (hence *lex conto sitae*).

3.2. Funds transfer in the United States: Article 4A of the Uniform Commercial Code

An interesting confirmation of certain trends which emerge from an analysis of the EU Settlement Finality Directive can be found if a comparison is made with Article 4A of the Uniform Commercial Code on Funds Transfer. The provision of the Uniform Commercial Code, pre-existing the Settlement Finality Directive, constitutes a meaningful point of reference for the European legislator.[60] Article 4A disciplines not only the various aspects of funds transfers but also regulates payment through funds-transfer systems; it thus allows a comparison with the EU legislation both on Payment Services (e.g. as far as the problems of

---

[58] See Vereecken, 'Reducing systemic risk in payment and securities settlement systems', p. 123.

[59] See Vereecken, 'Reducing systemic risk in payment and securities settlement systems', p. 125.

[60] Article 4A of the Uniform Commercial Code was approved for submission to the States for enactment in 1989.

liability in payments are concerned) and on Settlement Finality (especially as far as the role of agreement of the parties in defining rules of the system is concerned).

This section of the Uniform Commercial Code was drafted in order to fill the legislative gap in the discipline of non-consumer funds transfers and to provide a statutory framework for transfers of credit that are not governed by the Uniform Commercial Code or by the Electronic Funds Transfer Act.[61]

Article 4A aims at providing a comprehensive discipline to what are known as 'wholesale wire transfers'. These are transfers of large amounts of money through credits, which can be carried out intrabank, interbank and, in the United States, over two main systems: FedWire, operated by the Federal Reserve System (and disciplined by Federal Regulation J)[62] and the Clearing House Interbank Payments System (CHIPS) operated by the New York Clearing House (disciplined the New York Clearing House Rules for CHIPS). There are also further private systems for wire transfers among major banks (these transfers are disciplined by Federal Reserve Bank operating circulars or, in case of Automated Clearing Houses, by the uniform rules promulgated by the National Automated Clearing House Association).

The prudential scope underlying Article 4A of the Uniform Commercial Code can be summarised as the need to control the risks involved in the increasing flow of credit through non-paper-based systems. Article 4A applies to transfers of credit that flow from an originator to a beneficiary through the banking systems. Risks derive from the practice

---

[61]Indeed payments by cheque are regulated by Articles 3 and 4 of the Uniform Commercial Code. The exclusion of transactions governed by Articles 3 or 4 Uniform Commercial Code is accomplished by the exclusions of Article 4A-103(a)(1)UCC. Credit cards are governed in some respects by Truth in Lending Act (15 U.S.C. §§ 1601 et seq) and by state law (see, for example, 1974 Uniform Consumer Credit Code). Some aspects of electronic funds transfers to or from consumer accounts are governed by the Electronic Funds Transfer Act (EFTA) of 1978 (15 U.S.C. §§ 1693 et seq) or, to a limited extent in some states, by non-uniform consumer protection statutes. The Electronic Funds Transfer Act applies to any transfer of funds involving an account which is, among other things, 'established primarily for personal, family or household purposes' (15 U.S.C. § 1693a(2)). An account is defined in regulation E generally as a demand deposit, savings, or other consumer asset held by a financial institution and established primarily for personal, family, or household purposes (12 C.F.R. § 205.2(b)). The exclusion of transactions governed by the Electronic Funds Transfer Act is stated by Article 4A-108 Uniform Commercial Code. (See also P. Brumfield Fry 'Basic concepts in Article 4A: scope and definitions' *Business Lawyer*, 1990, vol. 45, p. 1401).

[62]12 C.F.R. pt. 210, subpart B (1989). Fedwire is the customary name used to refer to the automated payments network operated by the Federal Reserve System.

of banks involved in this type of transfer to extend short-term credit to their customers by making funds available before settlement; this poses significant risks to the payment system in the event a bank should fail to settle.[63] A party in a funds transfer has to face credit risk not only in relation to the party that has sent a payment order to it, but, according to the provisions contained in Article 4A of the Uniform Commercial Code, also in relation to any receiving bank which it has paid in a funds transfer that is not completed (i.e. no payment is made to the beneficiary of the funds transfer).[64]

The two principal obligations (within a possibly wider sequence of payment orders) that are relevant in analysing insolvency risks in a funds transfer are the obligation of a sender to pay a receiving bank and the obligation of a beneficiary's bank to pay a beneficiary.

These obligations arise with 'acceptance' of the payment order made respectively by the receiving bank and by the beneficiary's bank. 'Acceptance' by the receiving bank occurs with execution of the payment order, whereas a beneficiary's bank accepts a payment order either when it pays the beneficiary, or notifies the beneficiary of the receipt of the order, or the bank receives payment of the entire amount, or at the opening of the next funds-transfer business day of the bank following the payment date of the order if the amount of the sender's order is fully covered.[65]

Satisfaction of these obligations under Article 4A is also determined in a different manner, depending on the method of payment used.[66] Payment from the sender to the receiving bank can occur by Fedwire, by book transfer, or by settlement on a funds-transfer system. In these cases payment occurs, respectively, when the receiving bank receives final settlement of the obligation through a Federal Reserve Bank or through a funds transfer system; or when the credit on the account of the receiving bank is withdrawn; or when the sender's account with the receiving bank is debited.[67] If the sender and receiving bank are members of a funds-transfer system that nets obligations multi-laterally among participants,

---

[63] See Brumfield Fry, 'Basic concepts in article 4A: scope and definitions', pp. 1401–3.
[64] N.R. Nelson, 'Settlement obligations and bank insolvency', *Business Lawyer*, 1990, vol. 45, p. 1474.
[65] UCC § 4A-209 (a)(b). It is interesting to note that the EU Directive on Payment Services identifies the moment of 'receipt' of payment orders as the moment in which the service provider becomes liable, respectively, either to the payer or to the payee. Receipt, according to the EU legislation, is the moment in time when the payment order transmitted directly by the payer or indirectly by or through a payee is received by the payer's payment service provider (Article 64 Directive 2007/64/EC).
[66] UCC §§ 4A-403, 4A-405.
[67] UCC § 4A-403(a).

the receiving bank receives final settlement when settlement is complete in accordance with the rules of the system.[68]

As for the payment obligation from the beneficiary's bank to the beneficiary, there are two methods for payment. The beneficiary's bank can credit an account of the beneficiary (in which case payment is made when the beneficiary is notified of the right to withdraw the credit, or the bank lawfully applies the credit to a debt of the beneficiary, or funds are otherwise made available to the beneficiary by the bank); if no such credit occurs, the time when payment is made is governed by principles of law that determine when an obligation is satisfied.[69]

A further provision, relevant for the allocation of insolvency risk in the context of settlement obligations is the so-called Money Back Guarantee rule, according to which if the beneficiary's bank does not accept a payment order for the benefit of the beneficiary (the funds transfer has not been 'completed'), then the obligation of the sender to the receiving bank need not be paid.[70] The Money Back Guarantee rule changes a party's risk exposure: from an exposure to the party's sender to an exposure to the party's receiving bank if that bank has been paid.[71]

According to these rules on rise and discharge of the payment obligations as outlined in the provisions of Article 4A of the Uniform Commercial Code, insolvency risk in funds transfer thus lies for the receiving bank in the possibility that the party that has sent a payment order to the receiving bank fails before it has paid the receiving bank (if the funds transfer has been completed); and if the funds transfer has not been completed, in the risk for the bank sender, that a receiving bank which has already received payment fails.[72]

Article 4A Uniform Commercial Code also disciplines funds-transfer systems, defined as 'a wire transfer network, automated clearing house,

---

[68] UCC § 4A-403(b).

[69] UCC § 4A-405 (a) (b).

[70] UCC § 4A-402(c). This does not occur under the provisions of the Directive on Payment Services. Indeed, since there appears to be no direct liability between the payer and the payee, nor between the payer's service provider and the payee or between the payee's service provider and the payer; and since liability is only constructed in terms of the respective obligations of each user with its own payment service provider, in case of defective or non-execution where the payee's service provider can be held liable, the Directive does not provide for a refund but rather affirms that the payee's service provider shall immediately place the amount of the payment transaction at the payee's disposal (Article 75 Directive 2007/64/EC).

[71] Nelson, 'Settlement obligations and bank insolvency', p. 1476.

[72] Nelson, 'Settlement obligations and bank insolvency', p. 1477. In the latter case, if the insolvent bank was designated as an intermediary bank by another party, the loss will fall on the party that designated it (so-called 'Designated Intermediary Bank' rule, § 4A-204(e) UCC).

or other communication system of a clearing house or other association of banks through which a payment order by a bank may be transmitted to the bank to which the order is addressed'.[73]

An important analogy with the provisions set out by the EU Settlement Finality Directive can be found in the central role played by the rules of the funds-transfer system.[74] These rules govern the rights and obligations of participating banks (indeed the rights and obligations of a party to a funds transfer may be varied by agreement of the affected party) even if the rules conflict with Article 4A Uniform Commercial Code and even if the rights of third parties may be indirectly affected.[75] A significant example lies in the possibility that a funds-transfer system may provide that a payment to a beneficiary is provisional under certain conditions (i.e. until receipt of payment by the beneficiary's bank of the payment order is accepted).[76]

Another significant provision allows the funds-transfer system rule to govern choice of law issues. The default rule on choice of law provides that the rights and obligations between the sender of a payment order and the receiving bank are governed by the law of the jurisdiction in which the receiving bank is located; the rights and obligations between the beneficiary's bank and the beneficiary are governed by the law of the jurisdiction in which the beneficiary's bank is located; and the issue of when payment is made pursuant to a funds transfer by the originator to the beneficiary is governed by the law of the jurisdiction in which the beneficiary's bank is located.[77] According to Article 4A-507(b) Uniform Commercial Code, the parties can, by agreement, select a law of a particular jurisdiction to govern the rights and obligations between them, regardless of whether or not the payment order or the funds transfer bears a reasonable relation to that jurisdiction. A funds-transfer system rule may also select the law of a particular jurisdiction to govern rights and obligations between participating banks with respect to payment orders transmitted or processed through the system.[78]

---

[73] UCC § 4A-105(a)(5).

[74] These are defined as the rule(s) of 'an association of banks (a) governing transmission of payment orders by means of a funds-transfer system of the association or rights and obligations with respect to those orders, or (b) to the extent the rule governs rights and obligations between banks that are parties to a funds transfer in which a Federal Reserve Bank, acting as an intermediary bank, sends a payment order to the beneficiary's bank'(UCC § 4A-501(b)).

[75] UCC §4A 501(a)(b). See also Brumfield Fry, 'Basic concepts in Article 4A: scope and definitions', p. 1418.

[76] UCC § 4A-405(d).

[77] UCC §4A-507(a).

[78] UCC §4A-507(c).

The significant role played by the rules of the funds-transfer system, rules that are determined or varied by agreement of the participating parties to the system, confirms the impression that, in the regulation of rights and obligations of parties in complex mechanisms such as funds-transfer systems, a central source is private autonomy, and more specifically, a consolidated or formalised set of rules used in practice, that is, a form of *lex mercatoria*.

Finally, a further aspect of Article 4A of the Uniform Commercial Code merits attention. The choice of disciplining funds transfers through state legislation (as has occurred in the case of Article 4A of the Uniform Commercial Code) has drawn attention and in some cases criticisms. Observations in this regard include the consideration that most wire transfers are typically either interstate or international (and thus could be regulated at the federal level under the Interstate Commerce Clause[79]); that adherence to international conventions or treaties on international funds transfer can be dealt with more effectively by the federal government; and that insolvency issues are better dealt with at the federal level (in view, *inter alia*, of the fact that the extension of credit between participants in the wire transfer network due to the delay between the execution of a wire transfer and settlement is *de facto* in the case of FedWire guaranteed by the Federal Reserve and such protection could be extended to transactions through other wire transfer systems).[80] At the same time, however, Article 4A-107 of the Uniform Commercial Code directly allows operativity of pre-emption by providing that Federal Reserve Regulations and operating circulars of the Federal Reserve Banks supersede any inconsistent provision of Article 4A.

This issue can be of interest to the European observer. On the one hand the same problems of cross-border and international character of funds transfer suggest the importance of adopting a uniform supranational discipline (in this sense the Directive on Payment Services seems at least in part to accomplish this mission). On the other, whereas through the pre-emption doctrine the US legislation leaves an important regulatory power in the hands of a federal monetary institution (the Federal Reserve), by contrast, under the operativity of EU law, there is no such regulatory power (vested for example in the European Central Bank) and member states maintain the possibility of derogating from Directive provisions which are either inconsistent with certain requirements of national law, or

---

[79] Article 1, section 8, United States Constitution.
[80] See D.B. Goldstein, 'Federal versus state adoption of Article 4A', *Business Lawyer*, 1990, vol. 45, pp. 1514–16.

of implementing certain provisions of the Directive according to national policy choices.[81]

4. The Directive on Financial Collateral Arrangements[82]

The disruptive potential for harmonisation due to differences in substantive law is also particularly strong in another area of securities, the one regarding financial collateral arrangements. Indeed, the existence of a variety of different rules disciplining financial collateral undermines certainty in the market as to when and how collateral will be realised (especially in the case of insolvency), constituting one of the main obstacles to the cross-border use of collateral in financial transactions.

On the other side, economic studies have signalled that the use of collateral favours the reduction of systemic risk, since creditors who obtain valid and enforceable collateral can reduce their credit risks and free credit lines for further business.[83] The growth in the use of collateral in financial transactions (including capital market transactions, bank treasury and funding, payment and clearing systems, general bank lending) is demonstrated by the expansion of the EU Repo market.[84]

Collateral (in the form of cash or securities that are held in immobilised or dematerialised form by custodians and clearing systems) is also used for the reduction of systemic risk in payment and securities settlement systems.[85]

The provision of assets as a guarantee for the performance of an obligation can assume different forms, including a simple transfer of rights over assets, without a contextual transfer of ownership over the assets (as is the case of pledge, charge or lien), or the transfer of the full ownership of the assets from a collateral provider to a collateral taker, as is the case of a repurchase agreement or transfer of title agreement.[86] The collateral itself can be provided under a variety of

---

[81] See Article 86 Directive 2007/64/EC.

[82] Directive 2002/47/EC, of 6 June 2002, O.J. L168, 27 June 2002, p. 43.

[83] See Löber, 'The developing EU legal framework for clearing and settlement of financial instruments', p. 20.

[84] Ibid. See also the ICMA Repo Market Survey.

[85] Directive 2009/44/EC of 6 May 2009 has expanded the scope of the Financial Collateral Directive by including credit claims within the pool of available collateral (with the possible exclusion of credit claims arising from credit agreements for consumers as disciplined by Directive 2008/48/EC of 23 April 2008 on credit agreements for consumers, O.J. L133, 22 May 2008, p. 66).

[86] When there is simple transfer of rights over assets, the ownership of the collateral remains with the collateral giver (the debtor) but usually certain uses of the collateral

forms, including cash or securities. This concurs in explaining the possible conflict between the laws regulating the assets in the case of a cross-border collateral agreement, as national regulation of collateralisation procedures vary significantly. It is indeed possible that different laws govern different moments of a collateral arrangement, such as the law of the state in which the assets are located (*lex rei sitae*), which determines the modalities of the privilege, the law of the state disciplining the contract and the debt (the *lex contractus*), which determines whether a claim is privileged, and the law in which the debtor or the collateral taker respectively reside.[87] In the case of insolvency proceedings there will also be the *lex concursus*, which determines whether the privileges, attributed by the *lex contractus* and recognised by the *lex rei sitae*, can be effectively realised.[88] This multiplicity of national laws can significantly hamper the realisation of collateral, especially in the case of insolvency proceedings.

The EC legislator was well aware of these difficulties at the time in which the Settlement Finality Directive was enacted. The Settlement Finality Directive indeed contains a provision concerning the protection of collateral arrangements in the case of insolvency proceedings

---

are 'blocked' in favour of the creditor (the collateral taker). If the debtor fails to repay the debt, the creditor has the right to liquidate the collateral and thereby redeem a portion or all of the debt. The creditor has a security interest in the collateral assets which does not make those assets available to general creditors; however, until default occurs, the collateral giver-debtor retains the so-called 'equity of redemption', that is the right to have the assets redelivered upon repayment of the debt.

In a repurchase transaction (repo), if the debtor files for bankruptcy, the creditor simply cancels the obligation to sell back the collateral and then sets off the value of the defaulted debt against the remaining debt owed ('netting'). The creditor's protection lies in insolvency set off, therefore it is important for the creditor to ensure that the insolvency regime affecting the debtor permits such set-off. K. Alexander, 'Private law approaches to enhancing financial stability: The Hague Convention on indirectly held securities and European Union collateral directive,' in M. Andenas, Y. Avgerinos (eds), *Financial Markets in Europe. Towards a Single Regulator?*, The Hague, 2003, p. 124 and p. 129; Benjamin, *Interests in Securities*, p. 83.

[87] The determination of the modalities of the privilege includes which items can be collateralised; which registration requirements have to be observed to constitute valid collateral; how to perfect the collateral, e.g. which publicity requirements have to be respected to render the contract opposable to third parties; what is the rank of the privilege. See Löber, 'The developing EU legal framework for clearing and settlement of financial instruments', p. 20.

[88] Insolvency rules can prevent the realisation of privileges in order to safeguard equality among creditors; these rules include setting aside of contracts during the suspect period or establishing the modalities and terms within which privileges have to be perfected in case of insolvency. Vereecken, 'Reducing systemic risk in payment and securities settlement systems', p. 124.

(Article 9 Settlement Finality Directive), establishing that the laws that will govern the rights of the holders of securities as collateral will be those of the member state in which the register, account or centralised deposit system is located (*lex conto sitae*). However, this provision only concerns collateral in connection with a settlement system or the central banks of the member states but not collateral given to other financial market participants. The Collateral Directive extends the *lex conto sitae* rule to questions in relation to 'book entry securities collateral' (in general).[89]

The Directive on Financial Collateral Arrangements constitutes, like the preceding Settlement Finality Directive, an example of a change in Community legislation: it no longer operates through mutual recognition or minimum harmonisation, but provides, rather, for a substantive harmonisation of the rules.[90] It is also a significant instance of a reception, at the legislative level, of rules elaborated by market practice (financial market *lex mercatoria*).

The scope of the Collateral Directive is to limit credit risk in financial transactions by creating a more uniform legal regime for transfer of securities and cash as collateral under both pledge and title transfer structures. This is done by abolishing all formalities and administrative procedures required to create, validate, perfect or admit in evidence financial collateral arrangements or the provision of financial collateral under such an arrangement (Article 3).[91]

The Directive also provides that, in the case of an enforcement event, the collateral taker shall be able to realise any financial collateral provided under a security financial collateral arrangement either by sale or appropriation (if agreed upon) or set-off of their value against the relevant financial obligations (or applying their value in discharge of the relevant financial obligations), where financial instruments have been provided as collateral, and by set-off of the amount against or applying it in discharge of the relevant financial obligations where cash has been provided as collateral.[92]

---

[89] See also the 1st and 2nd recitals of the Financial Collateral Directive.

[90] See Löber, 'The developing EU legal framework for clearing and settlement of financial instruments' p. 21; F. Annunziata, 'Verso una disciplina comune delle garanzie finanziarie. Dalla Convenzione dell'Aja alla Collateral Directive', *Banca, borsa e titoli di credito*, 2003, I, p. 182.

[91] Such formalities may include, for example, notarial deeds, registration requirements, notification requirements, public announcements or other formal certification. See Löber, 'The developing EU legal framework for clearing and settlement of financial instruments', p. 23.

[92] Article 4, Directive 2002/47/EC.

Article 5 entitles a collateral taker to exercise a right of use in relation to financial collateral if the collateral arrangement so provides and that, where a collateral taker exercises right of use, he acquires a right to replace the original financial collateral with equivalent collateral at the latest on the due date for the performance of the relevant financial obligation covered by the arrangement. This provision aims at enhancing liquidity in the collateral market.[93]

The Directive recognises the validity of title transfer financial collateral arrangements, meaning that the definition of a collateral arrangement and its effects shall be determined (exclusively) on the basis of the arrangement between the parties (governed by the law identified according to the conflict of laws rule in Article 9 of the Directive) and shall not be undone by a possible different definition in national laws.[94] The Directive also recognises close-out netting provisions (which may otherwise be at risk under mandatory insolvency laws of some jurisdictions prohibiting or restricting insolvency set-off) 'notwithstanding the commencement or continuation of winding-up proceedings or reorganisation measures in respect of the collateral provider and/or the collateral taker and/or notwithstanding any purported assignment, judicial or other attachment or other disposition of or in respect of such rights' (Article 7).

This provision bears the signs of its origin: it constitutes a reception of a market practice, embodied and codified in the so-called Master Agreements.[95] Among the dispositions contained in the Master Agreements,

---

[93] See Alexander, *Private Law Approaches to Enhancing Financial Stability*, p. 130.

[94] Article 6, Directive 2002/47/EC. See also Annunziata *Verso una disciplina comune delle garanzie finanziarie*, p. 199.

[95] Master Agreements are uniform models prepared by different associations of the industry and disciplining certain financial instruments (including interest rate swaps, currency swaps, equity, commodity, credit default swaps and options, repo transactions, securities loans, forex spot, forward, futures and options, and collateral). The most common model is the 1992 ISDA (International Swaps Derivatives Association) Master Agreement (Multicurrency Cross-border), to which Europe has added in 2001 a specific European Master Agreement for Financial Transactions (EMA) prepared by the EBF (European Banking Federation) (and later modified in 2004) for repo transactions and securities loans. Other Master Agreements include those prepared by the Public Securities Association/International Securities Market Association (PSA/ISMA) and by the International Securities Lending Association (ISLA). Particularly interesting for close-out netting provisions is the Cross-Product Master Agreement (CPMA) created in 2000 by The Bond Market Association (TBMA) and other 'Publishing Associations', such as the British Bankers' Association (BBA), Emerging Markets Traders Association (EMTA), the Foreign Exchange Committee, the Investment Dealers Association of Canada (IDA), the International Primary Market Association (IPMA), the ISDA, the Japan Securities Dealers Association (JSDA) and

some indeed significantly aim at regulating the problem of protecting collateral arrangements from insolvency proceedings. These Agreements often express their choice of the law governing financial transactions in favour of legislation which allows contract clauses providing an automatic and anticipatory netting of the collateral and debit positions to the moment immediately preceding the opening of the insolvency procedure, as long as this anticipatory or automatic netting is admissible according to the rules governing the insolvency procedure and to those disciplining the collateral asset (usually the laws of the member state in which the collateral assets are located). Such clauses are permitted for instance by the laws of New York and by English law, often indicated as the law regulating financial derivatives.[96]

The reception of such a provision in the Financial Collateral Directive suggests a policy choice aiming at protecting the validity of those arrangements that ensure enforcement of financial collateral notwithstanding the commencement of insolvency procedures: a rule which favours financial creditors/collateral takers (the same actors which happen to be the promoters of these Master Agreements).[97] Insolvency law by contrast usually tends to 'freeze' payments made in the so-called suspect period before the opening of the insolvency procedure.

Analogous considerations can be made for another central provision of the Financial Collateral Directive: Article 8. This article provides for the disapplication of certain insolvency provisions (those establishing so-called 'zero-hour' rules, which allow the commencement of insolvency proceedings to have a retroactive effect, considering them to have begun at midnight of the day insolvency is declared); it also protects financial collateral which has been delivered on the date, but prior to the time, that proceedings were initiated.

The same article declares the validity of obligations to provide additional financial collateral (in order to take account of changes in the

---

the London Investment Banking Association (LIBA), and later amended in June 2003 (CPMA2) to manage risk across multiple entities. Certain provisions of CPMA2 will be examined further *infra*.

[96] Indeed, the most diffuse Master Agreements have an Anglo-American origin and indicate either English or New York law as the law applicable to the agreements. See S.M. Carbone, 'Derivati finanziari e diritto internazionale privato e processuale: alcune considerazioni', *Diritto del commercio internazionale*, 2000, pp. 8–9; See also F. Caputo Nassetti, *Profili civilistici dei contratti 'derivati' finanziari*, Milano, 1997, p. 108.

[97] The opposite will naturally be true in the cases of bank insolvency, where provisions allowing enforcement of netting arrangements favour the solvent party. However, usually netting (or insolvency set-off) is regarded as a measure to reduce risks in the banking system. See E. Hüpkes, *The Legal Aspects of Bank Insolvency*, p. 153.

value of the financial collateral or in the amount of the relevant financial obligations) or to substitute financial collateral with financial collateral having substantially the same value, even where such a provision was made on the day of the commencement of winding-up proceedings or reorganisation measures, but prior to the commencement of the proceedings.

This provision invites reflection on an analogy with the problems of revaluation in monetary obligations. The *ratio* of the norm lies in the implicit recognition of the possible disruptive effects of change in value of money. Whereas in the 'classical' discipline of monetary obligations the issue was that of allowing the defence of the value of a debt through the use of monetary clauses, in settlement and clearing regulation the concern is to defend the market from the risks of failure of the system (with a possible analogy between the need to defend 'debt' and 'collateral'). These risks may also in part depend on the interaction with the domestic insolvency laws; therefore the EU legislation (e.g. the Settlement Finality Directive and the Financial Collateral Directive) aims at protecting the systems from certain national rules of insolvency procedures.

Article 9 of the Directive deals with the problematic issue of the conflict of laws, adopting (in accordance with the provision contained in the Settlement Finality Directive) the Place of the Relevant InterMediary Approach (PRIMA approach), and thus confirming the abandonment of the traditional *lex rei sitae* rule.[98]

From the civil law perspective, the Directive on financial collateral poses a series of problems of substantive law. It introduces, for example, new rules on the ways in which collateral can be constituted and on the ways in which it can be enforced which are not always in accordance with the pre-existing national discipline. This may be the case for: the abolition of formalities for the constitution of collateral; the provision of direct appropriation as a way of ensuring enforcement; the recognition of the right of reuse of pledged collateral;[99] the problem of the mandatory nature of certain provisions

---

[98] The complex legal discipline concerning the conflict of laws has been the object of a specific international convention, the Hague Convention on the Law Applicable to Certain Rights in Respect of Securities Held with an Intermediary. The interaction between the Community legislation and this Convention will be examined further in Chapter 4.

[99] This constitutes another example of a rule adopted from market practice: from an economic point of view, the reuse of pledged collateral ensures a liquid and efficient securities market for financial intermediaries; however, this type of rule is new for the domestic law of most member states (see Löber, 'The developing EU legal framework for clearing and settlement of financial instruments', p. 23).

of domestic insolvency law and their contrast with the validity of close-out netting provisions pending after the commencement of insolvency procedures.

If one then considers that the origin of several of these new rules that are somewhat 'subversive' of national order is market-driven (even if incorporated and filtered through Community Law), this may tend to confirm the impression of the industry as the new legislator.

A second relevant problem of substantive law posed by this legislation is that the underlying notions of some of the fundamental institutions that enable settlement, clearing, netting and so on, differ among domestic rules, and the EU legislation does not provide a harmonised discipline. This is the case of the central institution of set-off, which has different operative rules in national legislation.[100] The same can be said

---

[100] These differences have been studied with a view to proposing a European uniform law of set-off (see R. Zimmermann, *Comparative Foundations of a European Law of Set-Off and Prescription*, Cambridge, 2002). Some of the basic elements which can be briefly recalled here include: (1) differences between a procedural notion of set-off (typical of the Common law systems) and a substantive notion of set-off (belonging to the civil law tradition), with ensuing differences in the moment of operativity of compensation; (2) differences between the systems allowing an extra judicial and unilateral declaration of set-off and those systems requiring that the *exceptio compensationis* be pleaded in court; (3) differences between a retroactive and an *ex nunc* effect of the declaration of set-off (Zimmermann, *Comparative Foundations of a European Law of Set-Off and Prescription*, pp. 22–44).

Recent additions to two of the most significant projects of soft law harmonisation, the Unidroit principles and the Principles of European Contract Law, include rules on set-off (i.e. Part II of the Unidroit Principles issued in 2004 and Part III of the Principles of European Contract Law issued in 2002). Important provisions concerning the foundations of the operativity of set-off are codified by both sets of rules with the scope of adopting a single harmonized solution which levels the differences between legal systems. For example, both the Unidroit Principles and the Principles of European Contract Law recognise a substantive notion of set-off, regardless of whether a legal procedure, in which the foundation of the exception of set-off has been verified, has been initiated (thus adopting the typical civil law notion). Both sets of rules also impose notice to the other party as a requirement for the exercise of the right of set-off (see Article 3 Unidroit Principles 2001 and Article 13:104 Principles of European Contract Law). As for the effects of set-off, both Unidroit Article 5 and Principles of European Contract Law Article 13:106 adopt the *ex nunc* rule, which in excluding the retroactive effects of the declaration of set-off (common to most legal systems), aim at ensuring legal certainty in a more effective way, given the recurring existence in practice of difficulties in determining the exact moment *a quo* in which all the requisites for the exercise of set-off are met. See R. Peleggi, 'La compensazione nei principi Unidroit dei contratti commerciali internazionali e nei principi di diritto europeo dei contratti: un primo confronto', *Diritto del commercio internazionale*, 2002, p. 492 et seq.

for fundamental insolvency institutions such as insolvency set-off and revocation.[101]

4.1. Impact of the lex mercatoria: master agreements, harmonised rules and monetary obligations

The Directive on financial collateral embodies several of the evolutionary trends in the law of monetary obligations that have been highlighted earlier. These include the reduction of complex financial transactions to a simple monetary obligation (justifying an initial wide definition of this type of obligation so as to include operations carried out in financial markets that *prima facie* may not be associated with the classical notion of monetary debts); the reception at the EU legislative level of rules elaborated by the market (financial market *lex mercatoria*); the visible incidence of market practice in the way these rules are formulated and in the policy choices they express. These aspects require further examination.

In the first place, the bond with the traditional 'simple' notion of a monetary obligation can be traced in the provision permitting close-out arrangements. According to these arrangements, which represent a reception of the provisions contained in the Master Agreements, in case of a close-out event, all the reciprocal obligations of the parties on derivatives are reduced to a single monetary obligation the value of which varies according to the variations of the indexes on which it depends. This means that through the operativity of a close-out netting provision, the parties can reduce their reciprocal positions to a single final settled amount: they can 'freeze' the variability and calculate their reciprocal exposures. The ensuing need of harmonisation depends on the necessity of employing a single tool for the calculations. The parties need the legal certainty of being able to 'potentially' calculate their reciprocal exposure at any moment in order to be able, *inter alia*, to adapt their credit risk

---

[101] Insolvency set-off (triggered by the insolvency of one of the parties and creating for the creditor a position that is analogous to that of a secured creditor without the need for a charge over assets) is not permitted in all jurisdictions (or not to the same extent in any case) because it is considered to violate the principle of *par condicio creditorum* without there being a publicised security interest. However, in most legal systems some form of insolvency set-off is recognised, in order to avoid the injustice following from the possibility that the creditor pay his debt to the bankrupt in full, while his own claim would be limited to a proportional share in the insolvent estate (See R. Zimmermann, *Comparative Foundations of a European Law of Set-Off and Prescription*, p. 43, and E. Hüpkes, *The Legal Aspects of Bank Insolvency*, p. 147; see also F. Nappi, *Studi sulla compensazione: esercizi di una europafreundliche auslegung*, Torino, 2004, p. 111).

according to variations in the market (often through the use of financial collateral).[102]

Certain provisions contained in the Master Agreements (other than those on validity of close-out netting and choice of law examined above) establish their relevance from the point of view of monetary obligations and constitute the reason that calls for a closer examination of these agreements. The fact is that the aspects which Master Agreements have found to be in need of regulation (and as such have been inserted in different sections of the Master Agreements) are indicative of those areas of monetary obligations which would require some form of substantial harmonisation. Indeed, after reducing legal and counterparty risk, and generating more liquidity on the market, the further step consists in rendering uniform certain recurring institutions of the various Master Agreements, such as the type of default events that allow close-out netting, or the different terms for notice of the intent to proceed with close-out netting.[103] Harmonisation of these institutions and of other significative substantive issues has been carried out in part in the provisions of the Cross-Product Master Agreement (CPMA).[104]

This is the case as far as the choice of a common 'base' currency is concerned and the consequent rule for determining its conversion in case a settlement amount is denominated in a currency other than the base currency: the equivalent amount in the base currency shall be determined at the spot exchange rate on the relevant settlement date (Article 3.2 Cross-Product Master Agreement).

The problem of the date in which liquidation and conversion of foreign money obligations should be carried out is indeed one of long standing in the (so far national) regulation of monetary obligations.

Once it is settled that the conversion has to be determined at the spot exchange rate, the issue is that of determining when is the relevant settlement date. As may be recalled, one of the most problematic questions in foreign money obligations is whether the conversion should be calculated at the rate on the date in which the debt is due or rather on the date of effective payment (in case of delay), with an ensuing different distribution of exchange rate risk between the parties in case of late

---

[102]F. Macario, 'I contratti di garanzia finanziaria nella direttiva 2002/47/CE', *I Contratti*, 2003, pp. 87–8.

[103]See De Biasi, *Un nuovo Master Agreement per strumenti finanziari sofisticati*, pp. 654–5.

[104]The Cross-Product Master Agreement serves as a reference framework, which includes within its sphere all those Principal Agreements that the parties shall choose to include.

payment.[105] Private autonomy normally regulates questions related to the determination of currency of payment and conversion rate on the assumption that the obligations are duly and correctly performed; the problems arise in case of pathologies in the contractual relationship (e.g. breach or delay). Indeed several problems have been raised for example in the US as to the guidelines that judges should follow in determining the liquidation of a debt expressed in foreign money without damaging the judgment creditor.[106]

In the case of financial instruments, these are exemplified by the hypothesis of default (or so-called 'Close-out event'), which triggers the operativity of a close-out netting provision. And it is precisely in this case that a uniform regulation may prove particularly useful.

Article 4 of the Cross-Product Master Agreement is central for, *inter alia*, the determination of the payment date (and the exchange rate at which the conversion into the Base currency should therefore be determined). It contains provisions on set-off, discharge of settlement accounts, determination and payment of the Final Net Settlement Amount(s) and Interest.

As far as the determination of the settlement amounts is concerned, if a close-out event occurs and close-out netting is carried out according to Cross-Product Master Agreement, the settlement amounts are not due immediately upon their calculation, but are deferred until the various set-off mechanisms have reduced the amounts due to one or more Final Net Settlement amounts.[107] This entails that a certain period of time elapses between the occurrence of the close-out event and the effective determination of the Final Net Settlement amount and its liquidation. The Master Agreement therefore provides that the various obligations (Settlement Amounts) between the parties that are progressively set off against each other (the various Net Set-off Amounts) are accrued according to the contractual overdue interest rate specified in the relevant Principal Agreement, or, if no such rate is specified, at the Base Rate, from the date on which the Amount would be due under the Principal Agreement until a date on which another Settlement Amount between

---

[105] In case of breach of contract, the issue is whether conversion should be determined on the day in which breach or default has occurred or on the day of the judgment for payment.

[106] See *Restatement Third of the Foreign Relations Law of the United States* §823, and the *Official Comment* (c); see also R.A. Brand, 'Restructuring the U.S. approach to judgments on foreign currency liabilities: building on the English experience', in *Yale Journal of International Law*, 1985–1986, vol. 11, p. 183.

[107] See the Cross-Product Master Agreement (Cross-Affiliate Version 2) Guidance Notes (June 2003), at p. 7.

the parties is owed, and so on, until the Final Net Settlement Amount is calculated and due.

The rules elaborated by the practice suggest that, while settlement and liquidation can be determined definitively only at the final payment date, however, in order to avoid charging the creditor with the risks of monetary depreciation from the date of close-out until the final payment date, the sums that are progressively set-off in order to arrive at the final amount due are automatically re-evaluated through the mechanism of the overdue interest rate. The same protective mechanism occurs for the conversion to the Base Currency (according to Article 3.2 Cross-Product Master Agreement), at the relevant settlement date.

Finally, the last point that requires a few brief observations regards the political orientation of the norms. As may be counterintuitive and as has already in part emerged with the analysis of certain provisions (e.g. those on the validity of close-out clauses notwithstanding the commencement of insolvency procedures), the norms adopted in the Community Legislation are visibly influenced by their origin and are express policy choices that may be defined as market-oriented.

The discipline of financial collateral contains a few emblematic provisions to this effect. The provision abolishing formalities (Article 3 Directive 2002/47/EC) for the realisation and enforcement of collateral, the possibility of realising collateral through direct appropriation in case of securities (if the parties have so agreed),[108] the possibility of allowing 'equivalent' collateral,[109] and especially the provision concerning enforcement of collateral notwithstanding the commencement of insolvency procedures (Article 4 n. 5 and Article 8 Directive 2002/47/EC on the disapplication of insolvency rules), indicate a financial-creditor-oriented policy.

Not surprisingly these provisions are often in conflict with mandatory national discipline on collateral that sacrifices part of the 'efficiency and rapidity' that the market would require for the sake of legal certainty (and to reduce the risk of fraud) and debtor protection. Such is the case, for example, with the abolition of formalities in the constitution of collateral: a problem that is also taken into consideration by the EC legislator in the 10th recital of the Directive on Financial Collateral that affirms that 'the Directive must provide a balance between market efficiency and the safety of the parties to the arrangement and third parties, thereby

---

[108] Member states can exclude the operativity of this norm if it is contrary to national rules (Article 4, 4.3 of the Directive); however, this opt out possibility is *de facto* later excluded through the provision in Article 7 Directive 2002/47/EC.

[109] This may be contrary to national mandatory rules. Such is the case in Italy, according to the provisions in Articles 2786 and 2787 of the Italian civil code.

avoiding, *inter alia* the risk of fraud'. Finally, an overall assessment of the two EC directives that have been examined seems to indicate that several substantive issues remain unresolved. It may be inferred that this important Community Legislation does not always provide a form of substantive harmonisation of the rules. Rather, the trend that may be highlighted in both the Directive on Settlement Finality and the Directive on Financial Collateral points at a double resort to external sources for legal integration: on the one hand to the rules of private international law, and on the other to private autonomy (where the main source is the financial *lex mercatoria*). These two sources will be further examined in the following chapters.

Chapter 4:
Private International Law
Perspective

1. Different instruments of legal harmonisation: uniform substantive law and private international law

Notwithstanding the harmonisatory efforts carried out by the European Union (EU) institutions in the field of settlement and clearing of securities, and in the field of the use of securities as collateral (namely through the enactment of the two Directives concerning these disciplines), a series of legal barriers still remain in place and have to be removed for a full liberalisation of the market. Some of these barriers have been highlighted above, and concern, for example, the absence of a common definition of certain key institutions or phases of the settlement procedures. Others concern differences in market practice conventions between member states that hamper cross-border transactions.

Further substantive law problems, such as the different 'interests' in securities (rights associated with the idea of 'ownership' of securities or 'entitlement against an intermediary or settlement system' to own such a security) that do not always correspond in domestic law notwithstanding the use of common expressions such as 'proprietary rights', have led to the drafting of a private international law convention, the Hague Convention on the Law Applicable to Certain Rights in Respect of Securities held with an Intermediary. This constitutes an indicative example of the different harmonisatory techniques available to legislators for the completion of legal integration of the markets.

Indeed, a very rough classification of harmonisation techniques allows a division according to their nature: adoption of uniform substantive law (with further subdistinctions within substantive law according to the source, institutional or market driven) or reliance on domestic laws through the technicalities of private international law.

What this study purports to show, however, is that in this particular field of clearing and settlement, whichever technique is chosen for the completion of the legal integration process, extensive use is made of *lex mercatoria* or other forms of soft law. Both harmonisation techniques bear a common feature in the field of financial transactions: the extreme volatility and necessary flexibility that characterise transactions in financial markets induce the legislators to assign significant normative power for the definition of harmonised rules to the market itself, under the different forms of soft law.

This consideration seems to be confirmed *inter alia* from an analysis of two texts that are representative of both the substantive law approach and the private international law approach. The first consists in the bottom line results of the two Giovannini Reports, expressly commissioned for the identification and study of the legal barriers in EU Settlement and Clearing Arrangements, which allocate to the market practice a relevant share in the responsibility for removing certain specific legal barriers.

The second text is the Hague Convention on the Law Applicable to Certain Rights in Respect of Securities Held with an Intermediary, which as a general rule (see Article 4.1) leaves it to the parties to determine the law applicable to securities held with an intermediary, with the consequence that the probability that parties will refer to some form of market-led regulation as the applicable law (soft law, master agreements) is higher than would be the case if the Convention were to identify as relevant the law that corresponds, for example, to the *lex rei sitae*.

What must be noted, however, is that, in defining the law applicable to securities held with an intermediary, it is often not so easy to keep the conflict of law issues separate from the substantive law ones, as the solutions envisaged by the former may be very similar to, or may even ultimately depend on, the underlying domestic substantive law rule.[1] The question revolves around the way in which interests in securities are defined and treated by different legal systems. The point however, will be examined further *infra*.

The legal discipline of important financial transactions is developed by market practice, international standards, private autonomy and standard master agreements and then often recalled or adopted directly by institutional hard law. A useful starting point for the analysis may therefore be the results of the first and second Giovannini Reports.

2. Remaining substantive law barriers

According to the 2001 Giovannini Report on EU Clearing and Settlement Arrangements, significant barriers (which relate more to settlement than to clearing) in the private sector are, *inter alia*, those concerning differences in national rules relating to corporate actions, differences

---

[1] See J.S. Rogers, 'Conflict of laws for transactions in securities held with intermediaries', *Boston College Law School Legal Studies Research Paper Series*, n. 80, 28 September 2005, p. 18; see also R. Potok (ed.), *Cross Border Collateral: Legal Risk and the Conflict of laws*, London, 2002.

in settlement periods, differences in operating hours and settlement deadlines.[2] The relevance of these particular barriers for this study is due to the fact that these technical impediments have not been resolved with the EU legislative interventions (i.e. The Settlement Finality Directive and the Financial Collateral Directive) and the suggestion made by both the First (2001) and the Second (2003) Giovannini Reports is that the industry should complete harmonisation through the predisposition of technical standards: soft law.

More specifically, differences in national rules relating to corporate actions, beneficial ownership and custody are due to the management of corporate actions, which often require a response from the securities owner, may necessitate specialised knowledge and/or local custody of physical documents, and may thus discourage the centralisation of securities settlement and custody. Differences may lie for example in the ways in which national legislation regulates compensation, cash accruals and payment of dividends on securities involved in open transactions. A soft-law market initiative in this area has been the proposal made by the G30 report to apply ISO 15022 message standards for communication between central securities depositories on corporate actions.

Significant differences also concern timing of transfer of ownership (i.e. on trade date, intended settlement date or actual settlement date). This type of legal barrier evidently has an impact beyond pure settlement issues. The Giovanni Report suggests once again that proposals be made by the private sector coordinated by the European Central Securities Depositories Association and the local agent banks through the Credit Sector Associations.

This recommendation is particularly indicative of the trend of abdicating substantive law competence to non-institutional actors. It is of course

---

[2] The First Giovannini Report on EU Clearing and Settlement Arrangements (2001) identified 15 barriers considered as sources of inefficiency in cross-border clearing and settlement arrangements across the EU. The Report categorised the 15 barriers by type and on the basis of private sector or government responsibility for their removal. Three types of barriers were identified: those relating to technical requirements/market practices; those relating to taxation; those relating to legal certainty. The Report correspondingly allocated the responsibility for the removal of these barriers. Responsibility for removing barriers relating to technical requirements/market practice was seen as falling either on the private sector (i.e. on settlement and clearing systems), or as shared between the private and the public sector; while responsibility for removal of both tax barriers and barriers relating to legal certainty was allocated to the government. However, for the purpose of this study, focus on the barriers due to market practices and to legal certainty proves particularly interesting because of the clear indication of the private sector as the most appropriate subject for the proposal and predisposition of harmonised rules (whereas clearly responsibility for harmonised taxation remains with national governments).

merely a suggestion, but issues such as timing of transfer of ownership affect domestic civil law and strongly characterise legal systems much more than a question of conventions on settlement periods or operating hours.

Signals of the deep impact of harmonisation efforts on domestic law lie in another example: the perplexities raised by the Financial Collateral Directive provision (Article 3) that abolishes all formalities and administrative procedures required to create, validate, perfect or admit in evidence financial collateral arrangements, affecting once again significant substantive provisions in domestic law. In the case of the quoted Article 3, however, a legitimation lies in the legislative competence of the EU, whereas in this hypothesis, the justification for such normative power could probably be sustained by the technical know-how of the private sector.

The differences in settlement periods referred to above are due to an inconsistency between national/local market conventions and the international settlement convention.[3] Another barrier is due to differences in operating hours and settlement deadlines (which can cause incompatibility of deadlines for matching and delivery in the different systems especially when different deadlines for the matching or delivery of the same instrument within a settlement system depend on where the instrument was traded) and should be harmonised using TARGET hours as the benchmark.[4] According to the Giovannini Report, the initiative of harmonising operating hours should be left to the private sector

---

[3] The technical difficulties arise from the fact that Germany settles on T+2, while other EU equity markets have a settlement period of T+3, which corresponds both to the international convention and to the US convention. In order to solve the mismatch in the settlement of obligations arising from these differences, market participants recur to funding arrangements, thus increasing the costs of cross-border transactions. Therefore a harmonised settlement period would be necessary. The G30 Recommendations stressed that harmonisation on a settlement period of T+2 would have the benefit of bringing the equity markets into line with the foreign exchange spot market (and a short settlement period limits credit risk); however, the 2003 Giovannini Report highlights that in view of international usages, and of those practised in the US, it may be useful to consider harmonisation on a T+3 settlement period. See '2001 Giovannini Report', p. 48; '2003 Giovannini Report' p. 9.

[4] According to the European Central Bank Users Standards (laid down in 1999), European settlement systems used by the Eurosystem for its monetary policy and intraday operations are required to conform to the operating hours of TARGET. However, since these standards only apply to monetary policy or intra-day credit operations, settlement systems may remain closed during TARGET operating hours in case the securities necessary to settle these operations have been pre-deposited with the local central bank, and thus differences in the opening days, hours and settlement deadlines still remain. See '2003 Giovannini Report', pp. 6–7.

(in particular to the European Central Securities Depository Association in coordination with the European System of Central Banks).[5]

The final example of identification of private sector competence for the removal of a legal barrier consists in the problem of the absence of intra-day settlement finality in all links between settlement systems within the EU (whereas such finality is required for European Central Bank operations) with consequences both for efficiency and systemic risk. According to the study group, removal of this barrier should be guaranteed by the private sector under the coordination of the European Central Securities Depositories Association with the European System of Central Banks/Committee of European Securities Regulators Joint Working Group.[6]

2.1. Barriers to competition and the TARGET2-Securities Project

A different set of barriers are those hampering competition, consisting, for example, and *inter alia* in rules that impose on market users an obligation to clear and settle through a particular system.[7] A significant debate has therefore followed the proposal made by the European Central Bank of creating a single European settlement platform, known as the TARGET2-Securities Project.

Given the difficulties in ensuring efficient cross-border settlement within the eurosystem,[8] the European Central Bank has elaborated a project that would link the TARGET2 payment system (the second version of the TARGET payment system created in 1999) with a securities settlement platform for the settlement of the cash legs of securities transactions. According to the project, settlement would be carried

---

[5] Ibid.

[6] Another practical barrier is due to the national differences in issuance practice and the absence of an efficient same-day distribution mechanism. The most significant difficulty of this type consists in the incapability of allocating ISIN numbers to securities issues in real-time across the securities markets in Europe. This problem could be solved through the introduction of standardised electronic links between issuing agents, dealers and settlement systems. ('2003 Giovannini Report', p. 10).

[7] '2001 Giovannini Report', p. 54.

[8] The current situation, well after the introduction of the euro, still does not provide an efficient settlement platform for euro-denominated securities (Euroclear has in part facilitated economies of scale deriving from the single currency, although its settlement platform only covers a limited number of national central securities depositories in the euro area). See speech by J-M.Godeffroy, Director General/Payment Systems and Market Infrastructure, ECB, British Bankers Association, London, 20 September 2006, available at http://www.ecb.int/paym/t2s/defining/outgoing/html/10faq.en.html#skipnavigation.

out through the delivery-versus-payment mechanism and cash settled on the same IT platform (so-called integrated model), without however transforming the settlement platform into a central securities depository.[9] The project has naturally raised the issue of whether a monopolistic concentration of settlement on a single platform would hamper competition.[10] There are several models of integration of securities

---

[9] The feasibility of separating settlement from custody has been the object of one of the public consultations with the market contemplated by the project.

[10] A series of studies has been conducted on the welfare benefits and competition issues arising from the merger of central securities depositories (See e.g. J. Tapking, 'Pricing of settlement link services and mergers of central securities depositories', ECB Working Paper Series, n. 710, 2007, according to whom the overall welfare effects due to reduction of operational costs deriving from a merger of two central securities depositories may vary according to the model, independent or interlinked, of operativity of the central securities depositories), and on the regulation of access to services provided by central securities depositories (although it must be noted that the TARGET2-Securities project excludes the possibility that the single platform will assume the functions of a central security depository).

An interesting study, for example (N. Linciano, G. Siciliano, G. Trovatore, 'The clearing and settlement industry. Structure, competition and regulatory issues', *Consob- Quaderni di finanza*, 2005, n. 58), holds that there are several similarities between access to the core services provided by central securities depositories and access to natural monopolies in the network industries. Therefore a possible rationalisation of the industry might be implemented through effective access price regulation and through 'the designation of non-discriminatory and homogenous tariffs that would allow investor central securities depositories, intermediaries and global custodians to access the network controlled by the issuer central securities depository', along with removal of legal, tax and regulatory barriers (Linciano, Siciliano and Trovatore, 'The Clearing and Settlement Industry', p. 3).

As for the welfare benefits, however, given that links in the settlement of cross-border transactions between central securities depositories operating in different countries can be either direct (when two central securities depositories interface with each other directly) or indirect (when the link is managed either by a local custodian or a global custodian as intermediaries); and that in the former case (direct link between two central securities depositaries) foreign central securities depositories can exert competitive pressure (just as local custodians and global custodians can) on issuer central securities depositories (once they reach a critical mass of clients such that they can settle an increasing number of transactions internally without accessing the issuer central securities depositories infrastructure), links with foreign central securities depositories can expose issuer central securities depositories to intense competition on the custody and settlement business.

If links between central securities depositories are created as a consequence of this competitive pressure and therefore induce central securities depositories to commit themselves to reasonable settlement fees (See K. Kauko, 'Interlinking securities settlement systems: a strategic commitment?', ECB Working Paper Series n. 427, 2005, pp. 24–30), and issuers are obliged to use the domestic central securities depository (because of different barriers to competition such as – in the case of

settlement infrastructures, and there is wide consensus among scholars and operators that integration would lead to more efficient and less risky securities processing.[11] What is missing is an agreement as to the model of integration that should be achieved in the European Union.[12]

---

trading of equities – legislative provisions, stock exchanges' rules or fiscal, regulatory or institutional differences such that only issuer central securities depositories are enabled in the management of corporate actions; or, in the case of non-equity instruments, exclusivity arrangements for post trade processing, IT and back office switching costs, or vertical ownership integration), then charging reasonable settlement fees enables central securities depositories to attract investors and charge higher fees to the issuers. It follows that 'the high settlement costs of cross-border trades in Europe, often regarded by academics and policy makers as signalling inefficiency in the industry structure and/or distortions resulting from technical and legal barriers (as suggested in the Giovannini Reports), may not in fact be in conflict with social welfare optimisation and that a regulatory intervention aiming at capping the cost of the link might in fact discourage the opening of the links, with detrimental effects for domestic investors' (Linciano, Siciliano and Trovatore, 'The clearing and settlement industry', pp. 12–13).

Following the same line of reasoning, the question is whether the removal of the barriers highlighted by the Giovannini Reports would actually drive down the price of the links; even if common standards that ensure perfect interoperability between central securities depositories were to be implemented, there would be no guarantee that central securities depositories would be given an incentive to efficiently price these interconnections, given that a reduction of price of the links would expose central securities depositories to competition from other central securities depositories, depriving them of some of their monopolistic rents (Linciano, Siciliano and Trovatore, 'The clearing and settlement industry', p. 14).

[11] The two basic models of cross-border integration are the interlink of the national infrastructures across countries, and the consolidation of the infrastructures due to mergers and alliances. See E. Kazarian, 'Integration of the securities market infrastructure in the European Union: policy and regulatory issues', IMF Working Paper n. 241, 2006, p. 9.

[12] Ibid. The consolidation process of securities infrastructures within Europe in recent years (which has occurred at the ownership level, not at the infrastructure level) has been implemented mainly through the creation of cross-border groups of stock-exchanges, clearing houses and securities settlement systems. The creation of a single European settlement system, such as the TARGET2-Securities, would have consequences for the entire securities and settlement sphere, especially in view of the fact that a single system, which has an implicit guarantee by a central bank and reduces the credit and liquidity risk by settling in central bank money, is likely to attract a large share of clearing and settlement in the European market, with the consequence of reducing the role of domestic systems to such depository functions as securities issuance and corporate events management (though they may still serve as settlement systems for domestic and/or low liquidity investors) (Kazarian, 'Integration of the securities market infrastructure in the European Union', pp. 12–13).

What must also be noted is that the influence of policy considerations and the origin (political or market-based) of legislators on regulatory outcome is visible, for example,

The European Central Bank has responded to these objections by highlighting that the existence of a multiplicity of central securities depositories (as is currently the case within the euro area) does not in itself warrant competition; on the contrary, central securities depositories often represent small local monopolies, and therefore the merger of the settlement function of central securities depositories into a single system may benefit the market from economies of scale without any meaningful reduction of competition.[13]

A further argument relies on the consideration that competition in the settlement business only exists between settlement in central bank money and settlement in commercial bank money (not between central securities depositories),[14] and the TARGET2-Securities project is limited to settlement in central bank money.

The legal foundation of the European Central Bank's competence to standardise settlement procedures against central bank money in the EU is found in Article 22 of the European Central Bank Statute which states that the European Central Bank and national central banks may 'provide facilities, and the European Central Bank may make regulations, to ensure efficient and sound clearing and payment systems within the Community and with other countries'.

Perplexities are due to the possibility that, given the role of the European Central Bank, the management of settlement on a single platform under its surveillance would not be totally neutral. An issue arises

---

in the tendency of securities market infrastructures in Europe to consolidate through the regrouping of national clearing and settlement systems under a holding company structure rather than closing some of the merged systems.

As has been pointed out (Ibid.), this is due to the direct participation of national policymakers in the mergers and alliances process, where they implement specific political choices which oppose the closure of the national system and the management of domestic securities in foreign systems. The financial community partly shares this viewpoint, albeit with a distinction depending on the size of the banks; large cross-border banks are interested in a consolidated infrastructure that leads to very few systems in Europe, while smaller local banks prefer local infrastructure. The legal framework governing the issue of national securities has also been used by governments to justify the maintenance of national central securities depositories. More specifically, policymakers have argued that for the sake of legal certainty, it is mandatory that the immobilisation and dematerialisation of listed national securities be governed by national legislation, and therefore be deposited at national central securities depositories even in the event of the merger of national and foreign systems.

[13] See Speech by J-M. Godeffroy, 20 September 2006.

[14] The European Central Bank cites the case of the settlement of German bonds, one of the most traded types of securities in Europe, a large part of which is done in the German central securities depository (Clearstream-Frankfurt) in central bank money, and another part of which is settled in Euroclear Bank in commercial bank money. See Speech by J-M. Godeffroy, 20 September 2006.

especially in view of the fact that the creation of TARGET 2 entails the realisation of a hypothesis of assigning regulation to an 'institutional' monetary source.[15]

Also, with reference to the related problem of the whether the European Central Bank can be a market player and a regulatory body at the same time, the European Central Bank has declared that the TARGET2-Securities project is to be realised in respect of regulatory-inspired measures such as the European System of Central Banks/Committee of European Securities Regulators Standards and the Code of Conduct proposed by the EU Commission. This constitutes an interesting perspective on the interaction of soft law and institutional law not only in the legislative, but also in the regulatory function.[16] A further example of this interaction between institutional law and soft law lies in the assessment and interpretation of another anti-distortionary provision, that contained in the European Market in Financial Instruments Directive (MiFID).

Indeed, another significant competitive barrier is the one denying foreign investment firms non-discriminatory access to central counterparty, clearing and settlement systems in a member state for the purpose of finalising transactions in financial instruments. The requirement that member states guarantee non-discriminatory access to central counterparties and clearing and investment facilities to foreign investment firms is the object of Article 34.1 of the Markets in Financial Instruments Directive.[17] The same Article (34.2) further provides that member states 'shall require that regulated markets in their territory offer all their members or participants the right to designate the system for the settlement of transactions in financial instruments undertaken on that regulated market' but nonetheless operators of central counterparty, clearing or securities settlement systems maintain the right 'to refuse on legitimate commercial grounds to make the requested services available' (Article 34.3) (therefore, presumably, also on different grounds than purely risk considerations).[18] The possible effects of this discretionary reserve left to central counterparties can be mitigated when construed under the light of a diffuse soft-law

---

[15] As has been noted above (see Chapter 3 *supra*), significant volumes of clearing processes carried out by central banks acting as multi-lateral central counterparties may indirectly influence the monetary aggregate.

[16] On the European Code of Conduct for Clearing and Settlement see *infra* Chapter 6.

[17] Directive 2004/39/EC of 21 April 2004 on Markets in Financial Instruments, *O.J.* L145, 30 April 2004, p. 1. Whilst liberalising the right of investment firms to access central counterparties, the Market in Financial Instruments Directive does not take the further step of allowing issuing firms to choose the central securities depositary by which they can dematerialise their securities.

[18] See K. M. Löber, 'The developing EU legal framework for clearing and settlement of financial instruments', ECB Legal Working Paper Series, n. 1, 2006, p. 27.

instrument. The Committee on Payment and Settlement Systems – International Organisation of Securities Commissions (CPSS-IOSCO) Recommendations for securities settlement systems and the European System of Central Banks-Committee of European Securities Regulators (ESCB-CESR) Recommendations for securities settlement systems and Recommendations for central counterparty in the European Union. have indeed formulated basic policy considerations for access rights. According to these standards, access criteria should be based only on risk considerations (see Recommendation n. 14, (3.71)), and could therefore be denied in case of insufficient technical, business and risk management expertise, insufficient legal powers or inadequate legal sources. However, this does not entail an absolute right for any participant to have access to any system; access criteria should be objective and publicly disclosed.

2.2. Legal certainty

A final important set of barriers is due to problems of legal certainty.[19] One of the most significant substantive law problems of this type concerns differences in rights recognised to securities owners. Some legal systems distinguish between ownership of a security and an entitlement against a settlement system or intermediary to own such a security, while in other states there is no such distinction. Furthermore, the underlying concept of 'ownership' may differ between member states even where the same expression is used.[20]

Difficulties due to different national concepts of property rights often arise when securities are used as collateral in financial market transactions. The main issue in these cases is that of distinguishing between transfer of full ownership, as in the case of sale of securities, and pledges, which involve different constituting techniques and pledging requirements.

This becomes fundamental in case of insolvency. If there is proper separation between client assets and proprietary assets, the insolvency

---

[19]The existence of an unsound legal framework increases transaction costs because of the additional time required to find measures to circumvent legal uncertainty; the problem becomes more stringent in the case of cross-border transactions where possible conflict of laws issues also have to be addressed. These additional costs may deter market participants from entering into securities transactions and may devaluate securities as objects of a security interest. The possible decrease in the volume of operations conducted in this market segment may also entail a general increase in the cost of credit and capital for securities issuers. See R. Goode, H. Kanda, K. Kreuzer, *Hague Securities Convention. Explanatory Report*, The Hague, 2005; see also the 'Explanatory notes to the preliminary draft UNIDROIT convention', *Uniform Law Review*, 2005, n. 1/2, p. 52.

[20]'2001 Giovannini Report', p. 55.

of the system or intermediary through which the securities are owned does not pose particular problems: there is no issue that the securities do not form part of the assets available to creditors of the insolvent system. Problems arise in determining whether the securities in question actually belong to those in whose names they were held. This depends on the regulation of finality which is disciplined in an inconsistent way across the member states, since each member state has different rules detracting from the finality of a transfer with the scope of protecting creditors or victims of dishonesty. These inconsistencies have not been quite levelled out by the Settlement Finality Directive either. Article 3.1 of the Directive, by stating that transfer orders and netting shall be binding on third parties in case of insolvency proceedings at the moment in which transfer orders were entered into the system, ultimately refers the definition of finality to the rules that govern that system (Article 3.3 Settlement Finality Directive), and thus not to a single harmonised rule.

These differences depend on the specific economic and social evolution that has taken place in member states and strongly reflect policy choices. A distinction must be drawn between cross-border transactions involving equities and those of debt securities. While debt securities can be issued more freely as to forms, terms and conditions of the debt, including where it falls to be paid and what its governing law is, equities, no matter where they are traded, remain tied to the national regime that created them.[21]

It becomes all the more evident that putting legislative power to determine circulatory rules of securities, for example, into the hands of market operators, constitutes a significant abdication of legislative power that may affect characterising institutions of civil or commercial law. Even the EU Commission, which had also considered the possibility of a 'Uniform Securities Code', finally suggested that such a uniform regime 'would be far from easy to design, especially for equities, because of the many links with national property, company, succession and insolvency law in Member States'.[22]

In response to the different treatment of rights in securities, both EU legislative initiatives (namely the Settlement Finality Directive and the Financial Collateral Arrangements Directive) and the Hague Securities

---

[21] '2001 Giovannini Report', pp. 54–5.
[22] Commission Communication on Clearing and settlement in the European Union. Main policy issues and future challenges, COM (2002), 257 final, 28 May 2002, p. 11. One of the most recent and significant examples lies in the crisis of the so-called subprime market that overwhelmed global financial markets in 2007. The core issue depends on the different mortgage designs and different collateral requirements provided under US law, which then affect the circulation of these mortgage-backed securities.

Convention have aimed at promoting equal treatment between entitlement against a settlement system or intermediary in respect of a security and a security itself.[23] The proposed solution comes through the Place of the Relevant InterMediary Approach (PRIMA approach), which uses the notion of location: where the security under a national law would be considered 'as issued', it is considered instead to be 'located' in the system (i.e. to be entitled against the system).

This rule can also be applied to intermediaries, in respect of entitlements against them recorded in their own accounting systems and is therefore a valid rule for every level of accounts. For each account holder, the relevant intermediary is the next one up the chain (hence the denomination PRIMA approach), and the security is considered subject to the legal system of the place where the account is held.[24]

The PRIMA approach however, is not uncontroversial. The main criticisms it has raised are due to the fact that is it based on a legal fiction, that does not resolve the need to potentially apply (and thus retain expertise in) all fifteen EU legal systems. Furthermore, the necessary 'dislocation' of securities from one jurisdiction to a different one (corresponding to the notion of the new location), can entail possible disadvantages for those owners whose rights were better under the original law where their securities were located.[25]

Furthermore, the PRIMA approach has not solved legal certainty issues which depend on the absence of uniform underlying laws (the conflict of laws solution is insufficient in this sense), especially as concerns the definition of what rights an account holder has. The recommendation on this problem made by the experts of the Giovannini Group is that a uniform substantive rule throughout all the member states on the legal nature of ownership of securities should be drafted. The experts are oriented towards recognising the status of a securities account held with an intermediary as constitutive of ownership and suggest that the rule be drafted by an 'EU Securities Account Certainty Project' nominated and backed by national governments. However, before examining the possible characteristics of a uniform substantive law, the most important conflict of laws convention in this field calls for a closer examination.

---

[23]'2001 Giovannini Report', p. 57.
[24]Ibid.
[25]'2003 Giovannini Report', p. 58.

3. The private international law approach to harmonisation: the Hague Convention on Securities[26]

As noted, in the field of intermediate-held securities, there is often a close tie between the conflict of laws approach and the substantive law that defines the rights to which a securities investor is entitled in respect of the securities holder.

The two issues can be logically separated but are as a matter of fact interdependent. The logical antecedent is that of defining what types of rights are recognised to an investor in securities. The following step is to identify which law will be applicable to these rights: more specifically, which law will apply to the electronic book-entries, which represent the way in which securities are held, transferred and pledged (often in cross-border transactions). The traditional *lex rei sitae* rule is an unworkable approach because of the evident difficulties in identifying the place of *rei sitae*: the place where the asset is located.[27]

The relationship between the two issues can be easily identified. Indeed, in those legal systems in which the substantive law defines the investor's property interest as a package of rights against the intermediary and the property held by the intermediary, often the conflict of laws approach will tend to determine the applicable law by factors limited to the arrangement between the intermediary and the account holder (i.e. through the PRIMA approach).

In other jurisdictions, where the substantive law defines the investor's property interest as a direct property interest in the underlying securities, treating all of the intermediaries as legally transparent, the conflict of laws approach will probably focus on factors related to the underlying

---

[26] The Convention on the Law Applicable to Certain Rights in Respect of Securities held with an Intermediary was drafted by the Hague Conference on Private International Law and concluded on the 5 of July 2006. It has not yet entered into force.

[27] According to the *lex rei sitae* rule, the 'effectiveness of a transfer of securities is determined by the law of the place where the securities are located at the time of transfer'. In the case of registered securities, 'the relevant law is either the law of the place of the issuer's incorporation or the law of the place where the register is maintained at the time of transfer' (Goode, Kanda, Kreuzer, *Hague Securities Convention. Explanatory Report*, p. 17). While these rules can be easily applied in case of direct holdings of securities, they become problematic in the case of intermediated holdings (as they would require the so-called 'look-through approach' that seeks to identify the applicable law by 'looking through' tiers of intermediaries down to the level of the issuer, register or actual certificates).

securities for the determination of the applicable law (i.e. the so-called 'look-through approach').[28]

The difficulties inherent in the look-through approach are due to the ways in which modern securities transactions take place, that is, by providing collateral in the form of diversified portfolios of securities regulated by the laws of different jurisdictions (which oblige a collateral taker to identify for every transaction a multitude of laws corresponding to perfection requirements of each State where securities issuers are organised).[29]

Given the close relation between the way in which interests in securities are construed and the relative conflict of laws rule, the question is whether the conflict of laws approach, under any form (i.e. the Hague Convention, the Unidroit Convention on Substantive Rules for Intermediated Securities, to quote two significant sources) is actually neutral towards substantive law. A meaningful example is that concerning the possible solution to the difficulties in applying the traditional *lex rei sitae* rule. If the proposal for determining the applicable law is to regard as the relevant property the account, instead of the underlying securities, the conflict of laws solution has *de facto* redefined the nature of the property, thus affecting substantive law.[30]

The issue was also posed when the Hague Convention on the Law Applicable to Certain Rights in Respect of Securities held with an Intermediary was drafted in 2002; however, the response seems to be negative. The Hague Convention does not prescribe any substantive

---

[28] See J.S. Rogers, 'Conflict of laws for transactions in securities held with intermediaries', p. 18.

[29] Goode, Kanda, Kreuzer, *Hague Securities Convention. Explanatory Report*, p. 18. In general, the conflict of law provisions concerning securities are articulated as follows: (1) the domestic law under which securities were issued (the *lex societatis*, or law of incorporation or of the main seat of the company for domestic issues in the form of equities or bonds; or the *lex contractus* in case of international bonds) governs securities in the direct relationship between the issuer and the end-investor; (2) the law applicable to listing and trading of securities listed on a particular stock exchange is the law of that stock exchange; (3) in case of intervention of a central counterparty (clearing) in a netting process, the applicable law is the law chosen to govern such contractual netting, usually through novation; (4) the law governing over-the-counter securities transactions is the *lex contractus* governing that transaction (Article 3(1) of the Rome Convention on the Law Applicable to contractual obligations in the EU). See D. Devos, *The Hague Convention on the Law Applicable to Book-Entry Securities – The Relevance for the European System of Central Banks in Legal Aspects of the ESCB.* Liber Amicorum Paolo Zamboni Garavelli, Frankfurt, 2005, pp. 379–80.

[30] See Rogers, 'Conflict of laws for transactions in securities held with intermediaries', pp. 19–20.

law provisions, and is meant to apply to all securities held with an intermediary, independent of how the legal system qualifies the interest deriving from a credit of securities to a securities account.[31]

One of the distinctive features of the Hague Convention is that of having adopted an alternative to the 'look-through approach' required *de facto* for the application of the *lex rei sitae* rule. Ultimately, however, the Convention drafters opted for a variation on the basic PRIMA approach rule.

The main rule of the Hague Convention, as expressed in Article 4.1, allows the account holder and the relevant intermediary to determine in the account agreement (with a so-called general governing clause), which will be the relevant law that will govern the account agreement (entailing that this *lex contractus* will govern both contractual aspects and proprietary aspects linked to the securities account); or to determine, again in the account agreement, a different law that will govern only the proprietary aspects of the holding and disposition of securities (those falling within the scope of the Convention), while there may or may not be a different choice of law for the account agreement generally.

The Convention does not seek therefore to 'locate' the securities account, the office that maintains the securities account, the issuer, and so forth, but rather leaves it to the agreement between the parties.[32] What must be noted, is that the agreement is between the *intermediary* and the account holder, not between the account holder and a transferee (the so-called pure agreement approach), which would otherwise raise doubts as to the legitimacy of a rule that allows an account holder and a transferee to agree on the law that could affect third parties' rights.[33]

However, in case the parties have not chosen a law to specifically govern the account agreement (under Article 4), Article 5 of the Hague Convention states a subsequent set of fall-back rules, according to which the applicable law will be the law of the place of the office through which the account was entered into (Article 5.1), or the law of the place under whose law the relevant intermediary is incorporated or organised at the

---

[31] Goode, Kanda, Kreuzer, *Hague Securities Convention. Explanatory Report*, p. 17.

[32] Goode, Kanda, Kreuzer, *Hague Securities Convention. Explanatory Report*, p. 20.

[33] Rogers, 'Conflict of laws for transactions in securities held with intermediaries' p. 30. It has also been noted (see Devos, *The Hague Convention on the Law Applicable to Book-Entry Securities*, p. 390) that the debate between the so-called 'subjective criterion' (law of the agreement) v. the 'objective criterion' (location of the account) is a theoretical discussion, since an 'account' is in essence an agreement between the account holder and the intermediary to record in book-entry form assets held by the intermediary in the name or on behalf of the account holder, and submitting to this purpose the entitlement to such assets to a specific law that will govern the correlative rights and interests of the account holder.

time the written account agreement is entered into (Article 5.2), or finally the law of the place where the intermediary has its place of business at the time the account agreement is entered into (Article 5.3). This represents an application of the PRIMA approach (see Articles 4, 5 and 6 of the Hague Convention), even if only as a fall-back rule.

The rule adopted by the Hague Convention is similar to Article 8 Uniform Commercial Code (after the 1994 revision). According to Article 8-110 Uniform Commercial Code, if litigation occurs in one of the states of the United States, and an issue arises concerning the law that governs the effectiveness of a security interest in indirectly held securities, the governing law is determined by the agreement between the account holder and intermediary.[34] The rule can be logically related to the underlying concept of the investor's entitlement interest in securities; an entitlement holder's property interest in an indirect holding system is a bundle of rights that can be asserted directly only against the entitlement holder's own intermediary.[35]

As emerges from a simple examination of the way in which the Hague Convention alternatively articulates conflict of laws rules, the role of the 'agreement' in this type of transactions, as is also the case for the definition of settlement and clearing procedures, is central. The Settlement Finality Directive, the Collateral Directive and an international conflict of laws convention (the Hague Convention) all leave it to private autonomy to determine the law that will govern the agreement, and to define such central institutions as the moment in which settlement is final, or the effects of insolvency on the obligations of a participant in a settlement system.[36]

---

[34] See Uniform Commercial Code § 8-110 (b)(e); See also Rogers, 'Conflict of laws for transactions in securities held with intermediaries', p. 6.

[35] See Uniform Commercial Code §§ 8-503 to 8-508. See J.S. Rogers, 'Policy perspectives on revised U.C.C. Article 8', *UCLA L.Rev.*, 1996, vol. 43, p. 1454.

[36] It is significant to note that in the discussions and Convention negotiations on the opportunity of opting for the law of the place of account or the law governing the account agreement, the first orientation of the securities industry tended towards the solution that finally prevailed (law governing the agreement). Subsequently, after the Draft of the Convention was presented, a legal opinion by the European Banking Federation was circulated which contended that the departure from the *lex rei sitae* rule to the *lex contractus* criterion would introduce legal risks, and could have important implications in the securities chain, on tax regimes, money laundering and fraud prevention (see Devos, *The Hague Convention on the Law Applicable to Book-Entry Securities*, p. 388). The European Central Bank in another opinion (ECB Opinion CON/2005/7 of 17 March 2005) also expressed concern and recommended a prior analysis of the possible impact on these areas.

This alternating orientation of the industry may indicate an acknowledgement of the existing trade-off between legal certainty deriving from mandatory rules set in a conflict of laws convention on the one side, and on the other, the potential for assuming an

If any indication is to be gathered from the observations above, it is that since the private international law solution does not purport to lay down any substantive law rules, several problems remain unresolved.[37] Rather, the task is conferred upon private autonomy (and as a residual rule to the PRIMA approach). The issues still in need of regulation may ultimately fall to the 'recommendations', 'principles' or 'standards' elaborated by one of the many organisations that produce soft law.

4. The Unidroit Convention on Substantive Rules for Intermediated Securities (the Geneva Securities Convention)

Another significant instance of a private international law instrument is represented by the Unidroit Convention on Substantive Rules for Intermediated Securities (to be known as the Geneva Securities Convention).[38]

---

active standard-setting role that may be conferred upon the industry when legal sources refer generally to 'agreement between the parties' (where the role of market operators in preparing quasi-normative contracts, such as Master Agreements, is decisive).

[37] The uncertainties deriving from the application of traditional domestic conflict of laws rules (due, for example, to the difficulties in determining not only the relevant domestic law, but also, at a further level, the relevant substantive law rules of that particular domestic law which have to be applied by the court, and the question whether these domestic rules have to be construed in a manner that takes into account the international character of the contract) have been at the basis of different theories, developed especially in the field of international commercial law, that purport to identify alternative approaches in the application of private international law. (See K. P. Berger, *The Creeping Codification of the Lex Mercatoria*, The Hague-London-Boston, 1999, pp. 9–10).

These include the so-called better-law approach (which looks at the quality of substantive law rules of the different systems); the 'comitas' doctrine (which aims at replacing traditional techniques of private international law with the so-called 'friendly admission of foreign economic law'); and 'hybrid' approaches such as the integration of classical conflict of law rules with substantive law rules, or the application to contracts that contain arbitration clauses of 'general principles of law' as opposed to the rules of any particular domestic legal system (see Berger, *The Creeping Codification*, p. 17 et seq.).

These theories have been criticised on several grounds, with the common conclusion that they do not provide an effective solution to the problem of legal certainty which is often a characterising element of international contracts and commercial transactions. What is relevant for the scope of this study, beyond the specific features of each of the purported solutions, is that all these theories indicate the growing dissatisfaction towards conflict of law rules as resolutive in the field of international commercial contracts.

[38] The Convention was adopted in Geneva on 9 October 2009 by the Diplomatic Conference to adopt a Convention on Substantive Rules regarding Intermediated Securities.

The interest of this project lies in the institutes that this Convention purports to regulate, once ratified and signed by a certain number of contracting States.[39]

As the name itself indicates, the Convention concerns substantive rules related to intermediated securities, and in this sense aims at covering a wider area compared with the pure conflict of law rules of the Hague Convention. This is due to the fact that conflict of laws rules do not always suffice to resolve cross-border issues when the underlying substantive law lacks harmonisation, or when the conflict of law rules may indicate the law of two or more jurisdictions as the law governing an institution or a legal relation. The case has been made for certain types of derivatives, which in some legal systems are considered as securities, whereas in others they are considered as contractual rights (which would therefore not benefit from the special discipline accorded to securities in case of insolvency, for example); or the case of certain special national statutory legislation which only applies to securities held with local central securities depositories.[40]

The Unidroit Convention on Substantive Rules for Intermediated Securities contains rules which are not considered by the EU legislation that has so far dealt with the regulation of securities, such as the Settlement Finality Directive or certain provisions of the Financial Collateral Arrangements Directive. This is the case for those articles disciplining the acquisition or disposition of intermediated securities by debts and credits, further specifying that this can be done on a net basis;[41] and those provisions covering the hypothesis of invalidity and reversal of a debt of securities to a securities account,[42] the acquisition by an innocent person of intermediated securities,[43] and the priority among competing interests.[44]

Notwithstanding the unresolved issue of the qualification of the nature of interests in securities, and notwithstanding a preliminary set of definitions set down in the first Article of the Unidroit Convention

---

[39] Article 2 of the Unidroit Convention on Substantive Rules for Intermediated Securities specifies that the Convention applies whenever 'the applicable conflict of laws rules designate the law in force in a Contracting State as the applicable law; or the circumstances do not lead to the application of any law other than the law in force in a Contracting State'.

[40] See the 'Explanatory Notes to the Preliminary Draft UNIDROIT Convention', p. 50.

[41] Article 11 Unidroit Convention on Substantive Rules for Intermediated Securities.

[42] Article 16 Unidroit Convention on Substantive Rules for Intermediated Securities.

[43] Article 18 Unidroit Convention on Substantive Rules for Intermediated Securities.

[44] Article 19 Unidroit Convention on Substantive Rules for Intermediated Securities.

for Intermediated Securities,[45] an explicit statement on the legal nature of interest in securities is absent.[46] However, an overall view of the contents of the Unidroit Convention provisions permits the assumption that the Convention provides a proprietary protection for this type of interest.[47]

Another indication of the broad regulatory scope of the Convention is found in the provisions regarding the 'Effectiveness in the insolvency of the relevant intermediary'.[48]

The Unidroit Convention for Intermediated Securities also includes provisions confirming the validity of close-out netting agreements[49] and of top-up or substitution of collateral[50] notwithstanding the commencement of insolvency proceedings in respect of the collateral provider. Finally, the Unidroit Convention contains a provision allowing the maintenance (where it pre-exists in domestic law) of the requirement that

---

[45] The Unidroit Convention often uses the same definitions used by the Hague Securities Convention; on the one hand, these definitions have been developed on the basis of a consensus among many countries, and on the other, the use of the same definitions is meant to promote interoperability between the two conventions. See the 'Explanatory notes to the preliminary draft UNIDROIT Convention', p. 78.

[46] This is due to the explicit choice of adopting, because of the different legal traditions and conceptual frameworks, a functional approach in drafting (i.e. adopting a neutral language and formulating rules only with reference to facts). The means by which the result is to be achieved in a concrete legal system remain within the legislator's discretion, as long as they are compatible with the other rules of the Unidroit Convention. See the 'Explanatory notes to the preliminary draft UNIDROIT Convention', p. 70.

[47] Indeed, Article 9 of the Convention, in defining the rights that the credit of securities to a securities account confers on the account holder, such as the 'right to receive and exercise any rights attached to the securities, including dividends, other distributions and voting rights', 'the right to effect a disposition under Article 11 or grant an interest under Article 12', specifies that these rights are effective against third parties. However (and this is a feature unique to the system of holding with intermediaries), in order to avoid disruptions in the system, an account holder may normally only exercise these rights against the 'relevant intermediary', i.e. its direct intermediary, and not against any intermediary which may be situated further up along the holding chain. This is because the latter upper-tier intermediary would generally have no knowledge or record of interests other than of its immediate own account holders. (On the last point see the 'Explanatory notes to the preliminary draft UNIDROIT Convention', pp. 86–8).

[48] Articles 21 'Effectiveness in the insolvency of the relevant intermediary' and 27 'Insolvency of system operator or participant' of the Unidroit Convention on Substantive Rules for Intermediated Securities protect, notwithstanding a different provision applicable in insolvency proceedings, the finality and irrevocability of a securities disposition within a securities settlement system when that disposition is final according to the uniform rules of the securities settlement or clearing system.

[49] Article 33 Unidroit Convention on Substantive Rules for Intermediated Securities.

[50] Article 36 Unidroit Convention on Substantive Rules for Intermediated Securities.

enforcement of collateral securities or obligations must be conducted in a 'commercially reasonable' manner.[51]

The Unidroit Convention on Substantive Rules for Intermediated Securities is an interesting instance of the tendency on the part of transnational institutions to develop instruments with which to regulate some of the same issues which have been the object of legislation (in this case of EU Directives), but which have nonetheless not yet found a uniform substantive discipline.[52] However, the harmonisatory efficacy of this type of instrument ultimately lies in the effective consensus (under the form of signature and ratification of the Convention) that it will be able to find.

A different instrument, of soft law, dealing with securities is the 2001 UNICTRAL Draft Legislative Guide on Secured Transactions, which addresses legislators who have to prepare domestic regulation on secured transactions. The Legislative Guide does not deal with security interests in securities, but rather with consensual security interests created by agreement.

However, even if the focus of the Guide is on security interests in key commercial assets such as goods, inventory equipment and receivables, it will also apply to bank accounts and may apply to other negotiable instruments, and may therefore affect issues related to securities settlement and clearing such as enforcement of security interests, including enforcement in case of insolvency of the debtor.

In such an hypothesis, it is interesting to observe, for example, that the Legislative Guide adopts a series of non-mandatory rules that would be applicable prior to default in the absence of agreement of the parties (and include, significantly and *inter alia*, the grantor's duty to make up for unexpected devaluation of the encumbered assets). In the event of insolvency, the Guide adopts the relevant principles of the UNCITRAL Guide on Insolvency Law and, while recognising that insolvency can affect assets subject to a security interest, recommends the pre-insolvency priority of a security interest and the respect of the pre-insolvency value of the security interest.[53]

---

[51] Article 35 Convention on Substantive Rules for Intermediated Securities.

[52] The Convention was drafted after the implementation in most member states of the EU legislation.

[53] See also the UNCITRAL Legislative Guide on Insolvency Law Recommendations n. 4, 7(e)). See S. V. Bazinas. 'The UNCITRAL Draft Legislative Guide on Secured Transactions' *Uniform Law Review*, 2005, vol. 10, n. 1–2, pp. 148–50.

Chapter 5:
Transfer of Monetary Sovereignty and Regulatory Issues

1. A regulatory perspective

As even a brief overview of the recent developments in the process of integration of both financial markets and of some of the rules concerning monetary obligations indicate, there is a bottom-up pressure, deriving from operators, that calls for rules to be made uniform.[1] The open issue remains that of the identification of the subjects that will be in charge of completing the integration process. For the markets, the debate focuses on the type, the functions, the role and the number of regulators. As for the discipline of monetary obligations, the questions concern the identification of a legitimate source for the adoption of uniform rules across member states, and the subjects who are to assume the role of the new supra-national legislator.

The first phenomenon that should be analysed under this perspective is the loss of sovereignty in the domain of market regulation and monetary obligations on behalf of the member states in favour of communitarian institutions. It will then be necessary to identify the emerging existence of new additional regulators, who are mainly private, and further examine how this transfer of sovereignty to new actors affects the characteristics of the rules that are adopted at the end of the legislative process.

---

[1] Over the past fifty years, different integration theories have been proposed to describe the building of the European Community, among them the most debated (and opposed to each other) being the neo-functionalist approach and the intergovernmentalist approach. (For a historical summary see A. Verdun, (ed.), *The Euro. European Integration Theory and Economic and Monetary Union*, Lanham, Boulder, New York, Oxford, 2002, pp. 10–11; A. Moravcsik, 'Preferences and power in the European Community: a liberal intergovernmentalist approach', *Journal of Common Market Studies*, 1993, vol. 31, p. 473). The debate can be here momentarily set aside to focus on the actors rather than on the modalities of integration.

1.1. The transfer of monetary sovereignty in the Economic and Monetary Union

With the creation of the Economic and Monetary Union and its grad-ual advancement through the different stages, member states have progressively lost their monetary sovereignty in favour of European supranational institutions. Monetary sovereignty is usually defined as the state's power to determine the value of its currency by; (a) setting its exchange rates against other currencies; (b) fixing the currency's convertibility (i.e. the use that can be made of the currency); and (c) controlling the supply of money.[2] The loss of monetary sovereignty can be emphatically summarised in the loss of the power by national governments to control exchange rates and interest rates.[3] The power to autonomously set the interest rates was *de facto* lost by the member states with the liberalisation of short-term capitals, following the entry into force of the Single European Act. Formerly, the existing restrictions on the exportation of national capital ensured that national savings would be reinvested within national boundaries under the form of credit to the state, and the state could authoritatively set the interest rate it was due to pay on the public loan titles.

Capital restrictions made it possible to pursue relatively autonomous monetary and credit policies, which depended on the possibility of main-taining an interest rate different from that of neighbouring countries.[4] With the liberalisation of the short-term capital markets within the common market area, this power to fix the interest rates authoritatively was lost in favour of competition.

Indeed, if the internal interest rate were inferior to the existing rate in the unified market, the state would no longer be able to keep the national

---

[2] See, for example, D. Carreau, 'Le système monétaire international privé', *Recueil des Cours de l'Académie de Droit International de l'Haye*, 1998, vol. 274, p. 372.

[3] See A. Chirico, *La sovranità monetaria tra ordine giuridico e processo economico*, Padova, 2003, p. 72.

[4] See M. Andenas, *Who is Going to Supervise Europe's Financial Markets?*, in M. Andenas, Y. Avgerinos (eds), *Financial Markets in Europe: Towards a Single Regulator*, The Hague, 2003, p. xvii. Capital inflows and outflows were limited by capital restrictions, and depended on the trends in other financial markets. By restricting capital outflows (and thus impeding savers and investors to go abroad), low interest rates could be preserved and downward pressures on the currency's exchange rate could be avoided in the short term, while in the long term domestic capital markets and savings were protected. The effects of restrictions on capital inflows (impeding lenders to raise capital on foreign markets) consisted in maintenance of price stability and protection against upward pressure on the exchange rates in the short term; while in the long term it permitted domestic control over key industries, especially in the area of financial institutions (Ibid.).

savings within its boundaries, and could no longer ensure that it be reinvested after its maturity, with the ensuing risk of having to reimburse consistent shares of its debt at every maturity date.[5] The consequence has been that, after the liberalisation of the short-term capital market, the interest rate for the renewal of public debt was perforce equal to that of the strongest currency, incremented by the differential of inflation and by a percentage point that would encourage savers to invest in national titles instead of foreign ones.[6]

The power to fix exchange rates unilaterally had been lost by member states with the creation of the European Monetary System (EMS) in 1979, which established bands above and below bilateral central exchange markets within which member currencies could float.[7] For national institutions governing monetary policy, the loss of power over control of interest rates and exchange rates (whether dating back to the commitment to the European Exchange Rate Mechanism peg or later to the European Central Bank) marked the effective transfer of monetary sovereignty, before the actual introduction of the single currency in Stage III of the Economic and Monetary Union.[8]

The singularity in the transfer of monetary sovereignty that has occurred with the Economic and Monetary Union is that is has been implemented without a contextual transfer of legislative and regulatory competence. Examples can be taken both from financial markets and from legislative competence for the discipline of monetary obligations *strictu sensu*.

As far as the former are concerned, whilst monetary policy has been transferred to the European Central Bank, the supervision of financial markets and of banking services has remained within the competences of domestic authorities and central banks, clearly entailing a dishomogeneity in the rules governing the markets and its principal operators. There has been an unprecedented separation between central banking and banking supervision, which has led to a growing debate over

---

[5] See G. Guarino, *Verso l'Europa: ovvero la fine della politica*, Milano, 1997, p. 38.

[6] Ibid.

[7] The fluctuation bands were initially fixed in the measure of 2.25 per cent above and below bilateral central exchange rates. See 'Resolution of the European Council on the establishment of the European Monetary System (EMS) and related matters', 5 December 1978. In 1993, in response to pressure on currency markets, the bands were widened to 15 per cent.

[8] See C.A.E. Goodhart, *The Transition to EMU*, in M. Andenas, L. Gormley, C. Hadjiemmanuil, I. Harden (eds), *European Economic and Monetary Union: The Institutional Framework*, London, The Hague, Boston, 1997, p. 7.

which type of regulator would best guarantee an efficient functioning of European financial markets.[9]

As for the regulatory competence concerning monetary obligations, the transfer of monetary sovereignty has also entailed to a duplication of sources. Whereas the regulation of *lex monetae* has been transferred to the European Union (EU) level, the *lex obligationis* remains at a national level. The consequence, however, has been that, *de facto*, the very concept of *lex monetae* has received a broader construction (so as to embrace, for example, the supervision of payments,[10] which strictly speaking should be considered as part of *lex obligationis*).[11]

At the same time the *lex obligationis*, deprived of the possible coordination with the national monetary policy, has been significantly curtailed, as its regulatory competence exists only where a communitarian discipline is not yet in force.[12] The operative space for national regulation, even in what is strictly speaking the domain of the civil regulation of monetary debts (*lex obligationis*), has thus been greatly reduced. It is therefore not unlikely that the trend will move towards a progressive unification at a

---

[9]See G. Di Giorgio and C. Di Noia, 'Appropriateness of regulation at the federal or state level: financial market regulation and supervision: how many peaks for the euro area?', *Brooklyn Journal of International Law*, 2003, vol. 28, p. 463, quoting T. Padoa Schioppa, *EMU and Banking Supervision*, Lecture at the London School of Economics Financial Markets Group, 24 February 1999, available at http://www.wcb.int/key/sp990224.htm and also quoting diffusely the different working groups, task forces and institutional initiatives studying the theme.

[10]*Ex* Article 105, paragraph 2(4) EC Treaty, one of the basic tasks of the European System of Central Banks shall be: 'to promote the smooth operation of payment systems'.

[11]The very concept of *lex monetae* has to be reinterpreted. Since the European Central Bank has the institutional scope of maintaining price stability and, since exchange rates between the euro and precedent national currencies are locked, the meaning of regulation of *lex monetae* has to be in part re-considered, as there is less room for manoeuvre on the value of currency. From the point of view of private law, this means that the regulatory competence relating to the basic principle of nominalism, which is traditionally interpreted as the most significant expression of the power to regulate the *lex monetae*, by imposing the solutory efficacy of legal tender, now has to be interpreted differently. The scope of nominalism, in the light of a stable currency, is that of guaranteeing the stability and efficiency of the system of payments. There is thus a further confirmation of the need, above mentioned and assumed as a basis, to interpret 'monetary obligations' in a broad sense.

[12]The coordination between monetary policy carried out by national central banks and the discipline of monetary obligations determined by legislators has been a historical constant; see, for example, the interaction between the adoption of currency devaluation measures and the correlative prohibition or admissibility of monetary clauses; or the admissibility of damages caused by monetary devaluation in case of delay in payment and the related modalities with which interest rates are calculated.

supra-national level of the rules governing transactions, and not only the concrete functioning of the market.

One of the most significant examples lies in Directive 2000/35/EC on combating late payments in commercial transactions.[13] While it is true that the Directive is only meant to apply to commercial transactions,[14] the incidence of this type of transaction on the overall volume of payments makes the relevance of the sphere of communitarian competence (and the often 'residual' nature of domestic competence) clear.

In its central provision (Article 3 n. 1, letter d) Directive 2000/35) the Directive, *inter alia*, sets the statutory interest rate in case of delay in payment.[15] Indeed, the power to determine statutory interest rates represents a typical hypothesis of a provision of monetary policy with microeconomic effects on the law of monetary obligations. The Directive, however, does not only contain provisions of *lex monetae*. Coherently with the need to harmonise those aspects of the *lex obligationis* that are closely tied to *lex monetae*, the Directive also disciplines those aspects of *lex obligationis* that are central to the implementation of the provisions of a monetary nature (such as the default terms from which a debtor is to be considered in delay,[16] the absence of a need to exercise a formal notice,[17] and the hypothesis of a 'grossly unfair' agreement on the date for payment or the consequences for late payment[18]).

However, even these harmonised Community provisions of *lex obligationis* often need to refer to those general domestic rules on monetary obligations that remain within the sphere of competence of the member states and have not yet been made uniform.[19] In the case of the Directive, for example, the particularly high interest rate has to be coordinated with the pre-existing national rules which determine if and how the statutory interest rate can be derogated by private autonomy, or the admissibility and measure of further compensation beyond the statutory interest rate for damage suffered from delay.

---

[13] Directive 2000/35/EC of 29 June 2000, O.J.L200, 8 August 2000, p. 35.

[14] See Recital n. 13 and Article 2 Directive 2000/35/EC.

[15] The level of interest for late payment which the debtor is obliged to pay shall be the sum of the interest rate applied by the European Central Bank to its most recent main refinancing operation carried out before the first calendar day of the half-year in question, plus at least seven percentage points, unless otherwise specified in the contract.

[16] Article 3, n. 1, lett. b) Directive 2000/35/EC.

[17] Article 3 n. 1 lett. b) Directive 2000/35/EC.

[18] Article 3 n. 3 Directive 2000/35/EC.

[19] The same occurs, for example, in the Directive 2007/64/EC on Payment Services as far as the moment of discharge of the debtor is concerned (see *supra* Chapter 2).

2. The new regulators

The analysis of the transfer of monetary sovereignty that has taken – and is still taking – place in the Economic and Monetary Union requires an identification of the institutional and operational actors of monetary policy in Europe. The institutional players at European level are: the Council of Ministers of the European Union, which holds both the legislative power in monetary matters, and has a fundamental role in deciding whether a member state fulfils the criteria to join the final stage of the Economic and Monetary Union;[20] the European Commission, with executive and regulatory powers, exercised upon delegation from the Council; [21] and the European Central Bank, which with the objective of pursuing price stability, has both regulatory powers and an operational role on the capital markets, governs the monetary policy for the euro-area, and forms, together with the national central banks of the member states participating in the Economic and Monetary Union, the European System of Central Banks.[22] The European Parliament only has a consultative role. At the level of the member states, national governments play a double role: institutional, as market supervisors, national legislators and regulators; and operational, as issuers of public debt. Finally, there are the operational players on the European capital markets, represented by the banking and investment communities.[23]

It is precisely with reference to the latter that one of the most significant aspects of the Economic and Monetary Union can be found: the emergence of a new source of monetary sovereignty. Contrary to the recurring phenomenon of international law, where states transfer part of their sovereignty in favour of international institutions, in the case of international monetary economics, the sovereignty of the single state yields before the financial markets.[24]

Financial markets, which are not institutional but rather composed of private agents and organisations, play a central role in judging the monetary policy of a state. The approval or disapproval judgment is expressed through investment or withdrawal of capital from the national market, and this control over the flow of capital clearly influences

---

[20] See EC Treaty, Articles 202–10.

[21] See EC Treaty, Articles 211–9.

[22] See EC Treaty, Articles 105–15.

[23] For this distinction between institutional and operational actors see R.G. Barresi, 'The European Union: The impact of monetary union and the euro on European capital markets: what may be achieved in capital market integration', *Fordham International Law Journal*, 2005, vol. 28, p. 1272.

[24] See Chirico, *La sovranità monetaria tra ordine giuridico e processo economico*, pp. 74–5.

the potential growth of the economy. Furthermore, the evaluations of financial markets are prospective and tend to estimate the future results of national monetary policies, thus assuming the role of controllers of the system.[25] The relation between the state and the markets is inverted; it is the market, in the form of international rating agencies, that evaluates public loan titles issued by the states, and thus influences national financial policies.[26]

The factual transfer of sovereignty to the markets indeed leads to the assumption that the markets too can be considered as normative sources. The norms will be produced in a bottom-up process, as opposed to the norms produced by the sovereign political power.[27] It is within the markets that the new rules are formed; the process of market globalisation has caused a decline in the centrality of national law as the primary regulatory source.[28] The state origin of the law is no longer the rule.

Rather, the ancient dualism between the business community (global, governed by the *lex mercatoria* and judged by arbitral courts) that operates on the markets on the one side, and the national states (which have progressively lost their normative and jurisdictional competences, as well as the control over the flow of capital and over monetary policy) on the other, seems to have found new vigour.[29]

The new source of law, however, is not opposed to the law-making power of national legislators. It has, conversely, developed *praeter legem*, in order to meet the needs of operators by creating new tools, such as options, swaps, financial instruments (which have also been defined as 'private usages') for the functioning of the markets.[30] It is with reference to the rule-making power of the operational players, the business community, that one can speak of a 'financial market *lex mercatoria*'.[31]

---

[25] Ibid.

[26] S. Cassese, *La crisi dello stato*, Bari, 2002, p. 37.

[27] The definition of the market as a normative source is formulated by Chirico, *La sovranità monetaria tra ordine giuridico e processo economico*, p. 76.

[28] See F. Galgano, *La globalizzazione nello specchio del diritto*, Bologna, 2005, p. 72, also quoting M.R. Ferrarese, *Le istituzioni della globalizzazione: diritto e diritti nella società transnazionale*, Bologna, 2000, p. 94.

[29] F. Galgano, *La globalizzazione nello specchio del diritto*, p. 73.

[30] D. Carreau, *Le système monétaire international privé*, p. 380.

[31] The expression '*lex mercatoria*' has been reproposed in a contemporary context, as the 'new doctrine of *lex mercatoria*', starting from the 1960s and has been developed especially by B. Goldman, 'Frontièrs du droit et la lex mercatoria', *Archives de philosophie du droit*, 1964, p. 177 and Goldman, 'La lex mercatoria dans les contrats et l'arbitrage internationaux: réalité et perspectives', *Journal du Droit International*, 1979, p. 475; C. Schmitthoff, *The Sources of the Law of International Trade, with*

The distinguishing characteristic of what is proposed as financial market *lex mercatoria*, construed within the wider notion of *lex mercatoria*, lies in the object of regulation. Whereas, when considering the contemporary rebirth of *lex mercatoria*, it has been observed that it is the contract that is both the object of regulation and the instrument that serves as the new vehicle promoting uniformity of rules,[32] the domain in which financial market *lex mercatoria* develops is that of the regulation of the markets. The aim of regulation has evolved from a search towards a uniform tool for transactions (international contracts), towards a common set of regulatory laws (and possibly a single regulator) for the efficient functioning of markets and financial services.[33]

Special Reference to East–West Trade, London, 1964; ID., 'Das neue Recht des Welthandels', *Rabels Zeitschrift für ausländisches und internationales Privatrecht,* 1964, vol. 28, p. 47; ID., in N. Horn-C. Schmitthoff (eds), *The Transnational Law of International Commercial Transactions,* Deventer, Boston, 1982; C. Fragistas, 'Arbitrage étranger et arbitrage international en droit privé', *Revue critique de droit international privé,* 1960, p. 1 et seq ; A. Goldstajn, 'The new law merchant', *Journal of Business Law,* 1961, p. 12 et seq; P. Kahn, *La vente commerciale internationale,* Paris, 1961; P. Fouchard, *L'Arbitrage Commercial International,* Paris, 1965. See also R. David, 'I diritto del commercio internazionale: un nuovo compito per i legislatori nazionali o una nuova lex mercatoria?', *Rivista di diritto civile,* 1976, I, p. 577; F. Galgano, *La globalizzazione nello specchio del diritto;* K.P. Berger, *The Creeping Codification of the Lex Mercatoria,* The Hague, London, Boston, 1999.
The expression describes the rebirth of a supranational and 'universal' law created by businessmen and operators without the intermediation of national legislators, with the scope of regulating in a uniform way the commercial relations within the economic unity of markets and beyond the political unity of the States (Galgano, *La globalizzazione nello specchio del diritto* p. 56). See *infra* Chapter 6.
[32] See Galgano, *La globalizzazione nello specchio del diritto,* p. 93 et seq.
[33] The neo-functionalist approach (assuming that the functional needs of an integrated European market would entail a transfer of policy-making powers to the EU level) has been suggested as a method justifying the rationale for a single regulator of the EU financial market (particularly for the securities market). See Y.V. Avgerinos, *The Need and Rationale for a European Securities Regulator,* in M. Andenas and Y. Avgerinos (eds.), *Financial Markets in Europe: Towards a Single Regulator,* pp. 147–8; G. Majone, *Regulating Europe,* London, 1996, p. 66.
According to this approach, 'minimum harmonisation should be seen today as a transitory stage on the way towards European legal unity' and centralisation (through the introduction of an EU supervisory authority in the field of investment services) would be useful in 'ensuring that rules are applied in the same way in all member states'. (Y.V. Avgerinos, *The Need and Rationale for a European Securities Regulator,* pp. 147–8).
Other authors, on the contrary, believe that minimum harmonisation safeguards national autonomy and competition among member states. See J. Köngden, *Rules of Conduct: Further Harmonisation?,* in G. Ferrarini (ed.), *European Securities Markets: The Investment Services Directive and Beyond,* London, 1998, p. 129.

The need for this common regulation of the markets derives from the atypical phenomenon observed above deriving from the implementation of Stage Three of the Economic and Monetary Union: on one side the transfer of monetary sovereignty to a single and supranational institution such as the European Central Bank; on the other, the maintenance of the supervisory competence on market functioning to domestic and national authorities and central banks.

Indeed, the problem of the level at which regulation should be implemented has become central with the development of globalised finance. On the one side, in the last few years there has been a growth in the tendency of regulation on a global or regional level (i.e. through international standards, agreements and conventions, on issues ranging from capital adequacy requirements to international supervision in different fields). However, the supervisory authorities who are called upon to enforce these regulations are still for the most part based on a national level.[34]

In Europe, given the possibility of ensuring a European jurisdiction, the debate revolves around the issue of whether to organise financial supervision on a national or on a European basis. Among the arguments in favour of a European supervisory structure there is the difficulty of achieving simultaneously a single financial market and stability in the financial system while maintaining a high degree of nationally based supervision.[35] Counters-arguments highlight that the current degree

---

Yet another interpretation sees the Economic and Monetary Union, in its two distinct parts, as an attempt to reconcile supra-nationalism and intergovernmentalism, where the economic policy-making (carried out through the Economic Union) tends towards intergovernmentalism, and monetary policy-making (realised through the Monetary Union) tends towards supra-nationalism. See F. Snyder, *EMU: Metaphor for European Union? Institutions, Rules and Types of Regulation*, in R. Dehousse (ed.), *Europe After Maastricht. An ever Closer Union?*, München, 1994, p. 64.

[34] This is due mainly to questions of political sovereignty and to the need of jurisdiction (i.e. for the enforcement of regulations, liquidation and winding-up procedures and taxation). See D. Schoenmaker, S. Osterloo, 'Cross-border issues in European financial supervision,' in D.G. Mayes, G.E. Wood (eds), *The Structure of Financial Regulation*, London, New York, 2007, p. 264.

[35] This is an application of the classical 'trilemma' in macro-economic policy, due to the fact that policy-makers are confronted with three incompatible objectives: (1) fixed exchange rates; (2) independent monetary policies; (3) perfect capital mobility. See Schoenmaker, Osterloo, 'Cross-border issues in European financial supervision', p. 265; N. Thygesen, 'Comments on the political economy of financial harmonisation in Europe', in J. Kremers, D. Schoenmaker, P. Wierts (eds) *Financial Supervision in Europe*, Cheltenham, 2003; A. Rose, 'Explaining exchange rate volatility: an empirical analysis of 'The Holy Trinity' of monetary independence,fixed exchange rates, and capital mobility', *Journal of International Money and Finance*, 1996, vol. 15, p. 925.

of integration of European financial markets does not yet require a European supervisory authority.[36]

The present system of prudential supervision in the EU is based on the principle of home-country control combined with minimum standards and mutual recognition.[37] The arguments in favour of home–country control are generally based on the consideration that it permits effective supervision (especially since it enables the supervisors to carry out the so-called consolidated supervision which will take into consideration a group-wide assessment of the risk profile and the required capital adequacy of financial institutions) and that it limits the regulatory burdens on financial institutions (whose subsidiaries in other countries are *de facto* under the control of the consolidated supervisor in the home country of the group or parent company, even though formally, *de jure*, it is the host country authorities which control the subsidiaries as separate legal entities).[38]

Home-country control, however, does not extend to financial stability of the host country, with the consequence that in an ever-increasingly integrated market, a failure in one country may have cross-border spill-over effects and may thus call into question whether home country control is the adequate regulatory solution for a market that is undergoing a process of integration.[39]

---

[36] Schoenmaker, Osterloo, 'Cross-border issues in European financial supervision', p. 265

[37] Once a financial institution is authorised and supervised in its home country, it can operate throughout the EU, either by offering cross-border services to other EU countries or by establishing branches in the other countries. See Schoenmaker, Osterloo, 'Cross-border issues in European financial supervision', p. 278.

[38] An example of the adoption of consolidated supervision is represented by the Directive on the supplementary supervision of credit institutions, insurance undertakings and investment firms in a a financial conglomerate (Directive 2002/87/EC of 16 December 2002, O.J. L35, 11 February 2003, p. 1). See Schoenmaker, Osterloo, 'Cross-border issues in European financial supervision', p. 278.

[39] Schoenmaker, Osterloo, 'Cross-border issues in European financial supervision', p. 279.

Other regulatory options for financial institutions have been summarised by the same authors into the following schemes. The first model is based on full supervision by the home supervisor for all EU-wide operations (thus including both branches and subsidiaries, whereas according to the current model, the home supervisor is responsible for a bank and its EU-wide branch network and it is the consolidated supervisor as well, while the host country is responsible for a bank's EU subsidiaries and controls the stability of the financial system). The home supervisor can act under either a national mandate (which entails that the supervisor will be predominantly responsive to the needs of domestic depositors and concerned with domestic financial stability) or under a European mandate.

2.1. New regulators, monetary policy and impact on harmonisation of the rules

The emergence of new regulators in the field of monetary obligations, payments and financial services implies the adoption of new policies, which can affect the harmonisation process both as to the type of rules that could be adopted and to the content of the rules.

The supra-national regulation, under the competence of the European Central Bank, concerns the macro-economic goals of the Economic and Monetary Union monetary policy which are defined in the EC Treaty.[40]

Another alternative is to create a central body within a European System of Financial Supervisors and to give this body full responsibility for the EU-wide operations, both branches and subsidiaries, of pan-European banks (having, clearly, a European mandate that aims at taking into consideration the interests of all depositors and countries). Under such a model, the European Central Bank would be in charge of the financial stability within the European System of Central Banks.

The ultimate alternative model is to give the host supervisor responsibility for all operations within its country, both for branches and for subsidiaries, and to limit the supervision to the scope of a strict national mandate. The European Financial Services Round Table (EFR, 2004) has suggested a model in which a clearly defined lead supervisor (usually the home supervisor), responsible for supervision on a consolidated, solo and sub-consolidated level, will be in charge of coordinating all reporting schemes, validating and authorising internal models, approving capital and liquidity allocation, approving cross-border set-up of specific functions and deciding about on-site inspections. See Schoenmaker and Oosterloo, 'Cross-border issues in European financial supervision', pp. 279–81.

[40] Article 105(2) of the EC Treaty assigns the task of defining and implementing monetary policy of the Community to the European System of Central Banks. The primary objective of the European System of Central Banks shall be to maintain price stability (Article 105(1)). Article 105 (1) continues by stating that 'Without prejudice to the objective of price stability, the ESCB shall support the general economic policies in the Community with a view to contributing to the achievement of the objectives of the Community as laid down in Article 2. The ESCB shall act in accordance with the principle of an open market economy with free competition, favouring an efficient allocation of resources, and in compliance with the principles set out in Article 4'. The European System of Central Banks is also competent for the conduct of foreign-exchange operations (intended to be non-inflationary, *ex* Article 105(2), 109 EC Treaty and Article 3.1 European System of Central Banks Statute; see C. Proctor, *The Euro and the Financial Markets. The Legal Impact of EMU*, Bristol, 1999, p. 32) in conformity with policies set by the Council according to the consultation procedures *ex* Article 111 EC Treaty; for the withholding and management of the official foreign reserves of the member states; for the promotion of smooth operation of payment systems.

Article 110 of the EC Treaty confers on the European Central Bank the power to enact Regulations for the promotion of the objectives assigned to the European System of Central Banks; Article 18 of the European System of Central Banks Statute, in view of the achievement of price stability and the other monetary policy objectives also assigns to the European Central Bank and to national central banks the power to: (1) buy/sell

The economic debates focus on the issues of independency of the European Central Bank especially with reference to the pursuit of price stability;[41] on the trade-off between 'rules versus discretion' as a remedy against the time-inconsistency problem of national monetary policy conduct on the one hand, and the risk of an excessive conservativism (especially in absence of a democratic accountability of the Central bank) in the adherence to strict pre-set non-inflationary objectives on the other;[42] on the problem of accountability and transparency of the Central Bank; and on the optimal monetary regime. A few very basic observations from the legal point of view should be made.

The macro-economic choices of monetary policy clearly affect the markets beyond the strict economic aspects. The credibility of a central bank (which according to many theories could be enhanced with an 'independent' authority[43]) is one of the first factors that determines the attractiveness of a market for investors. Secondly, in implementing its statutory goals, the European Central Bank will also have to regulate some concrete mechanisms for a more efficient functioning of the market.

From the strictly private law point of view, given the unprecedented separation between political sovereignty and monetary sovereignty, which can be summarised under the notion of separation of *lex monetae* and *lex obligationis*, the assumption is that a harmonisation of the *lex obligationis* will have to follow the unification of *lex monetae*. In the light of the objectives of monetary policy conferred on the European System

---

or lend/borrow any currencies, marketable instruments or precious metals; and (2) conduct credit operations with credit institutions and other market participants, with lending being based on adequate collateral; and it may also require financial institutions in the member states to hold minimum reserves on account with the European Central Bank or national central banks (Article 19 of the ESCB Statute). See also, for further comments, C. Proctor, *The Euro and the Financial Markets*, pp. 30–4 and pp. 74–80.

[41] See F. Amtenbrink, *The Democratic Accountability of Central Banks. A Comparative Study of the European Central Bank,* Oxford, Portland, 1999, pp. 11–26.

[42] See O. Issing, V. Gaspar, I. Angeloni, O. Tristani, *Monetary Policy in the Euro Area (Strategy and Decision-making at the Central European Bank)*, Cambridge, 2001, pp. 33 et seq.

[43] See *ex multis* Amtenbrink, *The Democratic Accountability*, p. 13; L. Wylie, 'EMU: a neoliberal construction', in A. Verdun (ed.), *The Euro. European Integration Theory and Economic and Monetary Union*, p. 77; P. H. Loedel, 'Multilevel governance and the independence of the ECB', in A. Verdun (ed.), *The Euro. European Integration Theory and Economic and Monetary Union*, pp. 128–9. The independence of a central bank is usually assessed with reference to four factors: (1) institutional independence; (2) functional independence; (3) organisational independence; (4) financial independence. See Amtenbrink, *The Democratic Accountability*, pp. 18–19.

of Central Banks and the European Central Bank, a few hypotheses can be made as to what type of harmonised legal rules could be enacted.[44]

With the creation of a monetary union, all the debts in legal tender in the participating member states are denominated in the same currency. While the determination of the effective value of the euro in the different member states may vary, as the purchase power of money depends on non-uniform factors such as production costs of goods and inflation, it is however necessary for the sake of legal certainty to ensure that all the debts determined in euros be performed in the same way, be it at the nominal value or at a different indexed value.[45] It will therefore be necessary to adopt common policies on the admissibility of value clauses and price indexation.[46] However, given the objectives of price stability and inflation control, these measures do not necessarily have to be in a prohibitive sense (as has been the case in the past), as the strenuous defence of nominalism may not be so stringent in stable economic conjunctures. There is no need to prohibit revaluation, as long as this occurs with harmonised rules throughout the common currency area.[47]

It may also be more difficult to conceive special national debt revaluation measures for certain categories of 'socially protected' creditors.[48]

---

[44] So far, Community legislation has obviously dealt with the regulation of the public monetary aspects, with the exception of a few provisions necessary for the implementation of the Third stage of the Economic and Monetary Union, such as Regulation n. 974/98 of 3 May 1998 on the introduction of the Euro, *O.J.* L139, 11 May 1998, p. 1, and Regulation n. 1103/97 of 17 June 1997 on certain provisions relating to the introduction of the euro, and particularly on continuity of contracts, *O.J.* L162 of 19 June 1997, p. 1.

[45] For example a debt of 1000 euros in France and a debt of 1000 euros in Spain should both be paid in the same amount at due date, be it 1000 euros, the nominal value, or 1010 euros, 1020 euros, etc. if the debt is indexed, for example.

[46] For example, the French legislature has recently changed the *Code monétaire et financier* (see *Loi no 2004–804* and *Loi no 2005–841*) to allow, in derogation from the general prohibition, price indexation for financial instruments and other enumerated categories of credits (Article L112-3 *Code monétaire et financier*). Germany has a similar special law prohibiting price indexation, with the exception of financial and capital market transactions and cross-border transactions between merchants (see §2 *Preisangaben-und Preisklauselgestetz* of 1998); however, it has been noted that with participation in the Economic and Monetary Union Germany has lost the competence to enact such a provision (see S. Grundmann, in *Münchener Kommentar Bürgerliches Gesetzbuch*, vol. 2, §§ 241-432, 4th edn, München, 2001, *sub* §§ 244, 245, par.75.), and these arguments can be extended to other euro-zone member states.

[47] The risk that private indexation may promote inflationary tendencies (although economists are not unanimous on the point: see C. Proctor, *Mann on the Legal Aspect of Money*, 6th edn, Oxford, 2005, p. 328), is greatly diminished.

[48] See, for example, Article, 429, 3rd paragraph, of the Italian civil procedure code, which provides an automatic indexation of employees' salaries. In Germany, under the

Indeed, these measures would necessarily have to be adopted on a case by case basis by the individual legislatures of the member states and thus sacrifice the nominal uniformity of debts denominated in euros, depending on what type of creditor is being paid and under which *lex obligationis*.

The pursuit of price stability, and thus the prospective of a stable non-inflationary conjuncture may also be decisive for national legislative choices between fixed or variable interest rates,[49] with ensuing consequences for common policy choices on anatocism and usury.

At the macro-economic level of monetary policy implementation, it is quite clear that there is little space for non-institutional actors and for the application of *lex mercatoria*. Rather, the novelty lies in the supranational and common source (the EC Treaty and the ensuing Regulations enacted by the European Central Bank), and in the greater independence of monetary policy from national political powers.

2.2. New regulators, soft law and the impact on market regulation

The second aspect that has to be examined with reference to new regulators concerns the policy choices made by non-institutional sources (market operators), which have been identified under the notion of financial market *lex mercatoria*. The policies here concern regulatory aspects, and particularly the choices regarding powers and characteristics of market regulators.

As has been pointed out, there are four levels at which a market can be regulated in aiming at the general objectives of stability, equitable resource distribution and efficiency: (1) the pursuit of macro-economic stability (carried out by Central Banks through macro-controls over currencies, interest rates, payments and possibly settlement systems); (2) prudential regulation of intermediaries; (3) transparency of the market and of intermediaries; and (4) safeguarding and promotion of competition in the financial sector.[50]

---

extremely severe monetary crisis between the two World Wars, the *Aufwertungsgesetz* of 1925 re-evaluated in a different measure different types of debts.

[49] The choice between a fixed or a variable interest rate differs widely across eurozone member states; common parameters will be clearly easier to achieve with a single Central Bank.

[50] See G. Di Giorgio and C. Di Noia, 'Appropriateness of regulation at the federal or state level: financial market regulation and supervision', pp. 469–70. One of the fundamental choices at the base of regulation policies is, however, the choice between regulatory harmonisation and regulatory competition (see *infra*). See diffusely *ex multis* G. Ferrarini, *Securities Regulation and Pan-European Securities Markets*, in

The issue of regulation, and of the best means of implementing regulation naturally requires an *ad hoc* study. A few very general observations suggest that, given a set of possible alternatives for the regulation of the market,[51] if the choices are suggested by soft law sources such as international financial standards, and are thus a product of the very business community (financial market *lex mercatoria*), the ensuing policies may be oriented to reflect the needs of only one set of actors on the market (the operators). The possible conflict of interests may, for example, concern the trade-off between market stability and competition, or between stability and transparency of the market. The objective of maintaining market stability in unfavourable economic conjunctures may lead to the adoption of measures limiting competition, such as barriers to new entries to the market or legal limitations on certain activities (as has occurred in the credit sector) thus impeding, for the sake of stability, the exit of inefficient actors from the market. The conflict of interest here may be accentuated when regulatory competences are assigned to a single agency[52] or when they are self-regulatory.[53]

As for transparency, the problem concerns investor protection in the banking sector: scarce transparency in fund-gathering activities may on the one hand result in application of lower interest rates (below market

---

G. Ferrarini, K.J. Hopt, E. Wymeersch (eds), *Capital Markets in the Age of the Euro. Cross-Border Transactions, Listed Companies and Regulation*, The Hague, London, New York, 2002, p. 249; see also W. Bratton, J. McCahery, S. Picciotto, C. Scott (eds), *International Regulatory Competition and Coordination. Perspectives in Economic Regulation in Europe and the United States*, Oxford, 1996. See also *supra*, Chapter 5.

[51] Key issues include *inter alia* the choice between externally imposed regulation or self-regulation and the means with which to ensure enforcement of self-regulation (e.g. through the use of law or of contracts); centralised or decentralised regulation; the different systemic issues underlying choices according to who the regulated subjects are (e.g. banking or non-banking financial services) (See C. Goodhart, P. Hartmann, D. Llewellyn et al., *Financial Regulation. Why, how and where now?*, London, New York, 1998, pp. 2–15); the choice between a single regulator or a multiple system of financial regulators, each being responsible for one or more regulatory objectives (See Di Giorgio and Di Noia, 'Appropriateness of regulation at the federal or state level: financial market regulation and supervision', *passim* and especially pp. 481–2); the choice between the different techniques for risk management (on the new techniques developed by banks for their risk taking within the market infrastructure, See Goodhart, Hartmann, Llewellyn, *Financial Regulation. Why, how and where now?*, pp. 73–97); the determination of the right degree of regulation (e.g. to avoid the risks of overregulation).

[52] See Di Giorgio and Di Noia, 'Appropriateness of regulation at the federal or state level: financial market regulation and supervision', p. 480.

[53] See Goodhart, Hartmann, Llewellyn, *Financial Regulation. Why, how and where now?*, p. 50.

rate), potentially strengthening banks' stability, but on the other, may work to the diasdvantage of investors.[54]

It may thus not be surprising that soft law (such as informal agreements implemented by banking and financial sectors, even restrictive in nature) is sometimes voluntarily submitted to by market operators in order to avoid more restrictive formal legislation or regulation.[55] This process may be classified as one of the forms of self-regulation, and more specifically, what has been defined as '*coerced* self-regulation, in which the industry formulates and imposes regulation but in response to threats by the government that if it does not the government will impose statutory regulation'.[56]

While this risk always exists in policy-making, it may perhaps be inferred that in the absence of a strong supra-national market regulator (as is the case in the European market[57]), and given a strong demand for a better and rapid integration of the common financial market, the soft law may have easier leeway to fill the *vacuum legis*, or at least to suggest some of the rules.

The growing reliance on soft law techniques and self-regulation in financial market policy on behalf of the EC institutions and particularly the Commission (exemplified by the importation into EC law of

---

[54] Di Giorgio, and Di Noia, 'Appropriateness of regulation at the federal or state level: financial market regulation and supervision', p. 480.

[55] See M. Giovanoli, 'Reflections on international financial standards as "Soft Law", *Essays in International Financial & Economic Law*, 2002, n.37, The London Institute of International Banking, Finance and Development Law, p. 9.

[56] J. Black, 'Constitutionalising self-regulation', *Modern Law Review*, 1996, vol. 59, p. 27 (italics in original). Other forms of self-regulation, according to the same classification which focuses on the relationship between the collective group and the state include '*mandated* self-regulation, in which a collective group, an industry or profession for example, is required or designated by the government to formulate and enforce norms within a framework defined by the government, usually in broad terms; *sanctioned* self-regulation, in which the collective group itself formulates the regulation, which is then subject to government approval; *voluntary* self-regulation, where there is no active state involvement, direct or indirect, in promoting or MANDATING self-regulation'. (Ibid.)

[57] The European legislator is mainly concerned with macro-economic policies. Furthermore, as has been observed (Di Giorgio and Di Noia, 'Appropriateness of regulation at the federal or state level: financial market regulation and supervision', p. 476), in the sector of financial regulation the principle of minimum harmonisation and the principle of mutual recognition do not seem to work. Or, if they are to provide a regulatory competition among member states (through mobility of financial intermediaries in transferring their headquarters), then the principle of mutual recognition would have to be applied in a much broader way than is currently the case. (See R. Petschnigg, 'The institutional framework for financial market policy in the USA seen from an EU perspective', ECB Occasional Paper Series n. 35, 2005, p. 5.)

several compilations of financial standards and by the encouragement expressed by EC institutions towards the adoption of codes of conduct prepared by the industry) is not without risks. The EC institutions themselves have manifested awareness of the trend adopted by the Commission, and with special reference to future governance, funding and political accountability of global standard setting bodies' have expressed the need for a strengthening of public oversight of these structures in order 'to ensure appropriate reflection of stakeholders, satisfactory transparency, due process and sustainable financing'[58] even suggesting that a coordinated position be taken by the EC where member states participate in international standard setting bodies such as the International Organisation of Securities Commissions, the International Association of Insurance Supervisors and the Basel Committee.[59]

3. The problem of regulation: risks and optional forms of intervention

The process of market integration involves both the removal of legal barriers and a series of regulation choices. However, the two aspects are closely linked. This emerges if one considers that the financial instruments that are traded on the market are contracts.[60] Therefore, the existence of a valid and enforceable contract under law ultimately conditions the financial instruments that are traded on the markets.[61]

---

[58] Green Paper on Financial Services Policy (2005–2010), COM (2005), 177, p. 7; see also the European Parliament's Van den Burg Report on the Current State of Integration of EU Financial Markets (April 2005), A6-0087, para. B.21.

[59] Commission White Paper on Financial Services Policy 2005-2010, COM (2005), 629 final, pp. 15–16. See N. Moloney, 'Innovation and risk in EC financial market regulation: new instruments of financial market intervention and the Committee of European Securities Regulators', *European Law Review*, 2007, vol. 32, p. 640, further noting, for example, that IOSCO 'is an international body without formal accountability links, with limited transparency as to its activities and decision-making procedures [....]' and whose 'dynamics of operation are not clear and the nature of the influence excercised by key market actors and powerful regulators is opaque'.

[60] For example, derivative markets permit the trading of contract rights or interests. A.M. Corcoran, 'Cross-border financial transactions: 25 questions to consider in making risk management decisions', in Ferrarini, Hopt, Wymeersch (eds), *Capital Markets in the Age of the Euro*, p. 318.

[61] Ibid. In a futures market, the product is a 'contract for future settlement' valued using a 'cash market' or 'calculated' reference price. The terms and conditions of this contract are based on cash market practices and are included in the rules of the market in case of membership exchanges. The knowledge of contract terms is therefore essential for the assessment of the effective pursuance of the trader's purposes and for the consequences in case of default. Both direct and indirect participants to the market, in order to access the market, agree to abide by all the present rules, terms

However, the *trait-d'union* with regulatory issues derives from the fact that a futures contract is also a financial trading instrument, which depends on the regulatory choices of the market. A parallel has been drawn in the EC securities regulation regime, between securities-settlement issues on one side, and the regulation of securities-trading markets on the other.[62] In both areas the relevant EC regime focuses on the macro-questions of stability and the management of the smooth operation of the market, whereas there seems to be a minor concern for the adoption of harmonised operating standards.[63]

Indeed, the issues emerging with the globalisation of markets concern the identification and management of a series of risks for cross-border transactions: transparency, liquidity, accountability, certainty.[64] These risks are generally related to the trading of services and the derivatives market, while other more specific risks concern the settlement and finality procedures and the use of collateral.

The types of risk in clearing and settlement, associated with both domestic and cross-border trades, include principal risk (the possibility that either counterparty will fail to meet his obligations); replacement risk (the risk borne by a counterparty of having to replace, at current market prices, the original transaction, if the other counterparty fails to meet his obligations at the due date); liquidity risk (the possibility that either counterparty will not settle an obligation for the full value on the due date but at some unspecified date thereafter) and cash deposit risk (the risk arising from the need to hold cash balances with an intermediary for settling security transactions).

However, in cross-border trades, because of the greater reliance on custodians or multiple custodians, there is an additional custody risk, consisting in the possible loss of securities held in custody in case of insolvency, fraud or negligence of the custodian or subcustodian.

The systemic risks of clearing and settlement represent a market failure which justifies the intervention of securities regulation and the subjection of these markets to supervision in order to ensure their stability and integrity.[65] One of the open issues, however, remains whether this

---

and conditions of the marketplace; and it is the market itself that usually indicates the national law under which its rules are articulated, or the different relevant national laws, in case of cross-border transactions involving trading or execution platforms in one jurisdiction with clearing and settling located in another. Corcoran, 'Cross-border financial transactions', pp. 319–22.

[62]See N. Moloney, *EC Securities Regulation*, Oxford, 2002, p. 712.
[63]Ibid.
[64]Corcoran, 'Cross-border financial transactions,' p. 317 et seq.
[65]N. Moloney, *EC Securities Regulation*, p. 11.

intervention should assume the form of harmonisation or of regulatory competition.[66]

3.1. Regulatory options and the EU legislator: harmonisation, regulatory competition and the Markets in Financial Instruments Directive

Regulation of European markets, especially in the process of implementation of the European Economic and Monetary Union, has undergone different phases, featuring both 'minimum harmonisation' efforts and maximum harmonisation, or 'high level' principles and the predisposition of conditions for the operativity of regulatory competition. This evolution is visible in two important legislative instruments, which over the decade that separates their respective issues have responded with changes in discipline to the evolving needs (and pressures) of progressively more integrated European markets. The first instrument is the Investment Services Directive, issued in 1993;[67] the second is the Markets in Financial Instruments Directive issued in 2004.[68] Before examining the current regulatory framework as designed by this legislation, it is necessary to provide an overview of some of the regulatory options at the disposal of policy-makers.

The economic theory underlying regulatory competition holds that the market will produce efficient arrangements between the parties, in order to prevent the transfer of firms to other jurisdictions which offer the laws they seek.[69] This 'market perspective', deriving from

---

[66]'Regulatory competition can be defined as the process whereby regulators deliberately set out to provide a more favourable regulatory environment in order either to promote the competitiveness of domestic industries or to attract more business activity from abroad'. See K. Gatsios, P. Holmes, *Palgrave Dictionary of Economics and the Law*, London, 1998, p. 271.

[67]Directive 93/22/EEC of 10 May1993 on investment services in the securities field, *O.J.* L141, 11 June 1993, p. 27.

[68]Directive 2004/39/EC of 21 April 2004 on markets in financial instruments, *O.J.* L145, 30 April 2004, p. 1.

[69]The first development of this theory is attributed to C. M. Tiebout, 'A pure theory of local expenditures', *Journal of Political Economy*, 1956, vol. 64, p. 416, according to which given a model of local governments with different levels of services and taxation, and in which citizens ('consumer voters') can 'vote with their feet' to choose the system that best suits their preferences, the local governments will be induced to allocate resources in an economically efficient way, and regulation will enhance economic welfare since competitive conditions diminish interest group influence and promote innovation. See also H. Søndergaard Birkmose, 'Regulatory competition and the European Harmonisation Process', *European Business Law Review*, 2006, vol. 17, p. 1077.

micro-economic theories according to which distributed decision-making and spontaneous order enhance economic welfare, holds that optimal regulation is most likely to result from competition between institutional orders.[70] As a consequence, other regulatory sources, such as governmental legislation will only be necessary in case of persisting market failures.

Especially in the case of international harmonisation, one of the widely shared theories in the debate holds that among the premises for harmonisation to be worthwhile, there must be some form of market failure existing beyond national boundaries, that remains unresolved notwithstanding efforts of national regulators.[71]

Efficient harmonisation should create a market in which operators can rely with some certainty as to the rules which apply[72] and should (through uniformity of rules) reduce transaction costs and lower protectionist barriers.[73] However, the risks of the harmonisation process lie in the possible outcome: the adoption of obsolete rules at the end of a slow decisional process (inherent in the adoption of international standards), whereas the securities market has a rapid pace of development and may require more flexible regulatory techniques.

Harmonisation may also hamper the development of efficient regulation at national level, in principle potentially better tailored to reflect the characteristics of local investors and market participants. When the harmonised standards are considered too high, for example in banking regulation, the principles of deregulation or strategic trade, as opposed to harmonisation, are often invoked to maintain the advantage of

---

[70] W. Bratton, J. McCahery, S. Picciotto, S. Scott,'Introduction: regulatory competition and institutional evolution', in Bratton, McCahery, Picciotto, Scott (eds), *International Regulatory Competition and Coordination*, p. 3.

[71] See G. Ferrarini, 'Securities regulation and pan-European securities markets', in Ferrarini, Hopt, Wymeersch (eds), *Capital Markets in the Age of the Euro*, p. 249, quoting White, 'Competition versus harmonization: an overview of international regulation of financial services', in C.E. Barfield (ed.), *International Financial Markets: Harmonization versus Competition*, Washington, DC, 1996, pp. 5–48.

The dilemma between regulatory competition and harmonisation can also be faced from the cost perspective. While harmonisation entails the risk of political distortion (where, for example, specific interests groups are favoured by specific regulations enacted by legislators for pure opportunistic reasons), regulatory competition can produce economic distortion. Assuming this perspective, harmonisation should be undertaken when the costs deriving from economic distortion outweigh the costs deriving from political distortion. See H. Søndergaard Birkmose, 'Regulatory competition and the European harmonisation process,' pp. 1079–80.

[72] Moloney, *EC Securities Regulation*, p. 11.

[73] Ferrarini, *Securities Regulation and Pan-European Securities Markets*, p. 249.

national regulation.[74] Furthermore, at the EC level specifically, every harmonisatory action has to comply with the principle of subsidiarity.[75]

These arguments have been used to sustain a different option: regulatory competition between member states. According to this system based on the premise of regulatory arbitrage, where regulatory regimes differ, market participants will prefer products or services which respond to their needs in terms of price and quality, but which originate from a state with a more efficient regulatory regime, over products or services originating under their own inefficient domestic regime. Accordingly, firms may choose to relocate in response to these signals, and further still, investors may choose to invest in a state in which the regulatory regime corresponds to the investor's perception of the optimal balance between risk and reward.[76]

As a result of regulatory competition, informational imbalance in the market may be reduced, thanks to the transmission of signals across the market and towards regulators. In response to these signals and in order to avoid migrations across the market, adopted regulation may also try to reflect the interests of as wide as possible a segment of the market (discouraging the adoption of inefficient regimes favouring a restricted number of subjects).[77] Finally, in view of the need to comply with principles of EU law, regulatory competition seems to be more compatible with subsidiarity as it encourages a centrifugal movement of regulation from centralised EC institutions towards member states.[78]

The conditions for the functioning of regulatory competition are a coordination with the principles of mutual recognition, home country control and minimum harmonisation.[79] On the one hand, in principle

---

[74] States will tend to support harmonisation when it is their standard that will be harmonised. See J. Braithwaite, P. Drahos, *Global Business Regulation*, Cambridge, 2000, p. 127.

[75] Moloney, *EC Securities Regulation*, p. 11.

[76] Moloney, *EC Securities Regulation*, p. 12.

[77] Bratton, McCahery, Picciotto, Scott, *Introduction: Regulatory Competition and Institutional Evolution*, p. 14.

[78] Moloney, *EC Securities Regulation*, p. 12.

[79] See Moloney, *EC Securities Regulation*, p. 14. A distinction has been drawn between the principle of mutual recognition as a conflict of laws rule (applied by the judiciary – the European Court of Justice) and the principle of home-country control (and home- country rule) provided for by the EC legislation. While the judicial principle of mutual recognition only has limitative effects (i.e. limiting the exercise of national functions, such as imposing additional requirements on a subject which while providing services in a host member state is already complying with the rules of another member state in which it is established), the legislative principle also provides for the allocation of specific competences (either rule making competences or supervision and enforcement competences) to a particular member state. See M. Ortino, 'The role

mutual recognition opens the market to those operators who comply with the minimum harmonisation standards which are imposed by the regulated subject's home–member state.[80] On the other, minimum harmonised standards encourage the mutual recognition principle as the latter generates confidence between member states as to the regulatory standards applied by each other (also promoting market stability) and avoids inefficient duplications of regulation. Finally, minimum standard harmonisation favours regulatory competition (as to the attractiveness of a member state as a primary regulator or home country) above the minimum level.[81]

The risks inherent in regulatory competition as to the possible (low) level to which competition drives regulation (so-called 'race to the bottom/race to the top dilemma') are seemingly avoided in the field of securities regulation because market participants tend to favour balanced systems of regulation which support market stability and do not damage investors.[82]

---

and functioning of mutual recognition in the European market of financial services', *International and Comparative Law Quarterly*, 2007, vol. 56, pp. 321–2).

A recent approach of the EC Commission to legislation in various fields and significantly in the field of financial services has been that of combining the principle of mutual recognition to a so-called 'essential harmonisation' or 'minimum harmonisation' of national laws. This is due to the fact that the judicial principle of mutual recognition has often been insufficient to integrate national markets in financial services. This insufficiency is due mainly to two reasons: (a) the traditional differences in national financial regulatory systems of member states (such that a lack of equivalence between national laws can be invoked as a reason for derogation from the obligation of mutual recognition), and (b) an often recurring absence of trust between member states as to their reciprocal national supervisory and enforcement activities (which are typical and essential, beyond substantive regulation, of financial services regulation). See Ortino, 'The role and functioning of mutual recognition in the European market of financial services', pp. 323–4.

[80] When the European Commission in its 1985 White Paper on the completion of the internal market (COM (85) 310 final) adopted the 'country of origin principle' (formulated by the European Court of Justice in the Cassis de Dijon judgment, case 120/78, 1979, *ECR* 649) as a new method of harmonisation not only for free movement of goods but also for the liberalisation of financial services, it actually accepted regulatory competition within the European Community. The first judicial application of the principle of mutual recognition to the field of services occurred in case 76/90, 1991, *ECR* 42221, *Saeger* v. *Dennemeyer*. See H. Søndergaard Birkmose, 'Regulatory competition and the European harmonisation process', p. 1092. However, the Lamafalussy Report has highlighted that the absence of clear EU-wide regulation has prevented the implementation of a mutual recognition system in the European securities market.

[81] Moloney, *EC Securities Regulation*, p. 14.

[82] Moloney, *EC Securities Regulation*, p. 13.

Regulatory competition is therefore grounded in the harmonisation regime. National differences are acknowledged through the principle of mutual recognition. While competition can be hampered by minimum standards and home-country control, it can on the contrary be encouraged by harmonisation (of the minimum standards) and mutual recognition. In order to ensure competition under these terms, however, a strong coordination between supervisors across the single market is necessary.[83] The effective degree of regulatory competition which can be ensured by minimum harmonisation also depends on the different market segments and regulatory areas involved.[84]

Problems with the regulatory competition are usually summarised under the disadvantages arising from an uncertain regulatory regime, the risk that protection barriers will remain in place, and the aforementioned 'race to the bottom/race to the top' dilemma on the level of regulation that may be finally adopted.[85]

Beyond the terms of the debate on harmonisation versus regulatory competition, what must be noted is that, in the field of securities regulation, harmonisation may assume different forms. These forms include: shared or key international standards promoted by market operators;[86] minimum harmonisation (where only some basic principles and requirements are made uniform, leaving it to the member states to specify the rules in detail) combined with the principle of mutual recognition (according to which member states recognise the regulatory regimes of other member states, and thus also implement the principle of home country control); and detailed or comprehensive or total

---

[83] Moloney, *EC Securities Regulation*, p. 15.

[84] It also depends on a set of factors such as mobility of market participants, their ability to choose regulatory regimes, the ability and degree to which regulators can interpret signals from the market, the absence of market failures requiring the adoption of harmonised common standards (see *supra*). Moloney, *EC Securities Regulation*, p. 13.

[85] In general, according to the regulatory competition theory, the race to the bottom will be avoided given a sufficient degree of decentralisation: applying the standard Darwinian evolutionary framework of macro-economics, competitive conditions will drive regulators to race to the top, since only efficient regulation continues in effect where the market remains dynamic. Bratton, McCahery, Picciotto, Scott, *Introduction: Regulatory Competition and Institutional Evolution*, p. 14.

[86] Such are the Committee on Payment and Settlement Systems–International Organisation of Securities Commissions (CPSS-IOSCO) Recommendations; the European code of conduct for clearing and settlement of cash equities prepared by the Federation of European Securities Exchanges (FESE), the European Association of Central Counterparty Clearing Houses (EACH) and the European Central Securities Depositories Association (ECSDA); the Committee of European Securities Regulators – European Central Bank Standards.

harmonisation, entailing the adoption of uniform law for the achievement of a completely integrated market.[87]

These theoretical considerations find a practical implementation in the regulatory choices made by the European legislator concerning markets and investment services. In the first place, the evolution embodied in the substitution of the Investment Services Directive by the Market in Financial Instruments Directive denotes a shift from minimum harmonisation (represented by minimum standards for post-trade transparency) to a set of high-level principles for market regulation. The Market in Financial Instruments Directive has been drafted according to the Lamfalussy process, with the intent of ensuring the enactment of a legislative instrument of sufficient flexibility to adapt to the necessary and rapid changes imposed by evolution of the markets and to the introduction of new markets and services.[88]

In line with a *topos* in securities regulation, the European legislative debates revolved around recurring central issues such as concentration rules, fragmentation and transparency requirements.

From the point of view of regulatory theory, there has been a step in the direction of implementing regulatory competition between markets in investment services, by repealing the 'concentration rule' contained in Article 14(3) of the Investment Services Directive and thus allowing

---

[87] See Ferrarini, *Securities Regulation and Pan-European Securities Markets*, p. 250. For a detailed survey of the various harmonisation methods that have been adopted for the construction of the single market, see P. J. Slot, *Harmonisation, European Law Review*, 1996, vol. 21, pp. 382–7, including in addition to the above quoted methods (and apart from definition of law and policy at Community level): optional harmonisation (where an option is left whether to apply the harmonised rules or the national rules); partial harmonisation (where the harmonised rule only applies for cross-border transactions); alternative harmonisation (which allows member states to choose between alternative methods of harmonisation); mutual recognition of controls (which in contrast to the principle of mutual recognition of national rules, is limited to member states' recognition of each other's control).

[88] See, however, G. Ferrarini and F. Recine, 'The MiFID and internalisation', in G. Ferrarini, E. Wymeersch (eds), *Investor Protection in Europe. Corporate Law Making, the MiFID and Beyond*, Oxford, 2006, pp. 268–9, according to whom the Lamfalussy structure's main goal (i.e. a flexible regulation for European securities markets) has not been reached, since level 1 provisions are too detailed and thus too rigid; level 2 implementing measures are often confined to residual issues; and at level 3 there is a mere implementation of level 1 and 2 provisions. According to the authors this is due to the fact that securities regulation in the EU is strongly dominated by politics (with a major role played by the European Commission) which dictates detailed measures of securities regulation (probably due to the combined needs of reconciling divergent national interests and of finding a compromise between diverging political and business interests at level 1 legislation), and does not leave sufficient space for specialised regulators.

retail investor orders to be executed not only on 'regulated markets' but also on alternative trading systems and by investment firms. Regulated markets will have to compete for order flow and liquidity with other regulated markets and trading systems. The Investment Services Directive implemented a model based on the 'European passport' approach, which by allowing intermediaries conditions of free access to all European markets was supposed to lead to the ideal conditions of pure competition among exchanges, and finally to the victory of the most efficient. Competition from alternative trading systems was scarcely taken into consideration.[89]

The Market on Financial Instruments Directive instead identifies three categories of trading services, disciplined by decreasing regulatory requirements: (1) regulated markets; (2) multilateral trading facilities; and (3) systematic internalisers.[90]

Whilst the abolition of the concentration rule seems to favour competition between markets, it has also caused debates on the risks of market fragmentation and especially on the consequences of internalisation. Fragmentation occurs where the same security trades in multiple venues and there is no mechanism to ensure interaction between orders submitted for the same security and between orders and best quotes posted on multiple venues. Market fragmentation results from different market mechanisms competing to provide low-cost and tailored services to different traders. The beneficial effects of fragmentation can, however, be offset by the impact on market quality, where the impossibility of quotes and orders interacting has negative effects on the production of price information and consequently on market and price efficiency. For these reasons it is traditionally held that, in most circumstances, competition amongst traders to obtain best price is best achieved in consolidated markets.[91] Therefore, there is tension between those in

---

[89] See B. Alemanni, G. Lusignani, M. Onado, 'The European securities industry', in Ferrarini, Wymeersch (eds), *Investor Protection in Europe*, p. 202.

[90] Article 4 (14) and (15) of the Directive on Markets in Financial Instruments defines regulated markets and multilateral trading facilities (MTF) as 'multilateral systems [...] which bring together multiple third-party buying and selling interests in financial instruments in the system and in accordance with non-discretionary rules'. The difference between these two types of systems lies in the fact that regulated markets require an authorisation by the competent authority. Systematic internalisers are defined as investment firms which 'on an organised, frequent and systematic basis, deal on own account by executing client orders outside a regulated market or a MTF' (Article 4 (7) MiFID).

[91] See R. Davies, A. Dufour, B. Scott-Quinn, 'The MiFID: competition in a new European equity market regulatory structure', in Ferrarini, Wymeersch (eds), *Investor Protection in Europe*, p. 164. See also T. Arnold, P. Hersch, J.H. Mulherin, J.M. Netter, 'Merging markets', *Journal of Finance*, 1999, vol. 54, p. 1083.

favour of consolidation of order flow on a single market and those demanding competition.[92] Indeed, from a theoretical point of view, fragmentation can have dangerous side effects. It has been predicted that order flows create externalities (liquidity attracts liquidity) that concentrate on the already largest market.[93]

According to conventional economic theories, concentration of order flow on a single market would improve market liquidity, and high liquidity would result in small bid-ask spreads. However, given a rise of alternative markets over the past decade, without any apparent detriment to market quality, it has been suggested that inter-market competition may in itself have a benign impact on overall market quality (offsetting the efficiency gains deriving from order flow concentration).[94]

As a consequence of competition from innovative market structures, or as a result of preferencing arrangements and in-house matching practices, order flow may be fragmented. A typical case of preferencing is internalisation of order flow, which refers to the situation in which broker-dealers execute retail client orders in-house against their own positions or against another client order.[95]

Possible problems related to internalisation of order flow arise from the fact that internalisation inhibits aggressive quoting and diverts away orders from the primary market, thus potentially affecting the quality of price discovery and leading to higher spreads.[96] Internalisation may

---

[92] From a practical and political point of view, the issue sees stock exchanges (especially those operating in Continental Europe), which fight to defend their national dominant positions, opposed to investment banks (often consolidated in conglomerates or ready to create multilateral trading facilities, such as the Turquoise project, announced in 2007) which seek wider spaces of operativity. See Ferrarini, Recine, 'The MiFID and Internalisation', in Ferrarini, Wymeersch (eds), *Investor Protection in Europe*, p. 240.

[93] M. Pagano 'Trading volume and asset liquidity', *The Quarterly Journal of Economics*, 1989, vol. 104, pp. 260–4. See also B. Chowdry and V. Nanda, 'Multimarket trading and market liquidity', *Review of Financial Studies*, 1991, vol. 4, p. 483; A.R. Admati and P. Pfleiderer, 'Sunshine trading and financial market equilibrium', *Review of Financial Studies*, 1991, vol. 4, p. 443.

[94] See H.R. Stoll, 'Organization of the stock market: competition or fragmentation', *J. Appl. Corporate Finance*, 1993, vol. 5, p. 91; J. Köngden, E. Thiessen, 'Internalisation under the MiFID', in Ferrarini, Wymeersch (eds), *Investor Protection in Europe*, p. 274. Advantages possibly arising from inter-market competition, such as lower transaction costs, refer to competition between stock exchanges (and are largely derived from empirical experience on US markets); they do not necessarily apply in case of competition between organised markets and internalisers. (Köngden, Thiessen, 'Internalisation under the MiFID', p. 274).

[95] Davies, Dufour, Scott-Quinn, 'The MiFID: competition in a new European equity market regulatory structure', pp. 166–7.

[96] See Davies, Dufour, Scott-Quinn, 'The MiFID: competition in a new European equity market regulatory structure', p.164. Indeed, if a large fraction of the order flow is

also produce a conflict of interest between the broker/dealer's own profit-maximising goals and the broker/dealer's obligation to provide the best price to the client.[97]

As a response to these concerns deriving from the possible negative effects of market fragmentation caused by preferencing and internalisation ensuing from repeal of the concentration rule, the Market in Financial Instruments Directive has imposed the best-execution rule and rigid pre- and post-trade transparency rules. Indeed, orders will be processed sequentially and best possible execution must be provided (Article 21 Market in Financial Instruments Directive); information about a firm's execution practice and post-trade information have to be provided to the investors (Articles 19 and 28 Market in Financial Instruments Directive); and prices for trades executed at different trading venues will be disclosed so that market information can be consolidated and price discovery increased (Articles 28 and 30 Market in Financial Instruments Directive). From a theoretical point of view, however, the imposition of maximum pre-trade transparency, while optimising the price-discovery process, may also negatively affect liquidity, where possible market participants could refrain from trading to avoid possible reactions from other traders.[98]

The final version of the Markets in Financial Instruments Directive reflects these tradeoffs. On the one hand investors can access alternative trading systems under a regime of internalisation; on the other, while the

---

internalised, dealers have little incentive to compete by narrowing the spread because this would reduce overall dealer rents (i.e. supernormal profits) and would not attract the order flow already allocated to other dealers, i.e. internalisation may reduce the level of competition. (Davies, Dufour, Scott-Quinn, 'The MiFID: competition in a new European equity market regulatory structure', p. 167.)

[97] With internalisation, while current market prices are used as a reference, investment firms are executing their clients' orders away from the market. Opponents of internalisation believe that it leads to a lower degree of pre-trade transparency (since these orders cannot interact with other pools of liquidity and possibly receive improved execution) and has a negative impact on the price discovery process (Davies, Dufour, Scott-Quinn, 'The MiFID: competition in a new European equity market regulatory structure', pp.167–8). Proponents of internalisation of order flow on the other hand believe that internalisation may create positive competition for traditional market centres. Banks internalise the order flow to avoid the costs of executing orders on the order book (exchange and in some cases, clearing and settlement fees) and to earn bid-ask spreads (Ibid.).

[98] See Alemanni, Lusignani, Onado, *The European Securities Industry*, p. 205. This risk is further complicated where regulated markets (typically based on order-driven systems which gain from maximum pre- and post-trade transparency) compete with broker-dealers who internalise orders (and being typically quote-driven, require a certain degree of opacity).

Market in Financial Instruments Directive as a general rule requires the maximum pre-trade transparency from all possible trading venues, it also allows for a variety of possible exceptions according to the type of trades and/or intermediaries involved.[99]

Beyond regulating investor protection and transparency with the provisions mentioned above, the Market in Financial Instruments Directive also concentrates on a third area of regulation: market access. The coordination between competition and mutual recognition is implemented through the confirmation of the home-country control principle and of the EU passport principle. More specifically, investment firms authorised by a member state may provide services in any other member state (Article 31 Market in Financial Instruments Directive) and member states have to ensure that investment firms authorised by other member states have access to regulated markets established in their territory either directly by setting up branches in the host state, or by remote membership, or by having remote access to the regulated market (Article 33 Market in Financial Instruments Directive). Furthermore, investment firms have the right of access to central counterparty, clearing and settlement systems in other member states (Article 34 Market in Financial Instruments Directive).

3.2. Reciprocity and the principle of the Most Favoured Nation

Other regulatory issues in financial services involve the choice between the application of the principle of reciprocity (and Conditional Most Favoured Nation) as opposed to that of Most Favoured Nation and National Treatment.[100]

The principle of reciprocity in the regulation of trade in financial services entails that states require as a matter of positive law reciprocal concessions from other states before making concessions of their own (similar effects derive *de facto* from the principle of Conditional Most Favoured Nation); whereas according to the principle of Most Favoured Nation (implemented in the field of financial services by some regional agreements such as NAFTA), 'any regulatory benefit accorded to importers or exporters from one nation should be accorded to importers

---

[99]See Articles 29(2) and 44(2) Market in Financial Instruments Directive allowing competent authorities to be able to waive pre-trade transparency obligations respectively for investment firms or market operators operating a multilateral trading facility (Article 29(2)) and regulated markets (Article 44(2)) 'in respect of transactions that are large compared with normal market size for the share or type of share in question'.

[100]See J. Braithwaite, P. Drahos, 'Financial regulation', in Braithwaite, Drahos (eds.) *Global Business Regulation*, p. 126.

or exporters from other nations'.[101] The principle of National Treatment prescribes that 'a state should regulate foreign corporations according to the same rules as national corporations'.[102]

Translated into the field of financial services, these key regulatory principles have implications in the field of banking and financial services, for example, and can affect the functioning and reciprocal relations between major financial markets. Indeed, the US (under the negotiations on financial services following the Final Act of the Uruguay Round in which the General Agreement on Trade in Services (GATS) was signed in 1994) have adopted conditional Most Favoured Nation to persuade, through reciprocity in its large domestic market, other states to improve their position on trade in financial services.

In the field of banking, the fact that the US have traditionally adopted the principle of National Treatment but that their own system of banking regulation has been highly regulated (impeding, for example, US banks from entering into the business of securities) implies that foreign banks are also restricted in their activities (i.e. as in the case of entering securities business). As a consequence, both European and US banks have fewer restrictions when operating in markets outside the US (and more specifically in the European market).

As a regulatory response, in the Second Banking Directive, the European Union maintained the possibility for operation of the principle of reciprocity, according to which Europe could impede US banks from pursuing securities activities in the European market unless European banks could reciprocally do the same in the US market. The adoption of the principle of national treatment merely entails an equalisation of the conditions of regulation (including restrictions) and therefore does not necessarily produce satisfactory results for those who wish to enter a specific market. However, this principle is widely and increasingly adopted in financial regulation.[103]

3.3. Legal sources for market operativeness: an overview

A proper assessment of the terms of the debate on harmonisation and regulatory competition also requires a brief classification of the existing legal sources of securities market regulation. A first general distinction must be made between general laws and special laws regarding the operation of the market. With reference to the first, laws of general application include laws regarding property, contract, torts, general

---

[101] Braithwaite, Drahos, 'Financial regulation,' p. 25.
[102] Ibid.
[103] See Braithwaite, Drahos, 'Financial regulation', pp. 126–7.

commercial law, banking and insolvency.[104] One can also refer to the relevant substantive (national) law in this case. The settlement process provides once again a good example. In the trading process, the interest rights of the purchaser after trade and before settlement is carried out, are merely personal (contractual) rights; after settlement, the purchaser owns interests in securities and his rights are proprietary.[105]

The rules which are instead necessary for the proper functioning of the market (the special rules), include laws regarding the legal relationship between customers, brokers, exchanges, clearing corporations and settlement banks, property and contractual rights created or held through the market, and rules in case of insolvency of one of the market participants.[106] Within the rules for the functioning of the market, a further distinction can be made between technical requirements and market practice. The former are typically the responsibility of clearing and settlement systems; while market practice is often based in law.[107] A distinction must also be made between the origins of these different regulatory sources; these include both the private sector (e.g. management of the clearing and settlement sector, establishment of market practices and requirements) and public legislators/national legislators (e.g. taxation of securities, regulatory choices, imposition of certain requirements with possible anticompetitive effects, etc.).[108]

Finally, the last source that may be cited is private party autonomy. Certain market arrangements, especially those involving multi-lateral clearing, exchange and settlement processes, may be regulated by contract (and generally all jurisdictions support an express choice of law as a method for resolving conflict of law issues in cross-border transactions, especially where multi-lateral contractual arrangements are involved).[109] This variety in normative types confirms the emergence of the so-called financial market *lex mercatoria* as a key regulatory source of these markets, with the consequence of the emerging role of market operators and of the business community as legislators. A preference for this type of source has sometimes even been suggested by the experts studying legal barriers to cross-border securities transactions.[110]

---

[104] See Corcoran, 'Cross-border financial transactions', p. 334.

[105] J. Benjamin, *Interests in Securities. A Proprietary Law Analysis of the International Securities Markets*, Oxford, 2000, p. 22. It is only the proprietary rights that will normally not be affected by the insolvency of the vendor.

[106] Corcoran, 'Cross-border financial transactions', p. 334.

[107] See '2001 Giovannini Report', p. 45.

[108] For this distinction, see the '2001 Giovannini Report', p. 42.

[109] Corcoran, 'Cross-border financial transactions', p. 334.

[110] According to the Lamafalussy Final Report, the restructuring of EU clearing and settlement 'should largely be in the hands of the private sector'. 'Market forces

This soft law is of both a public and a private nature. Indeed, when it is elaborated at the international level, international soft law (as opposed to national soft law) is not addressed to the general public or the final destinataries of the norms; rather, it consists of understandings between regulators, recommending the application of certain rules to the sectors they supervise.[111] In other cases, this soft law involves the formulation of technical standards, which are then issued as recommendations, financial standards or principles.

The standard setting carried out by international financial institutions has been divided into three categories of 'international agreements': (1) model contracts or agreements to facilitate cross-border financial transactions (such as the International Swaps and Derivatives Association Master Agreement) or technical standards to facilitate payments between banks; (2) interstate agreements to promote cross-border competition in banking and financial services; and (3) agreements to enhance and maintain financial stability through the efficient management of systemic risk.[112]

3.4. A further regulatory dilemma: the public/private divide

Especially with reference to the adoption of shared or key international standards, another regulatory dilemma is that concerning the public/private divide. The problems arise because of the special tie between regulation of financial markets, monetary sovereignty and the process of market internationalisation. Given the progressive loss of monetary sovereignty with the consolidation of the Economic and Monetary Union, the open issue remains whether the substitute regulatory power should be vested by a public or by a private source.

First of all, in order for supranational legislation (whichever its nature) to be effective within a national market in the case of cross-border transactions, the legislation of the member state where the market is located must allow for this interference, by permitting, for instance, that a foreign law regulate the international activities of national undertakings

---

should mainly determine the contours of European clearing and settlement such as the extent of linkage between post-trading bodies (clearing, settlement, central securities depositories, etc.) and the possible emergence of a single European central counterparty', while 'public policy should focus on competition issues and removing the kinds of obstacles and impediments that make consolidation difficult'. (Lamfalussy Final Report, cit., p. 16).

[111] M. Giovanoli, *International Monetary Law: Issues for the New Millenium*, Oxford, 2000, p. 39.

[112] K. Alexander, R. Dhumale, J. Eatwell, *Global Governance of Financial Systems. The International Regulation of Systemic Risk*, Oxford, 2006, p. 35.

according to the rules of private international law.[113] The issue then becomes whether this remand can apply to voluntary, non-binding, private law.

The solution may seem contradictory. On the one hand, *de facto* a large area of international financial relations has been left to regulation by conduct codes, international standards and voluntary soft law, all constituting what has been defined as a form of 'international co-operation *below* the level of formal juridification'.[114] Surprisingly, this soft law, or financial *lex mercatoria*, has been implemented at national level in a very effective way.

International standards do not have, strictly speaking, binding legal force (not even as international customary law); however, various national jurisdictions have chosen to incorporate these standards into their domestic legislation, either spontaneously or through mechanisms of 'peer pressure' or 'official incentives' or 'market incentives'.[115]

An overview of the different instruments used for regulation of financial markets indicates that there is a wide variety of tools which go beyond the strict dualist option public/private or state/self-regulation. The wide range of types of regulatory tools in financial services regulation comprises: written norms (legal and non-legal) and accompanying sanctions; economic or market-based instruments; social norms and accompanying sanctions; and technologies and processes.[116] On the other hand,

---

[113] See T. Marauhn, 'Introduction: the regulatory dilemma in international financial relations', in R. Grote, T. Marauhn (eds), *The Regulation of International Financial Markets. Perspectives for Reform*, Cambridge, 2006, p. 9.

[114] See Marauhn, *Introduction: the regulatory dilemma in international financial relations*, p. 10.

[115] M. Giovanoli, *International Monetary Law: Issues for the New Millenium*, p. 35 et seq. Examples of 'peer pressure' include the practice of 'cold-shouldering' and 'naming and shaming' those market operators who refuse to comply with market-based regulations (in the UK the rulings of the Takeover Panel are an example; other examples are the rules on money-laundering). See J. Black, 'Mapping the contours of contemporary financial services regulation', *Journal of Corporate Law Studies*, 2002, vol. 2, p. 258.

[116] Black, 'Mapping the contours of contemporary financial services', p. 256. The author further quotes as an example of a widely used instrument the Command and Control model (CAC), which is based on 'legal rules backed by civil, criminal and administrative sanctions monitored and enforced by a government-empowered body'. Legal norms also confer power on private subjects to create or alter private rights. Allowing, for example, as the UK Financial Services and Markets Act of 2000 does, a private action for breach of the rules conferred in the same Act, could serve as an incentive to firms to comply with the rules. The same considerations can be extended to the provision of the power conferred on regulators to enforce rights granted to individuals (i.e. the right conferred upon the UK Financial Services Authority to bring actions under the Unfair Terms in Consumer Contracts Regulations). Private law rules

however, certain issues should not be left to private actors precisely because of the strong tie between financial markets and monetary sovereignty.

The strategic implications of the choice are demonstrated, for example, by the traditional public interference with financial markets, implemented through the supervision of banking and insurance activities and securities (such supervisory powers have often permitted the preservation of a certain degree of national sovereignty over national markets, by regulating the entrance of foreign actors and supervising the activity of national actors abroad).[117] Similar concerns could be expressed, for example, in the case of clearing and settlement procedures, which, as has been observed, can be considered to a certain extent as substitutes for monetary circulation.

Concerns are especially relevant in the hypothesis of a crisis (stability considerations are often at the basis of public supervisory competence). Indeed, one of the questions is whether soft law as such can be 'crisis-proofed', that is, if voluntarily adopted standards would continue to be implemented in a crisis.[118]

---

can also be used by market operators to create more limited rights, such as demand of collateral or disclosure requirements. (Ibid.).

As far as non-legal norms are concerned, these too have been widely used in financial services regulation, as is demonstrated by the existence of guidance rules issued by market authorities which are not legally binding, and by the proliferation of codes of conduct. Another set of tools are economic and market instruments, used both by government and non-governmental actors. These comprise, for example, capital adequacy requirements (imposed by governments) and the activities of credit and fund management ratings agencies (a typical example of market-based regulation). In certain areas government-imposed instruments can operate in such a way as to stimulate the development of market-based regulation: this is the case of mandatory disclosure requirements that are meant to facilitate and enhance the (presumably) rational choices that the market operators are making. (Black, 'Mapping the contours of contemporary financial services', p. 257).

[117] See Marauhn, 'Introduction: the regulatory dilemma in international financial relations', p. 9.

[118] Giovanoli, *International Monetary Law: Issues for the New Millenium*, p. 51.

Chapter 6:
Soft Law and Financial *Lex Mercatoria*

1. Soft law: subjects, rules, status

The expression 'soft law' is indefinitely wide and comprises different types of sources. The common feature lies in the non-binding nature of the rules that are elaborated and in the absence of conferral of legislative competence to the actors that prepare these rules and/or standards.[1]

A first distinction that should be made concerns the subjects that elaborate soft law: these include a variety of institutional, social and academic actors, which can be further divided into international/institutional organisations and private subjects.[2] The legal status of these bodies, especially with reference to international organisations, varies greatly, comprising both institutional and fully recognised international organisations such as the international financial institutions (International Monetary Fund and World Bank), and *de facto* groupings promoted at government and sectorial level (such as the G-7, G-10, G-20 groups),

---

[1] Often in the juxtaposition between soft law and hard law (with special reference to the process of harmonisation of European law) a distinction must be drawn between the agendas that the soft law advocates aim at pursuing. On the one hand there is a movement that perceives soft law as the means to implement a Social European Agenda, where soft law could serve as the tool to modernise the European social model and to foster social integration (using governance methods that are alternative to compulsory regulation, such as the European Employment Strategy and the Open Method of Coordination). According to other supporters of the role and efficacy of soft law, the added value of this non-binding instrument lies in its potential for enhancing market efficiency. Soft law could strengthen the European Single market and respond to the needs of the global merchant class. The privilege of private autonomy, freedom of contract and the pursuit of uniformity of rules constitute the means for removing cross-border obstacles to trade, eliminating the distortions resulting from different national laws and reducing costs of legal services (See A. Di Robilant, 'Genealogies of soft law', *American Journal of Comparative Law*, 2006, vol. 54, pp. 504–9). The aspects analysed so far in this work, and those that will now be examined, clearly refer to the latter perception of soft law.

[2] See Di Robilant, 'Genealogies of soft law', p. 500; V. Lemma, '"Soft law" e regolazione finanziaria', *La nuova giurisprudenza civile commentata*, 2006, II, p. 607.

regulatory and supervisory sector-specific experts and committees, and professional associations.[3]

The second distinction concerns the type of texts and instruments that are issued by international organisations or private associations. These include intergovernmental trade and service agreements, inter-regulator agreements, international technical agreements, industry codes of conduct,[4] standards of good practice and recommendations.

Private subjects, for example, multi-national corporations, often issue codes of conduct; these may also be issued by para-public subjects such as trade associations. The Unidroit Principles and the standard contracts developed by the International Chamber of Commerce (ICC) can furthermore be considered as evidence of a new *lex mercatoria*.

Certain normative products of the European Union (EU) institutions may be regarded as forms of soft law as well. These are the Commission's Communications and Guidelines, Inter-Institutional Agreements, and to a certain extent even opinions and Recommendations of the EU institutions.[5]

Starting with the subjective distinction, among the international organisations that create soft law, a pivotal position is held by the Bank for International Settlements (BIS), which hosts permanent secretariats that are extremely active in the generation of financial standards.[6] The relevance of the BIS as a producer of soft law lies in the reports that are issued every year containing disciplinary solutions for several domains of financial relations. The BIS publishes a significant number of so-called standards of good practice. These standards are not legally binding and refer to market operators (i.e. banks) as their destinataries (therefore not to legislators nor to central banks as supervisors of

---

[3] See M. Giovanoli, 'A new architecture for the global financial market: legal aspects of international financial standard setting,' in M.Giovanoli, (ed.) *International Monetary Law. Issues for the New Millennium*, Oxford, 2000, p. 11.

[4] See D. Sabalot, 'International agreements and supranational bodies', in M. Blair, G. Walker (eds), *Financial Services Law,* Oxford, 2006, p. 785.

[5] See K.C. Wellens and G.M. Borchardt, 'Soft law in European Community law', *European Law Review*, 1989, vol. 14, pp. 289, 298–300.

[6] These include the Basel Committee on Banking Supervision (BCBS), the International Association of Insurance Supervisors (IAIS), the Committee on the Global Financial System (CGFS), the secretariat of the Financial Stability Forum (FSF) and the Committee on Payment and Settlement Systems (CPSS). Other international organisations which are engaged in the promotion of financial integration and economic development at different levels are the Organisation for Economic Co-operation and Development (OECD) and the World Trade Organisation (WTO). The creation of the Bank for International Settlements dates back to 1930, when its task was to handle the payment of First World War reparations by Germany. It then became a meeting place for European central bankers, after the Second World War.

the markets). However, even before these recommendations are (if ever) transformed into binding law (as is the case, for example, with several recommendations issued by the Bank for International Settlements, which have later been incorporated into 'hard law' under the form of EU legislation or of EU public documents),[7] they are often complied with by market operators. This is due to different factors which will be examined *infra*.

Of central importance in the field of payments and securities settlement regulation is the Committee on Payment and Settlement Systems (CPSS), which is hosted by the Bank for International Settlements, and the International Organisation of Securities Commissions (IOSCO).

The CPSS was established in 1990 by the Governors of the Central banks of the G-10 countries as a follow-up to the work of the Committee on Interbank Netting Schemes (created in 1989 to study the policy issues relating to cross-border and multi-currency interbank netting schemes) and more generally to the activities of the Group of Experts of Payment Systems (also established by the G-10 Governors in 1980). The main scope of the CPSS is the analysis of risks and the development of minimum standards or best practices. It serves as an important forum for the study and development of domestic payments, settlement and clearing systems in cross-border and multi-currency settlement schemes. In association with the IOSCO, the CPSS in 2001 issued the Core Principles for Systematically Important Payment Systems[8] and the CPSS/International Organisation of Securities Commissions Recommendations for Securities Settlement Systems[9] and, in 2004, the CPSS/International Organisation of Securities Commissions Recommendations for Central Counterparties.[10]

---

[7] See, for example, the issue of several key standards for sound financial systems, among which the International Accounting Standards (IAS) issued by the International Accounting Standards Board, (then converted into EC Regulation 108/2006 of 11 January 2006 amending Regulation 1725/2003 adopting certain international accounting standards in accordance with Regulation 1606/2002 as regards International Financial Reporting Standards and International Accounting Standards, O.J.L24, 27 January 2006, p. 1) and the International Standards on Auditing (ISA), issued by the International Auditing and Assurance Standards Board (IAASB). See also the adoption of the Basel II capital adequacy requirements through the Capital Requirements Directive (comprising Directive 2006/48/EC of 14 June 2006 relating to the taking up and pursuit of the business of credit institutions, O.J. L177, 30 June 2006, p. 1, and Directive 2006/49/EC of 14 June 2006 on the capital adequacy of investment firms and credit institutions, O.J.L177, 30 June 2006, p. 201).

[8] Available at http://www.bis.org/publ/cpss43.htm.

[9] Available at http://www.bis.org/publ/cpss46.htm.

[10] Available at http://www.bis.org/publ/cpss64.htm.

The IOSCO is an international organisation of securities exchange regulators who cooperate in setting guiding principles for global capital markets. Members of the IOSCO regulate over 90 per cent of the world's securities markets, hence the importance of the organisation as one of the global standard-setting bodies. The methods for the implementation of the standards enacted by these securities commissions vary (as they are not endowed with normative force) and have to be implemented at the national level under the relevant legal frameworks.

Among the standards it has released, mention should be made of the Principles of Securities Regulation of 2003, which are grouped into eight different categories: Principles Relating to the Regulator; Principles for Self-Regulation; Principles for the Enforcement of Securities Regulation; Principles for Cooperation in Regulation; Principles for Issuers; Principles for Collective Investment Schemes; Principles for Market Intermediaries; Principles for the Secondary Market.[11]

Two other significant professional associations are the International Swaps and Derivatives Association (ISDA) and the International Securities Market Association (ISMA). The ISDA has over 650 member institutions and is the global trade association representing participants in privately negotiated derivatives markets such as swaps and options in all asset classes (including interest rate, currency, commodity and energy, credit and equity derivatives). The ISDA serves an important harmonisatory function in the field of derivatives contracts and repurchase transactions through the predisposition of Master Agreements. The role and influence of these Master Agreements not only for private operators, but also for legislators enacting new or reforming old rules, has been examined previously (see *supra* Chapter 3). The ISDA has also issued legal opinions on the enforceability of netting and collateral arrangements and acts to secure recognition of the risk-reducing effects of netting in determining capital requirements.[12]

Another important international committee enacting financial standards is the Committee of European Securities Regulators (CESR). The Committee of European Securities Regulators is a network of member-state securities regulators whose remit is to improve coordination among securities regulators and oversee the correct and timely implementation and enforcement of directives across member states.[13] One of the techniques adopted by the Committee of European Securities Regulators

---

[11] See OICV-IOSCO, 'Objectives and principles of securities regulation', May 2003, available at http://www.iosco.org.

[12] See Sabalot, *International Agreements and Supranational Bodies*, p. 789.

[13] The Committee of European Securities Regulators was established under the terms of the European Commission's Decision of 6 June 2001 and it is one of the two committees (the Committee of European Securities Regulators with an advisory function, the

to ensure that directives on regulated entities are implemented, applied and enforced in as convergent as possible manner is the issuance of soft codes and guidelines. The Committee of European Securities Regulators/European System of Central Banks Standards for Securities Clearing and Settlement in the European Union (which focus on the adaptation of the CPSS/International Organisation of Securities Commissions Recommendations for securities settlement systems to the EU environment) have been used as a reference for the interpretation of the Market in Financial Instruments Directive, for example.[14] A further instrument used to enhance consistent supervision and enforcement of the Single Market for financial services is that of a Multilateral Memorandum of Understanding on the Exchange of Information and Surveillance of Securities Activities.[15]

Memoranda of Understanding and inter-regulator agreements are often used both in the areas of international cooperation and information sharing and as regulatory devices. The use of Memoranda of Understanding for the latter purpose has been promoted by the International Organisation of Securities Commissions, which in 1991 issued its Principles for Memoranda of Understanding, providing a blueprint to be used by securities and futures regulators when developing Memoranda of Understanding with their counterparts.[16]

The role of these Recommendations and standards is threefold. First of all, they can be referred to by private parties when the latter are left to choose, for example, the law that will govern their agreement or the applicable law in a cross-border transaction. In the second place, institutional law or general principles can also be interpreted in the light of some of these principles. One example is the construction of access criteria to clearing and settlement systems, which according to the parameters formulated in some of these standards, should only be based on risk considerations. Third and finally, these standards can play an important role by formulating and encouraging the adoption of certain institutions that are then transferred into institutional law. The fact that

---

European Securities Committee (ESC) with a regulatory function) envisaged in the Final Report of the Lamfalussy Committee.

[14] See *supra* Chapter 4.

[15] The text of the Memorandum is available at http://www.cesr-eu.org.

[16] The Principles include provisions on the subject matter of the Memoranda of Understanding, confidentiality, implementation procedures, the rights of persons subject to a Memoranda of Understanding request, consultation, public policy exception, types of assistance, participation by the requesting authority, cost-sharing. See the IOSCO Principles for Memoranda of Understanding, Sept. 1991 (available at http://www.iosco.org/library/pubdocs/pdf/IOSCOPD17.pdf). See also Sabalot, *International Agreements and Supranational Bodies*, p. 785.

many of these recommendations (prepared both by institutional and non-institutional bodies, such as study groups and professional associations of the different market segments) have served as a framework or a basis on which communitarian legislators have then enacted directives and regulations indicates that the instruments for the regulation of the market are created through a double ascending and descending phase. The market operators press for regulation and sometimes prepare the 'soft-law' drafts; these are then adopted by the EU legislator and enacted under forms of binding law, which are finally applied by the very operators that pressed for regulation.[17]

Another typical characteristic of soft law is its reliance on arbitration for the resolution of disputes. Just as the rules are no longer a product of national legislators (whose role is that of implementing regulations enacted elsewhere), the judicial power over disputes tends to be removed from the national courts.

Recent trends indicate that the financial community, which traditionally has not been as apt as the commercial and the insurance communities to refer to arbitration, is increasingly turning to arbitral courts for the solution of disputes concerning securities transactions, guarantees, documentary credits, consumer loans and public sector lending.[18] Moreover, institutional sources (e.g. the European Commission) have also recommended the establishment of 'a Community-wide network of financial services complaints bodies [...] to provide effective and rapid out of court redress on a cross-border basis'[19] and which was launched as the FIN-NET network for settling cross-border financial disputes out of court.[20]

The transfer of judicial competences to alternative and non-institutional bodies is both a consequence of the source of law (created by private actors who wish to be judged by peers with a swift and efficient

---

[17] The abovementioned phenomenon is the recurring scheme under which legislative models circulate in European law. The interesting specificity of the field of financial services lies in the fact that the models that are put up for circulation are not national legislative models consolidated in the stronger member states, but rather the rules proposed by transnational operators of the market, who are motivated in promoting the rules for the most efficient realisation of cross-border transactions.

[18] See W.W. Park, 'Arbitration in banking and finance', *Essays in International Financial & Economic Law*, 1997, n. 10, The London Institute of International Banking, Finance & Development Law, p. 6.

[19] See Commission Communication on e-commerce and financial services, COM(2001) 66 fin., p. 3.

[20] See European Commission Internal Market and Services DG 'FSAP Evaluation', p. 28.

procedure), and also a contributory factor in the process towards uniformity.

On the one hand, rules created by transnational operators will necessarily search for the solutions common to most operators, therefore to the market, with an implicit codification of the rules. On the other, there is also a spontaneous process of adherence to the solutions adopted by international arbitral courts, whose judgments tend to implicitly assume the value of binding precedents that other international courts are likely to follow in the future. The business community will therefore tend to adopt the rule in the knowledge that it reflects the orientation of the courts and that, in the event of a future controversy, it would be the probable outcome.[21]

2. Examples of soft law: the European Code of Conduct on Clearing and Settlement

A further example of soft law regulation, which provides an interesting case of interaction with other institutional legislative sources, is the European Code of Conduct on Clearing and Settlement. The code of conduct, presented in November 2006, is a market-led initiative by the exchange and post-custody industry (comprising the Federation of European Securities Exchanges (FESE), the European Association of Central Counterparty Clearing Houses (EACH) and the European Central Securities Depositories Association (ECSDA)) aiming at creating 'an efficient European framework for cash equities trading, clearing, settlement and custody' and offering 'market participants the freedom to choose their preferred provider of services separately at each layer of the transaction chain (trading, clearing and settlement)'.

The code covers post-trading activities in cash equities in Europe and deals with price transparency, access and interoperability, and service unbundling and accounting separation.

For the implementation of the objective of price transparency, the adherent organisations agree *inter alia* to publish all offered services and their respective prices including applicable terms and conditions, all discount and rebate schemes and the applicable eligibility criteria, and price examples that facilitate comparability between offers of services.[22]

---

[21] See F. Marella, 'La nuova lex mercatoria. Principi Unidroit ed usi dei contratti del commercio internazionale,' in *Trattato di diritto commerciale e di diritto pubblico dell'economia diretto da F. Galgano*, vol. XXX, Padova, 2003, pp. 246–50; F. Galgano, *La globalizzazione nello specchio del diritto*, Bologna, 2005, p. 59.

[22] See Code of Conduct n.9- 15. The London Stock Exchange agreed to sign the Code in November 2006 and has accordingly published some examples of the typical application of its trading tariffs.

The code takes into account the provisions in the Markets in Financial Instruments Directive, which grant some access rights in the post-trade area to regulated markets and to investment firms[23] and purports to extend access rights to the relationships between infrastructures and organisations (i.e. access rights between central counterparties and central securities depositories), and to ensure that this access is granted on the basis of non-discriminatory and transparent criteria and prices.[24]

As for the implementation of service unbundling and accounting separation, which aim respectively at giving customers flexibility when choosing which services to purchase and providing relevant information on the services provided, Article 39 of the code sets down the unbundling of the services of account provision, clearing and settlement, credit provision, securities lending and borrowing and collateral management, while Articles 42 and 43 provide for separate disclosure of the costs and revenues for each unbundled service.

As observed earlier, an interesting feature of the code of conduct lies in the attempt to operate within the existing legislative sources (i.e. the Market in Financial Instruments Directive) and from that basis, to extend rights or fill in certain gaps that the market considers relevant. Therefore, whilst the Market in Financial Instruments Directive takes into account the access rights of market participants, the market operators feel the need to ensure that the organisations will have the same access rights and the possibility of interoperability as well. The code is not simply a set of rules of conduct; the implementation of the objectives it purports to further has a concrete regulatory content. Under certain aspects it moves along the path set by the Market in Financial Instruments Directive, and constitutes a significant example of a soft-law instrument aiming at interventions in the structure and operation of the market and not simply (despite its name) at laying down principles or recommendations concerning the conduct of operators when carrying out their activities.[25]

In this regard, it is an example of the growing importance of non-institutional bodies as regulatory sources, all the more so in view of the fact that the EU Commission has seemingly welcomed the code and agreed to promote its implementation.[26]

---

[23] See Articles 34 and 36 of the Market in Financial Instruments Directive.

[24] Articles 22, 25–27 of the code of conduct.

[25] Even though the status of the code is 'voluntary in nature and the provisions ...shall not grant any legal rights to, or duties for, the Organisations signing it or third parties' (Article 47 of the European Code of conduct for clearing and settlement).

[26] In July 2006, the EU Commissioner for the Internal Market C. McCreevy announced that he favours an industry-led approach to a more efficient and integrated post-trading market in the EU, as opposed to proposing a Directive, and called upon the industry to provide a suitable solution. The code of conduct was the response and it was presented

3. Effectiveness and efficiency of soft law mechanism; legitimation of privatised law-making

As has been highlighted before, the main common feature of all the different forms of soft law is their non-binding nature. However, non-bindingness does not imply non-effectiveness. On the contrary, the very fact that operators often adhere spontaneously to many of these standards, recommendations and codes of practice, gives this form of law a stronger efficacy than its 'softness' would suggest. Why this occurs and whether this is the most efficient solution remains now to be examined.

Compliance with soft law rules is not followed by any possibility of enforcement. In general, action for the pursuance of judicial enforcement

---

to Commissioner McCreevy in November 2006. The European Commission declared that it welcomed the clearing and settlement industry's new code of conduct and that it expected the scope of the code, at first limited to cash equities, to be gradually extended to include other financial instruments such as bonds and derivatives. It also agreed to chair an ad-hoc monitoring committee for the implementation of the code. See the press release of 7 November 2006 on the code of conduct, available on the EU Commission's website.

Another example of reliance on market discipline by EC institutions (of growing importance in the post-Financial Services Action Plan policy making of the Commission) is represented by the recommendation made by the EC Commission that the industry comply with the Code of Conduct for Credit Rating Agencies drafted by the International Organisation of Securities Commissions in 2004 (see the Commission's Communication on Credit Rating Agencies of January 2006, *O.J.* C59, 2006, p. 2). Observance of the code, under supervision of the Committee of European Securities Regulators, is to be ensured through the so-called 'comply or explain' principle, according to which the four major rating agencies in the EC, which voluntarily agree to submit to the Committee of European Securities Regulators' review, are to publically illustrate how they complied with the Code, participate in annual meetings with the Committee of European Securities Regulators to discuss implementation and report to their national regulator where a substantial incident has occurred.

Although the code of conduct on credit rating agencies is not directly concerned with the problems of clearing and settlement, however, the informal endorsement made by the EC Commission of what are considered to be best-practice standards developed by an international (market) organisation is indicative of the emerging trend in the regulatory approach of the EC institutions: that of 'harnessing industry goodwill and expertise to the threat of regulation' (N. Moloney, 'Innovation and risk in EC financial market regulation: new instruments of financial market intervention and the Committee of European Securities Regulators', *European Law Review*, 2007, vol. 32, p. 639). Indeed, whereas in response to recent high-profile defaults on inappropriately rated bonds – the United States for example have adopted a regulatory approach to rating agency risk (see the U.S. 2006 Credit Rating Agency Reform Act) represented by the conflict of interest management and gatekeeper risk – the EC seems in this phase to rely on a market-led approach.

entails costs for the plaintiff; the possibility of success of a non-binding rule therefore in part also depends on the possibility of ensuring compliance, without the burden of costs of access to justice. The advantage of soft law in this sense derives from the fact that the sanction for non-compliance lies with the market operators themselves.

The idea underlying the efficacy of soft law is that the choice of adherence or non-adherence is made solely on the basis of an evaluation of the advantages deriving from compliance to the destinataries of the rule. However, since it is often the same destinataries (market operators) that elaborate or help elaborate the rule, its observance and efficacy are based on the expectancy interest that the rule has been created for the advantage of its destinataries and that it often supplements for deficiencies of hard law. Therefore the market expects all its operators to comply with the soft law rules created under their own initiative and for their own benefit.[27]

Often it is precisely the 'private' origin of these rules that legitimates the perception that private law-making may be a response to failures of politics and/or law. Indeed, any liberal market community will reasonably feel bound by such fundamental principles as freedom of contract, faith in contract, precise definition and certainty of property rights, conflict conciliation procedures and bindingness of law; where, however, these basic institutions are weak, private substitutes such as private supervision, information networks and informal guarantees for compliance with contracts proliferate.[28]

According to some theories, this may be especially true for international commercial transactions. The uncertainty in the applicable law in cross-border transactions has been identified by some economists as entailing a problem of 'constitutional uncertainty' and low confidence in the enforcement of contracts by a protective state, with the consequence that compensatory private cooperative arrangements (comprising such mechanisms as letters of credit or arbitration and sometimes identified as 'private ordering' or *lex mercatoria*) are necessary for international trade

---

[27] See Lemma, '"Soft Law" e regolazione finanziaria' p. 605; R. Goode, 'Rule, practice, and pragmatism in transnational commercial law', *International and Comparative Law Quarterly*, 2005, vol. 54, p. 549. On the expectation interest created by soft law, see J. Gold, 'Strengthening the soft international law of exchange agreements', *American Journal of International Law*, 1983, vol. 77, p. 443; T. Gruchalla-Wesierski, 'A framework for understanding "Soft Law"', *McGill Law Journal*, 1984–1985, vol. 30, pp. 46–7.

[28] See J. Köngden, 'Privatisierung des Rechts', *Archiv für die Civilistische Praxis*, 2006, n. 2/3, vol. 206, p. 511.

to take place in an efficient way, i.e. with a reduction of transaction costs.[29]

There are different ways in which the market ensures observance of soft law. One example is excluding from the market those who do not comply (i.e. by refusing to conclude transactions with non-complying operators); another is imposing negotiations on the economic conditions of the transactions in order to cover the enhanced potential risks deriving from non-compliance with the soft law rules. Compliance with soft law thus becomes the economic incentive for lowering negotiation costs and the final price of the financial instrument.[30] Further incentives derive from the pressures that can be exercised over certain operators by others: in particular, auditors, rating agencies and the private companies who own stock exchanges.[31]

The first hypothesis is that of pressure made by auditors so that clients follow soft law standards of accounting and that this be signalled in their balance sheets. Where the majority of auditors encourage this type of enforcement, operators may have little choice whether to adhere or not, if the consequence of non-compliance is the impossibility of obtaining auditing of their financial statements.

On the same grounds, rating agencies may take into account compliance with soft law standards as one of the indicators of financial stability that influences the final rating of the company. The effectiveness of these pressures is often based on the so-called 'comply or explain' principle, according to which non-compliance can provoke a negative impression in the evaluation of an undertaking or operator.

The final outcome of these pressures is analogous to the effects of traditional hard law enforcement measures. A lower rating of a company entails an increase in the costs it incurs in obtaining its financing capital (and thus a general increase in its expenses): the infliction of a traditional pecuniary sanction would produce the same final result.[32]

Similar pressure for compliance with soft law rules may also be the consequence of their application in sector-specific arbitration procedures,

---

[29] See H.J. Schmidt-Trenz, *Außenhandel un Territorialität des Rechts - Grundlegung einer neuen Institutionenökonmik des Außenhandels*, Baden Baden, 1990, pp. 242 et seq. and 282 et seq.; D. Schmidtchen, 'Territorialität des Rechts, Internationales Privatrecht und die privatautonome Regelung internationaler Sachverhalte', *Rabels Zeitschrift für ausländisches und internationales Privatrecht*, 1995, vol. 59, p. 71 et seq.

[30] See Lemma,'"Soft Law" e regolazione finanziaria', pp. 605–6. See also Giovanoli, *International Monetary Law: Issues for the New Millenium*, Oxford, 2000, pp. 35 et seq.

[31] Lemma,'"Soft Law" e regolazione finanziaria', pp. 605–6; M.J. Bonell, *Le regole oggettive del commercio internazionale*, Milano, 1976, pp. 165–6.

[32] Lemma, '"Soft Law" e regolazione finanziaria', p. 608.

organised by professional or trade associations (usually those which have previously laid down the rules), where non-compliance with the awards may be sanctioned by exclusion from the association or imposition of pecuniary fines, or the proposal of commercial boycott of the undisciplined party on behalf of the other members of the association.[33]

A further, albeit different, factor that encourages adherence to soft law standards is the process of privatisation of markets, which is often accompanied by a wide delegation of regulatory competence to auto-regulation. In this case, compliance to certain standards of soft law may become an access requirement.[34]

As these examples illustrate, compliance with soft law depends on techniques of 'self-supervision' (carried out by arbitral tribunals, black-lists, withdrawal of trade associations' members' rights, risks of damage to the commercial reputation of the parties).[35] Whilst this compliance is ensured from a practical point of view through these different techniques of pressure and suasion, from the theoretical point of view, the issue of the absence of legal legitimation is often posed.[36] The problem seems all

---

[33] M. J. Bonell, *Le regole oggettive del commercio internazionale*, pp. 163–5; P. Fouchard, *L'arbitrage commercial international*, Paris, 1965, p. 466 et seq.

[34] The Italian Consob, for example, has adhered to the Committee of European Securities Regulators standards, and as far as rules of corporate governance are concerned, the new regulation on the market of this stock exchange provides that the companies that intend to request admission to listing in this market are required 'to compare their own model of corporate governance with the model proposed by the Code of conduct of listed companies and are required to communicate to the Consob the results of this comparison' (section I A.2.10 Istruzioni al Regolamento dei mercati and section I A.2.11 Istruzioni al Regolamento del Nuovo Mercato). A further consequence of this provision is that of extending a soft law regulation to all companies who seek admission to listing, regardless of what would be the proper international private law rule that would govern a foreign company (usually the *lex loci incorporationis*). See S. M. Carbone, 'Strumenti finanziari, *corporate governance* e diritto internazionale privato tra disciplina dei mercati finanziari e ordinamenti nazionali', *Rivista delle società*, 2000, pp. 471–2.

[35] See K. P. Berger, *The Creeping Codification of the Lex Mercatoria*, The Hague, London, Boston, p. 29. For further details on the different theories justifying the autonomous nature of international commercial law and on different suasion techniques, see M.J. Bonell, 'Das Autonome Recht des Welthandels-Rechtsdogmatische und Rechtspolitische Aspekte', *Rabels Zeitschrift für Auslandisches und Internationales Privatrecht*, 1978, vol. 42, pp. 491–2.

[36] One of the main arguments against the recognition of privatised law-making is that it constitutes a disguised attempt to ignore the contents of codified law, under the methodological justification of the normative force of facts. See Berger, *The Creeping Codification of the Lex Mercatoria*, p. 30. Further criticisms as to the application of this privately created law, under the name of *lex mercatoria*, recurrently highlight that parties may not conclude a 'contract without law', declaring themselves *legibus soluti*

the more delicate given the expansion of the role of soft law as a key source in the regulation of such voluminous transactions as those that take place daily in financial markets.

The evidence of the phenomenon that takes place on the market has led some authors to speak of a 'sociological transformation of the traditional theory of legal sources' that takes into consideration the specific needs of international commerce, where it is no longer the national sovereign who creates and enforces the law, but rather the law itself which evidences rules of behaviour enforced by sanctions.[37]

The proliferation of private soft law is, not surprisingly, a phenomenon triggered by globalisation of markets. The process of integration of previously separate national markets entails that international business transactions are no longer performed within national borders and international contracts are often concluded irrespective of the applicable domestic law. In such a globalised context (which naturally also comprises new technological means for the conclusion of transactions) businessmen seek a reduction of transaction costs and an increase of economic efficiency. The anchorage of transnational commercial transactions to domestic rules, bearing high transaction costs, is often perceived as an obstacle to the realisation of efficient and globalised markets.[38] While on the one hand globalisation has weakened the territoriality of the law, which has always been one of the principal guarantees of the effective application of state law and regulation, on the other, in globalised markets what is often missing is a national or supranational competence for law-making (not only for enforcement).

(thus placing their contract in 'a legal vacuum'). See Berger, *The Creeping Codification of the Lex Mercatoria*, p. 43, also quoting case law (French *Cour de Cassation*, 21 June 1950, *Messageries Maritimes, Rec. crit. dr. int. priv*, 1950, p. 609; English House of Lords, *Amin Rashed Shipping Corporation* v. *Kuwait Insurance Co.*, 1983, WLR 241, p. 249; Permanent Court of International Justice, *Serbian Loans Case*, 1929, P.C.I.J., Ser.A. No. 20, p. 41; Vienna Court of Appeal of January 26, 1982, *NORSOLOR* v. *Pabalk Ticaret*, AG 1982, p. 166). See also F.A. Mann, 'England rejects "delocalised" contracts and arbitration', *International and Comparative Law Quarterly*, 1984, vol. 33, p. 193.

[37] See C. Joerges, 'Vorüberlegungen zu einer Theorie des Internationalen Wirtschaftsrechts', *Rabels Zeitschrift für Auslandisches und Internationales Privatrecht*, 1979, vol. 43, p. 41; Berger, *The Creeping Codification of the Lex Mercatoria*, p. 29.

[38] See K.P. Berger, *Transnational Law in the Age of Globalization*, Rome, 2001, pp. 2–3, who also indicates the economic and geopolitical factors which influence the process of transnationalization of commercial law.

A remedy for this default can often be found precisely in private rules (such as business contracts or cooperation under national insolvency procedures, elaborated by multi-national undertakings involved more and more often in international and cross-border insolvency procedures).[39]

The globalisation of financial markets has led to a growing demand for common financial instruments. Only the possibility of accessing different markets from which to choose the best form of financing for the undertakings ensures competition,[40] and only competition can trigger the efficiency that market operators invoke. Also, in a privatised process of law-making, the possible comparative advantages of the legal process become more decentralised, the rules may be adjusted more quickly to the needs of those subject to them and, from an economic analysis point of view, the 'failing economic productivity of private international law' posited by some scholars and practitioners can be replaced.[41] Under this perspective, as economies grow more complex, the role of decentralisation in the law-making process and the enforcement of custom on the business community are two of the keys for achieving efficiency.[42] The issues of integration of the markets, uniformity of substantive legal rules on financial instruments, and realisation of efficient competition mechanisms are closely inter-related.

In this context, the role of soft law is pivotal and has an important interplay with private international law. Indeed, as a consequence of globalised markets, voluminous exchanges of securities and payments take place in cross-border transactions through complex systems of clearing and settlement. Through the multi-lateral netting processes, the sources of acquisitions and payments are lost, thus entailing that these transactions are no longer disciplined by national rules, but rather by complex contracts.[43] Indeed, clearing and settlement systems are governed by 'agreements', that is, contracts. These cross-border contracts have opened the path to the application of soft law, adopted where, according to private international law rules, private autonomy can determine the applicable law.

It can thus be observed that the substantive content of financial instruments is increasingly determined by the usages and practice of

---

[39] Köngden, 'Privatisierung des Rechts', p. 512.

[40] The underlying assumption is that the very essence of soft law, especially where structured according to the opt-in model, lies in the opportunity for the parties to choose a certain set of rules.

[41] See Berger, *The Creeping Codification of the Lex Mercatoria*, p. 28.

[42] See R. D. Cooter, 'Decentralized law for a complex economy: the structural approach to adjudicating the new law merchant', *University of Pennsylvania Law Review*, 1996, vol. 144, pp. 1645–6.

[43] See Goode, 'Rule, practice, and pragmatism in transnational commercial law', p. 540.

international commercial law, and the possibility of incorporating these substantive contents depends in part also on the mechanisms developed by conflict of law rules, which leave ample space for the operation of the parties' private autonomy by encouraging so-called self-contained contracts. Parties can thus choose the applicable law and competent *lex fori* and tend to adopt accepted standard principles developed by the market.[44]

One of the most significant examples is that related to the development of derivative instruments. The expansion of these financial instruments has led to their circulation being considered equivalent to that of money in international commerce;[45] hence the need to ensure uniform rules for all derivatives, which must be autonomous from the underlying legal relations and independent of the legal system in which they originated. These needs have been to a certain extent satisfied by acting precisely on some of the private international law aspects of these instruments, by allowing, for example, in the over-the-counter negotiation of derivatives, the reception, through private autonomy, of the common contractual practice of international commerce (exemplified by the use of the so-called Master Agreements elaborated by the International Swaps and Derivatives Association).[46]

The adoption of uniform standard rules is only possible once the debts underlying the financial instruments are 'objectivised' and rendered autonomous in order to allow their transferability. This is done through the adoption of provisions such as close-out netting, which allow anticipated performance of the debt in case of risks of insolvency. The debts can therefore no longer be referred to the national rules of a specific legal system, and to the extent that their uniform discipline (especially with reference to the conditions under which the holder is entitled to performance) allows their circulation, these instruments can be assimilated to one of the functions of money.[47]

---

[44] See Carbone, 'Strumenti finanziari, *corporate governance* e diritto internazionale privato', pp. 461–2.

[45] Carbone, 'Strumenti finanziari, *corporate governance* e diritto internazionale privato' p. 461.

[46] See *supra* Chapter 4. See also, on the use of master netting agreements and credit support agreements as methods for the reduction of credit risk in over-the-counter derivatives market and on the problems of conflicts of laws, N. Hval, 'Credit risk reduction in the international over-the-counter derivatives market: collateralizing the net exposure with support agreements', *The International Lawyer*, 1997, vol. 31, p. 801.

[47] See Carbone, 'Strumenti finanziari, *corporate governance* e diritto internazionale privato', p. 465.

While it may be misleading to speak of financial transactions governed by a body of 'general rules', it is undeniable that these transactions are disciplined by a set of specific and complex rules, which have been developed by the market and which can be assimilated in their application, validity and efficiency problems to the set of rules developed for international commercial contracts, often referred to as '*lex mercatoria*'.

4. International financial standards applied as *lex mercatoria*?

An issue requiring further attention is whether the 'financial soft law' examined above can be considered as part of the *lex mercatoria* in its technical meaning. That is to say, whether these standards can be applied where parties have chosen *lex mercatoria* or 'general usages of trade' or similar notions as the law governing their contract or their legal relations.[48] Opponents of such a wide notion of *lex mercatoria* contend that to include standard-term contracts, codes of practice promulgated

---

[48] For a reconstruction of the different phases of development of *lex mercatoria* and of its relation with modern international commercial law, see *ex multis* C. Schmitthoff, 'Das neues Recht des Welthandels', *Rabels Zeitschrift für Auslandisches und Internationales Privatrecht*, 1964, vol. 28, pp. 53–4.

The different theories as to the (substantive) meaning of the term *lex mercatoria* can be generally categorised into three groups. According to the first, *lex mercatoria* indicates a legal mass of rules and principles deprived of systematicity, which serves as a complement to domestic law and which from domestic law derives its validity and enforceability (under the principle of party autonomy in contract law). Party autonomy is thus linked to domestic law.

A second theory defines *lex mercatoria* as the totality of trade usages that are tailored according to the needs of international commerce (sometimes referred to as a 'factual *ius commune*' or as 'autonomous law of world trade') (see Berger, *The Creeping Codification of the Lex Mercatoria*, p. 40 and citations *ibidem*).

Finally, a third notion identifies the *lex mercatoria* as an independent, supra-national legal system which derives its validity either from its autonomous existence or from the principle of party autonomy as a meta-legal rule (Schmitthoff, 'Das neues Recht des Welthandels', p. 68 et seq.; Berger, *The Creeping Codification of the Lex Mercatoria*, pp. 40–1).

As for the basis of legitimation for the applicability of *lex mercatoria*, from the theoretical point of view, traditional doctrine is divided between a 'statal-positivistic notion', according to which the rules find application *vigore proprio* as positive rules belonging to a legal system and an 'autonomistic notion', according to which these rules find application when they are invoked through the private autonomy of the parties. In both cases, however, these theories assume the existence of a 'legal system' to which these rules belong (See Bonell, *Le regole oggettive del commercio internazionale*, p. 86 et seq.) The autonomistic notion of *lex mercatoria* can be further divided into two theories: (1) the notion according to which the rules which make up the *lex mercatoria* represent the objective and general legislation of hypothetical supranational

by international business organisations and international conventions in the notion of *lex mercatoria* is to confuse the character of customary law belonging to *lex mercatoria* with contract law and treaty law. Furthermore, *lex mercatoria* does not have the objective of harmonisation which is instead typical of international conventions and standard-term international contracts.[49] However, first of all the content of *lex mercatoria* is by its very nature neither crystallised nor closed.[50] On the contrary, *lex mercatoria* is an open source that is ready to include

---

private legal systems or of international legal systems, which are independent both of national legal systems and of public international law; (2) the notion according to which these rules remain contractual rules, whose validity and efficacy depend on the express reference made to them by private parties, but which can ultimately lead to the formation of contracts that are 'self-regulatory'. (Ibid.)

    A general classification is also possible with reference to the content of these rules. They may be divided into: (1) 'general principles of law', or 'principles of international law' (whose status is often assimilated to that of one of the sources of international law *ex* Article 38 of the Charter of the International Court of Justice), that are recalled in international contracts and comprise such fundamental principles on the formation or performance of contract as that of *pacta sunt servanda*; (2) certain standard contracts that are commonly used in international commercial or financial practice; (3) certain standard clauses, such as those on hardship or *force majeur*, whose extremely wide adoption suggests their promotion to the nature of a usage, and that can thus sometimes be implied in contracts even in the absence of an express term inserted by the parties; (4) certain principles that are the outcome of interpretation and construction processes carried out by arbitrators (i.e. the principles regarding the capacity of States to stipulate arbitral conventions, the autonomy of the arbitral clause, the principle of *rebus sic stantibus*); (5) uniform laws (i.e. Conventions on the International Sale of Goods); (6) the rules of international organisations (resolutions, recommendations, and codes of conduct); (7) customs and usages of international trade (see P. Bernardini, 'Contratti internazionali e diritto applicabile', *Diritto del commercio internazionale*, 1987, p. 401; O. Lando, 'The *Lex Mercatoria* in international commercial arbitration', *International and Comparative Law Quarterly*, 1985, vol. 34, pp. 749–51; see also B. Goldman, 'La lex mercatoria dans les contrats et l'arbitrage internationaux: réalité et perspectives', *Journal du Droit International*, 1979, pp. 477–9; C. Schmitthoff, 'The law of international trade, its growth, formulation and operation', in *Sources of the Law of International Trade*, London, 1964. For an extensive analysis of the content of the rules of international commercial transactions, see Bonell, *Le regole oggettive del commercio internazionale*; F. Osman, *Les principes généraux de la* lex mercatoria: *contribution à l'étude d'un ordre juridique anational*, Paris, 1992).

[49] See Goode, 'Rule, practice, and pragmatism in transnational commercial law', p. 547, also recalling A.M. Slaughter, 'International law and international relations theory: a prospectus', in E. Benvenisti, M. Hirsch (eds), *The Impact of International Law on International Cooperation*, Cambridge, 2004, p. 41 and L.J. M. Mustill, 'The new lex mercatoria: the first twenty-five years', in M. Bos, I. Brownlie (eds), *Liber Amicorum for Lord Wilberforce*, Oxford, 1987, pp. 152–3.

[50] See Goldman, 'La lex mercatoria dans les contrats et l'arbitrage internationaux', p. 487, describing the progressive inclusion within *lex mercatoria* of new general

and adopt, under the condition of their repetition and effectivity, not only the 'general principles' of international commercial law, but also (and this is relevant in the financial field), the most common usages and other forms of soft law, such as specialised standard terms, contracts and agreements, model laws and legislative guides. In the second place, the object of adopting a wider notion of *lex mercatoria*, which can be defined as 'financial *lex mercatoria*', is that of allowing the operativity of the same mechanisms of application and reception which have been developed for the application of those general rules commonly qualified as *lex mercatoria*.

From a practical point of view, application of *lex mercatoria* traditionally occurs in two ways: it is either recalled in international contracts or it is applied in international arbitration procedures.[51] International contracts can refer to 'the general principles of international commerce', to the Unidroit principles, to the 'usages of international commerce' and so forth. The common denominator of these general indications made by the parties is that they exclude any particular national law as the applicable one, and refer to those principles that are developed in the practice of international commerce (such as usages, rules, general clauses and standard contracts).[52]

Reference to the *lex mercatoria* can also be implicit. In those contractual clauses which refer to *amiable compositions* and thus defer to a decision according to equity (which strictly speaking does not constitute an arbitration), the arbitrator/third party may take into consideration the usages of international commerce.[53] Furthermore, *lex mercatoria* is sometimes applied spontaneously in arbitrations: this is the case where

---

principles, standard contractual models, specific contractual solutions which are repeated over time.

[51] Goldman, 'La lex mercatoria dans les contrats et l'arbitrage internationaux', p. 479. For an overview of the attitude of national rules towards arbitral awards based on *lex mercatoria* see O. Lando, 'The *lex mercatoria* in international commercial arbitration', pp. 756 et seq.

[52] Both national arbitral regimes and international arbitral conventions recognise the possibility for parties to refer to these 'rules of law' as opposed to reference simply to applicable 'law' (e.g. Article 1496 French new code of civil procedure; Article 187 Swiss International Private Law of 1987; Article 834 Italian code of civil procedure; Section 46(1)(b) UK Arbitration Act of 1996; Section 1051(1) German code of civil procedure; Article 42(1) Washington Convention of 1965. See also Article 13 of the 1975 Regulation of the International Chamber of Commerce Arbitral Tribunal). See P. Bernardini, *L'arbitrato commerciale internazionale*, Milano, 2000, p. 196; Goldman, 'La lex mercatoria dans les contrats et l'arbitrage internationaux', p. 480.

[53] See F.A. Mann, 'The proper conflict of laws', *International and Comparative Law Quarterly*, 1987, vol. 36, p. 448, limiting this hypothesis as the only one in which reference can be made to '*lex mercatoria*'.

in the absence of an indication by the parties of the applicable law, the arbitrators will apply 'the rules of law, and in default, commercial uses'.[54]

The issue is whether, in the absence of party choice, an arbitrator can invoke the *lex mercatoria* either in addition or in substitution of the applicable law. This can be done either through the dispositive provisions on the applicable law in the conflict of laws rules which yield to international contract and usage, or by applying an appropriate conflict of laws rule in such a way as to remand to *lex mercatoria* itself as the applicable law. The theoretical legitimation for such an adoption of the *lex mercatoria*, confirmed in some instances by case law, is that 'to the extent that *lex mercatoria* represents general principles of law common to relevant States, there seems to be no reason why it cannot be applied as the proper law governing the rights of the parties'.[55] The acceptance of this recourse by the parties to *lex mercatoria* is also demonstrated by the fact that permanent international arbitral tribunals, such as the International Chamber of Commerce, have relied on this source in their awards.[56]

---

[54] See International Chamber of Commerce case n. 1641/69, *Journal du Droit International*, 1974, p. 888. See also Goldman,'La lex mercatoria dans les contrats et l'arbitrage internationaux', pp. 481–2. One of the solutions proposed by scholars to the problems (of uncertainty) deriving from the application of conflict of laws rules is that of the development and application to international contracts that contain arbitration clauses of general principles of substantive national law (see e.g. R.B. Schlesinger and H.-J. Gundisch, 'Allgemeine Rechtsgrundsätze als Sachnormen in Schiedsgerichtsverfahren', *RabelsZeitschrift für Auslandisches und Internationales Privatrecht*, 1964, vol. 28, p. 9 et seq). However, the power of arbitrators to apply national rules in the absence of a specific indication by the parties is not unanimously accepted. Indeed, the formulation of numerous arbitration regulations and conventions (Article 13(3) of the International Chamber of Commerce; Article 33 (1) of UNCITRAL; Article VII of the 1961 Geneve Convention) obliges the arbitral judge to apply, in the absence of any indication of the applicable law by the parties, the 'law' which he deems appropriate according to the conflict of laws rules. This reference to 'the law' should be read, according to some theories, as implying a law which is part of a national legal system (see Y. Derains, 'Possible conflict of law rules and the rules applicable to the substance of the dispute,' in *UNCITRAL's Project for a Model Law on International Commercial Arbitration*, ICCA Congress series n. 2, Deventer 1984, pp. 173–4. See also, for a reconstruction, Bernardini, 'Contratti internazionali e diritto applicabile', p. 403).

[55] R. Goode, 'Usage and its reception in transnational commercial law', *International and Comparative Law Quarterly*, 1997, vol. 46, p. 29, further quoting the decision of the English Court of Appeal in *Deutsche Schachtbau-und Tiebohrgesellschaft gmbH v. R'As al-Khaimah National Oil Co.* (1987) 3 W.L.R. p. 1023.

[56] Bernardini, *L'arbitrato commerciale internazionale*, pp. 193–4. Arbitral courts have accepted both contractual clauses which exclude *a priori* the application of any national law in favour of general principles and usages of commercial law (see International Chamber of Commerce Case n.1569/70, quoted by Goldman, 'La lex

The acknowledgement of the *lex mercatoria* as an independent body of rules is not free from criticism. The construction of *lex mercatoria* as an autonomous source of law often goes hand in hand with theories that highlight the inefficiencies of private international law in resolving certain specific problems of international commercial transactions.[57] These theories sometimes go as far as proposing the superiority of *lex mercatoria* to private international law as the key to solving the problems of uncertainty in international trade.[58] However, these theories have been contested on the grounds of the insufficient autonomy of the *lex mercatoria* both from the point of view of its completeness and from the point of view of its applicability as an alternative to private international law.

It has been highlighted that *lex mercatoria* is no more than a vague expression which can be summarised *inter alia* as 'a collective name for a bottom-up regulation of commerce which is separate from the top-down regulation by state law and state courts'.[59] Though useful in many aspects of foreign trade, *lex mercatoria* cannot be regarded as an alternative to state law because it is not a comprehensive legal system which would allow a solution to be found for any question of commercial law (it is rather a sum of its components, such as standard terms and contract forms which must be incorporated into the contract in order to be applicable). *Lex mercatoria* is furthermore made up of very general principles that do not form a coordinated set of rules such as those which normally characterise the interaction between legislative sources in a normative system, and the application of *lex mercatoria* to a contract free from any relation with other rules of domestic law may often be problematic.[60] Furthermore, since *lex mercatoria* is not recognised as an autonomous body of principles (as it is ultimately

---

mercatoria dans les contrats et l'arbitrage internationaux', p. 479), and agreements having the same content which have arisen *ex post* during the course of arbitral proceedings (International Chamber of Commerce Case n. 2152/72, in *Journal du Droit International*, 1974, p. 889).

[57] Goode, 'Rule, practice, and pragmatism in transnational commercial law', p. 541; Schmidt-Trenz, 'Außenhandel un Territorialität des Rechts- Grundlegung einer neuen Institutionenökonmik des Außenhandels', p. 242 et seq. and p. 282 et seq; Schmidtchen, 'Territorialität des Rechts, Internationales Privatrecht' p. 71 et seq.

[58] See Schmidtchen, 'Territorialität des Rechts, Internationales Privatrecht', p. 101 et seq.; M.E. Streit, A. Mangles,'Privatautonomes Recht und grenzüberschreitende Transaktionen', *ORDO*, 1996, vol. 47, p. 73.

[59] See J. Basedow, 'Lex Mercatoria and the private international law of contracts,' in J. Basedow, T. Kono (eds), *An Economic Analysis of Private International Law*, Tübingen, 2006, pp. 63–4.

[60] For an overview of some of the most recurring criticisms to the theory of the autonomous character of *lex mercatoria*, see Bernardini, *L'arbitrato commerciale*

under the control of public policy and national mandatory rules), the normative force of every international usage depends on recognition by national law.[61] Therefore, international contracts, even where they refer to terms that can be considered as part of the *lex mercatoria*, must nevertheless be supplemented by state law; private international law is still indispensable.[62]

Other authoritative views in private international law recognise the choice of *lex mercatoria* as the applicable law only within a given legal system, as an expression of choice-of-law principles, but not as an alternative which would avoid national law altogether.[63]

A response to these criticisms is that the designation by the parties of the *lex mercatoria* as the law applicable to the contract may not be futile, to the extent that where the *lex mercatoria* is incomplete, it will be necessary and sufficient to refer to another applicable law.[64]

The point, however, to which attention should be drawn here is that the concept of *lex mercatoria*, with all the ensuing implications on the ways and instances in which it can be applied, should be extended so as to comprise not only rules developed in international commercial contracts (so far the main realm where reference to it has been successfully made) but also those applied in international financial transactions. The most recurring clauses in Master Agreements, for example, such as close-out netting, may well develop into consolidated principles which parties will be able to refer to simply as 'financial *lex mercatoria*'. The same could be said for modern usages in relation to documentary credits, demand

---

internazionale, p. 195, and Goode, 'Usage and its reception in transnational commercial law', p. 33 et seq.

[61]The problem of recognition of the normative force for international usages (apart from those usages that are so widespread as to have acquired the status of general principles of law, such as *pacta sunt servanda*) has been confined ultimately not to what the national law says about the usage, 'but upon whether the power to decide on the existence and content of such usage has been exercised by a tribunal having competence under the *lex loci arbitri* and conforming with its procedural requirements'. Goode, 'Usage and its reception in transnational commercial law', p. 34; see also Schmitthoff, *The Sources of the Law of International Trade*, pp. 4–5; and with reference to the autonomy of *lex mercatoria* from national law, Bernardini, 'Contratti internazionali e diritto applicabile', pp. 406–7.

[62]See J. Basedow, *Lex Mercatoria and the Private International Law of Contracts*, p. 65.

[63]See C. von Bar, P. Mankowski, *Internationales Privatrecht*, I, München, 2003, p. 87; H. Batiffol, P. Lagarde, *Droit international privé*, I, Paris, 1993, pp. 422–3; P. North, J. Fawcett, *Cheshire's and North's Private International Law*, London, 1999, p. 559 et seq.

[64]Goode, 'Usage and its reception in transnational commercial law', p. 34.

guarantees, clearing and settlement systems for the transfer of funds and investment securities.[65]

A certain pressure in this sense also emerges from an overview of the recommendations and reports on existing legal barriers and need for harmonisation examined above (see Chapters 3 and 4). The very fact that these studies seek an amalgamation of the most common terms, times, clauses and so forth, used in practice (and identifies, for example, the Custodians of Banking associations as those who should codify these usages) is no more than a recognition of this financial soft law and an encouragement towards its consolidation.

Furthermore, the rules and discipline concerning financial instruments already constitute a practical application of this common transnational soft law. The significant similarity in the regulation of swaps, options, futures, is both an effect of the origin and use of these instruments, and at the same time an indication of the continuing denationalisation of their discipline.

---

[65] See Goode, 'Rule, practice, and pragmatism in transnational commercial law', p. 548, quoting these usages as central in modern financial trade but not considered – correctly from the author's point of view – as part of *lex mercatoria*.

Concluding remarks 1

The aim of this study has been the identification and characterisation of the legal sources which regulate transactions in European financial markets. After examining these markets at different levels, and taking into consideration both the legal institutes at the basis of the transactions and some aspects of the macro-economic and regulatory context in which financial transactions take place, a few conclusions can be drawn and a tentative answer to some of the initial questions can be provided. The most important element that must be highlighted is that of the growing role of a financial *lex mercatoria* as the technical and specific set of rules that governs financial transactions. Increasingly complex cross-border transactions, which are the result of globalised markets, are increasingly less disciplined by norms ensuing from national legislative activity; rather, they are governed by rules which under different forms derive from practitioners.

To the initial issue concerning the need for a general set of rules for the discipline of the common institutes at the basis of financial transactions, we can offer a compromise. On the one hand, a common set of norms is indeed necessary, as emerges both from the pressure exercised by the market operators in this sense and by the initiatives taken by the market operators themselves through the development of a body of soft law containing international standards. On the other, it may not be necessary to reformulate the general notions of monetary obligations and debts, which, in those civil codes where they exist, are central to the construction of the discipline of payments and financial transactions.

The conclusions emerging from this study indicate that some of the fundamental general rules concerning debts involved in cross-border transactions have *de facto* already been harmonised by forms of soft law. The open problem remains that of recognising these rules. National laws should leave space for the operativity of special rules whenever transactions related to the market are concerned. The specific rules of financial instruments can be considered, from the point of view of the hierarchy of legal sources, as the *lex specialis*, which can prevail over the *lex generalis*. The issue is whether and under which form this *lex specialis* can become part of national laws.

One possible path, which seems in part to have been undertaken by supra-national legislators such as the European Union (EU), is the adoption of these technical rules and their insertion into EU legislation which will then be transformed into national law. The other path is leaving a wide range of operativity to private autonomy, which through mechanisms of the choice of the applicable law can refer to at least some of the forms of soft law. Indeed, as emerges from the observation of recent historical trends and current orientations of many legislators, who are managing important processes of transfer of competence in extremely technical aspects concerning the functioning of market transactions, as long as national legislators accept the operativity of international financial soft law through different techniques (which do not, however, entail a formal recognition of the autonomous and independent character of this body of *lex mercatoria*), the modification of the general national rules governing monetary obligations may not be an absolute necessity.

Indeed, whilst experiments in providing general rules on payments have been carried out by non-legislative bodies (see for example the Unidroit principles and the Principles of European Contract Law), it is significant that national legislators have not tried to 'modernise' the old rules where they exist (maybe under the assumption that these rules can still be valid if interpreted in a certain way). The consequence seems to be that the general rules disciplining the notions of debts and payments are gradually becoming a residual default set of rules, given the relative importance of simple cash transactions between private parties within national borders. Similarly to what has occurred for international commercial contracts, which have developed their specific usages without necessarily entailing a modification of national disciplines of the same types of contracts, it may be possible that a similar process can be carried out for financial instruments. The rules governing the regulation of financial transactions will not be found in general rules on obligations, just like the rules governing international commercial contracts are often not found in national disciplines.

In the second place, it may not be without significance to note that the two major legal systems whose rules are often relevant as the applicable law of international financial transactions (i.e. the laws of the State of New York and of the United Kingdom) both lack a general set of rules on monetary obligations. However, this reception of market-originated rules cannot be an uncritical acceptance either. What must be borne in mind is that these rules respond to the demands of only one set of actors: market operators. The origin of the discipline is necessarily reflected in the construction of the legal institutes and may, in many cases, lack a balance between the needs of the different parties involved in market transactions: a balance which may, on the contrary, be expected from a legislator taking into account wider policy issues.

The conclusions concerning the legal sources in financial markets that can be drawn from these brief observations are twofold. They relate on the subjective side to the emergence of new authorities and new competences; on the objective side to the content of the rules, which move from general principles to technical rules, and from the point of view of cross-border transactions from conflict of law rules to uniform substantive rules. Indeed the law of financial transactions, being made up in large part of cross-border transactions, is an area where tools of private international law can be invoked. However, these tools will not necessarily lead to an application of national substantive laws as the applicable laws. Rather, through party autonomy and the recognition of some form of operativity of international financial standards and usages, the final rules which may find application may be rules of soft law.

Given this trend, and given the reality of recent financial crisis, in which the role of legal disparities is far from being secondary, the problems which legislators and regulators are forced to tackle concern the mechanisms through which this soft law is recognised as a source. Its contents will first of all need to be analysed and clarified, and secondly put under some form of supervision. It seems that the task of policy-makers and legislators in the near future will have to focus precisely on the acknowledgement of the source which *de facto* disciplines legal content of financial transactions and on a deeper analysis and control of its contents. It is only through this bottom-up process that problems of transparency in securitisation processes, difficulties in identifying the interests underlying securities which are commercialised on global markets, and subsequent falls in the confidence in the markets can be avoided – or at least some of the damage can be controlled. Since financial markets can undoubtedly be classified as global scenarios, this process will necessarily require international and cross-border legal coordination.

Bibliography

Admati, A.R. and Pfleiderer, P., 'Sunshine trading and financial market equilibrium', *Review of Financial Studies*, 1991, Vol. 4, p. 443.

Alexander, K., Dhumale, R. and Eatwell, J., *Global Governance of Financial Systems. The International Regulation of Systemic Risk*, Oxford: Oxford University Press, 2006.

Amorosino, S. and Rabitti Bedogni, C. (eds), *Manuale di diritto dei mercati finanziari*, Milano: Giuffrè, 2004.

Amtenbrink, F., *The Democratic Accountability of Central Banks. A Comparative Study of the European Central Bank*, Oxford: Hart, 1999.

Andenas, M. and Avgerinos Y. (eds), *Financial Markets in Europe: Towards a Single Regulator*, The Hague: Kluwer Law International, 2003.

Andenas, M., Gormley, L., Hadjiemmanuil, C. and Harden, I. (eds), *European Economic and Monetary Union: The Institutional Framework*, London, Boston: Kluwer Law International, 1997.

Annunziata, F., 'Verso una disciplina comune delle garanzie finanziarie. Dalla Convenzione dell'Aja alla Collateral Directive', *Banca, borsa e titoli di credito*, 2003, Vol. I, p. 177.

Ascarelli, T., 'Obbligazioni pecuniarie', in *Commentario del codice civile* a cura di Scialoja e Branca, Libro IV, Delle obbligazioni, artt. 1277–1284, Bologna, Roma: Zanichelli, 1959.

Baele, L., Ferrando, A., Hördahl, P., Krylova, E. and Monnet, C., *Measuring Financial Integration in the Euro Area*, European Central Bank Occasional Papers n. 2004.

Barfield, C.E. (ed.), *International Financial Markets: Harmonization versus Competition*, Washington D.C.: AEI Press, 1996.

Barresi R.G., 'The European Union: The Impact of Monetary Union and the Euro on European Capital Markets: What may be achieved in capital market integration', *Fordham International Law Journal*, 2005, Vol. 28, p. 1257.

Basedow, J. and Kono, T., (eds), *An Economic Analysis of Private International Law*, Tübingen: Mohr Siebeck, 2006.

Bazinas, S.V., 'The UNCITRAL Draft Legislative Guide on Secured Transactions', *Uniform Law Review*, 2005, Vol. 10, n. 1–2, p. 148.

Benjamin, J., *Interests in Securities. A Proprietary Law Analysis of the International Securities Markets*, Oxford: Oxford University Press, 2000.

Berger, K.P., *The Creeping Codification of the Lex Mercatoria*, The Hague, London, Boston: Kluwer Law International, 1999.

Bernardini, P., 'Contratti internazionali e diritto applicabile', *Diritto del commercio internazionale*, 1987, p. 393.

Bernardini, P., *L'arbitrato commerciale internazionale*, Milano: Giuffrè, 2000.

Black, J., 'Constitutionalising self-regulation', *Modern Law Review*, 1996, Vol. 59, p. 24.

Black, J., 'Mapping the contours of contemporary financial services regulation', *Journal of Corporate Law Studies*, 2002, Vol. 2, p. 253.

Blair M. and Walker G. (eds), *Financial Services Law*, Oxford: Oxford University Press, 2006.

Bonell, M.J., *Le regole oggettive del commercio internazionale*, Milano: Giuffrè, 1976.

Bonell, M.J., Das Autonome Recht des Welthandels- Rechtsdogmatische und Rechtspolitische Aspekte', *Rabels Zeitschrift für Auslandisches und Internationales Privatrecht*, 1978, Vol. 42, p. 485.

Bonell, M.J., *An International Restatement of Contract Law. The UNIDROIT Principles of International Commercial Contracts*, 3rd edn, Irvington: Transnational Publishers Inc., 2005.

Braithwaite, J. and Drahos, P., *Global Business Regulation*, Cambridge: Cambridge University Press, 2000.

Brand, R.A., 'Restructuring the U.S. approach to judgments on foreign currency liabilites: building on the English experience', *Yale Journal of International Law*, 1985–1986, Vol. 11, p. 157.

Bratton, W., McCahery, J., Picciotto, S. and Scott, S. (eds), *International Regulatory Competition and Coordination. Perspectives in economic regulation in Europe and the United States*, Oxford, New York: Clarendon Press, 1996.

Brumfield Fry, P., 'Basic concepts in article 4A: scope and definitions', *Business Lawyer*, 1990, Vol. 45, p. 1401.

Caputo Nassetti, F., *Profili civilistici dei contratti 'derivati' finanziari*, Milano: Giuffè, 1997.

Caputo Nassetti, F., *I contratti derivati finanziari*, Milano: Giuffrè, 2007.

Carbone, S.M., 'Derivati finanziari e diritto internazionale privato e processuale: alcune considerazioni', *Diritto del commercio internazionale*, 2000, p. 3.

Carbone, S.M., 'Strumenti finanziari, *corporate governance* e diritto internazionale privato tra disciplina dei mercati finanziari e ordinamenti nazionali', *Rivista delle società*, 2000, p. 457.

Carbonnier, J., *Droit civil*, 3, *Les biens*, 19th edn, Paris: Presses Universitaries de France, 2000.

Carbonnier, J., *Droit civil*, 4, *Les obligations*, 22nd edn, Paris: Presses Universitaires de France, 2000.

Carreau, D., 'Le système monétaire international privé', *Recueil des Cours de l'Académie de Droit International de l'Haye*, 1998, Vol. 274.

Carrière, P., 'La nuova normativa sui contratti di garanzia finanziari. Analisi critica', *Banca, borsa e titoli di credito*, 2005, I, p. 184.

Cassese, S., *La crisi dello stato*, Bari: Laterza, 2002.

Chirico, A., *La sovranità monetaria tra ordine giuridico e processo economico*, Padova, 2003.

Chiu, I. H.-Y., 'Three challenges ahead for the new EU securities regulation directives', *European Business Law Review*, 2006, Vol. 17, p. 121.

Chowdry, B. and Nanda, V., 'Multimarket trading and market liquidity', *Review of Financial Studies*, 1991, Vol. 4, p. 483.

Cooter, R.D., 'Decentralized law for a complex economy: the structural approach to adjudicating the new law merchant', *University of Pennsylvania Law Review*, 1996, Vol. 144, p. 1643.

Corbin, A.L., *Corbin on Contracts*, V, rev. ed., St Paul, Minnesota: West Publishing Co., 1999.

Costi, R. and Enriques, L., 'I mercato mobiliare', in *Trattato di diritto commerciale* diretto da Cottino, Vol. VIII, Padova: Cedam, 2004.

Crowther, G., *An Outline of Money*, rev. edn, London, Edinburg, Paris, Melbourne, Toronto, New York: Nelson, 1955.

David, R., 'Il diritto del commercio internazionale: un nuovo compito per i legislatori nazionali o una nuova lex mercatoria?', *Rivista di diritto civile*, 1976, I, p. 577.

Dawson, J.P. and Cooper, F.E., 'The effect of inflation on private contracts: United States 1861–1879', *Michigan Law Review*, 1935, Vol. 33, p. 706.

De Biasi, P., 'Un nuovo Master Agreement per strumenti finanziari sofisticati', *Banca, borsa e titoli di credito*, 2001, I, p. 644.

Dehousse, R., (ed.), *Europe After Maastricht. An ever closer Union?*, München: Law Books in Europe, 1994.

De Ly, F., '*Lex mercatoria* (new law merchant): globalization and international self-regulation', *Diritto del commercio internazionale*, 2000, p. 555.

Derains, Y., 'Possible conflict of law rules and the rules applicable to the substance of the dispute, in UNCITRAL's project for a model law on international commercial arbitration', ICCA Congress series n. 2, Deventer, 1984.

Di Giorgio, G. and Di Noia, C., 'Appropriateness of regulation at the Federak or State Level: financial market regulation and supervision: how many peaks for the euro area?', *Brooklyn Journal of International Law*, 2003, Vol. 28, p. 463.

Di Majo, A., *Le obbligazioni pecuniarie*, Torino: Giappichelli, 1996.

Di Robilant, A., 'Genealogies of soft law', *American Journal of Comparative Law*, 2006, Vol. 54, p. 499.

European Central Bank, *Legal Aspects of the European System of Central Banks. Liber Amicorum Paolo Zamboni Garavelli*, Frankfurt-am-Main: European Central Bank, 2005.

Esser, J. and Schmidt, E., *Schuldrecht*, Bd. I, 5th edn, Karlsruhe: C.F. Müller, 1975.

Fabozzi, F.J. (ed.), *The Handbook of Financial Instruments*, Hoboken, New Jersey: Wiley, 2002.

Ferran, E., *Building an EU Securities Market*, Cambridge: Cambridge University Press, 2004.

Ferrarese, M.R., *Le istituzioni della globalizzazione: diritto e diritti nella società transnazionale*, Bologna: Il Mulino, 2000.

Ferrari, A., Gualandri, E., Landi, A. and Vezzani, P., *Strumenti, mercati, intermediari finanziari*, 3rd edn, Torino: Giappichelli, 2001.

Ferrarini, G. (ed.), *European Securities Markets: The Investment Services Directive and Beyond*, London, Boston: Kluwer Law International, 1998.

Ferrarini, G. and Giudici, P., 'Le garanzie su strumenti finanziari nel diritto comunitario: orientamenti e prospettive', *Il Fallimento*, 2002, p. 999.

Ferrarini, G. and Wymeersch, E. (eds), *Investor Protection in Europe. Corporate Law Making, the MiFID and Beyond*, Oxford: Oxford University Press, 2006.

Ferrarini, G., Hopt, K.J. and Wymeersch, E. (eds), *Capital Markets in the Age of the Euro. Cross-Border Transactions, Listed Companies and Regulation*, The Hague, London, New York: Kluwer Law International, 2002.

Forssbaeck, J. and Oxelheim, L., *Money Markets and Politics. A Study of European Financial Integration and Monetary Policy Options*, Cheltenham, UK, Northampton, MA: Elgar, 2003.

Fouchard, P., *L'Arbitrage Commercial International*, Paris: Dalloz, 1965.

Fragistas C., 'Arbitrage étranger et arbitrage international en droit privé', *Revue critique de droit international privé*, 1960, p. 1.

Gaillard, E. (ed.), *Transnational rules in international commercial arbitration*, Paris: ICC Publication, 1993.

Galgano, F., *La globalizzazione nello specchio del diritto*, Bologna: IP Mulino, 2005.

Giovanoli, M. (ed.), *International Monetary Law: Issues for the New Millenium*, Oxford: Oxford University Press, 2000.

Giovanoli, M., 'Reflections on international financial standards as "soft law"', *Essays in International Financial and Economic Law*, 2002, n. 37, The London Institute of International Banking, Finance and Development Law Ltd.

Giovanoli, M. and Heinrich, G. (eds), *International Bank Insolvencies. A Central Bank Perspective*, The Hague, London, Boston: Kluwer Law International, 1999.

Goebel, R.J., 'Legal framework: European Economic and Monetary Union: will EMU ever fly?', *Columbia Journal of European Law*, 1998, Vol. 4, p. 249.

Gold, J., 'Strengthening the soft international law of exchange agreements', *The American Journal of International Law*, 1983, Vol. 77, p. 443.

Goldman, B., 'Frontières du droit et la lex mercatoria', *Archives de philosophie du droit*, 1964, p. 177.

Goldman, B., 'La lex mercatoria dans les contrats et l'arbitrage internationaux: réalité et perspectives', *Journal du Droit International*, 1979, p. 475.

Goldstajn, A., 'The New Law Merchant', *Journal of Business Law*, 1961, p. 12.

Goldstein, D.B., 'Federal versus state adoption of article 4A', *Business Lawyer*, 1990, Vol. 45, p. 1513.

Goode, R.M., *Payment Obligations in Commercial and Financial Transactions*, London: Sweet & Maxwell, 1983.

Goode, R.M., *Usage and its Reception in Transnational Commercial Law*, International and Comparative Law Quarterly, 1997, Vol. 46, p. 1.

Goode, R.M., *Commercial Law*, 3rd edn, Trowbridge: LexisNexis UK, 2004.

Goode, R.M., Kanda, H. and Kreuzer, K., *Hague Securities Convention. Explanatory Report*, The Hague: Brill, 2005.

Goodhart, C., Hartmann, P., Llewellyn, D., Rojas-Suárez, L. and Weisbrod, S., *Financial Regulation. Why, how, and where now?*, London, New York: Routledge, 1998, reprinted 2001.

Grote, R. and Marauhn, T. (eds), *The Regulation of International Financial Markets. Perspectives for Reform*, Cambridge: Cambridge University Press, 2006.

Gruchalla-Wesierski, T., 'A framework for understanding "soft law"', *McGill Law Journal*, 1984–1985, Vol. 30, p. 37.

Guarino, G., *Verso l'Europa: ovvero la fine della politica*, Milano: Mondadori, 1997.

Guzman, A.T., 'Choice of law: new foundations', *Georgetown Law Journal*, 2002, Vol. 90, p. 883.

Hammond, B., *Banks and Politics in America: From the Revolution to the Civil War*, Princeton: Princeton University Press, 1991.

Hawtrey, R.G., *The Gold Standard in Theory and Practice*, London: Longmans, Green, 1927.

Hirata de Carvalho, C., 'Cross-border securities clearing and settlement infrastructure in the European Union as a pre-requisite to financial markets integration: challenges and perspectives', HWWA Discussion Paper (Hamburgisches Welt-Wirtschafts-Archiv), 2004, n. 287.

Hirschberg, E., *The Nominalistic Principle: a legal approach to inflation, deflation, devaluation and revaluation*, Ramat-Gan: Bar-Ilan University, 1971.

Horn, N. and Schmitthoff, C.M. (eds), *The Transnational Law of International Commercial Transactions*, Deventer, Boston: Kluwer, 1982.

Hüpkes, E.H.G., *The Legal Aspects of Bank Insolvency. A Comparative Analysis of Western Europe, the United States and Canada*, The Hague, London, Boston: Kluwer Law International, 2000.

Hurst, J.W., *A Legal History of Money in the United States, 1774–1970*, Nebraska: Nebraska University Press, 1973.

Hval, N., 'Credit risk reduction in the international over-the-counter derivatives market: collateralizing the net exposure with support agreements', *The International Lawyer*, 1997, Vol. 31, p. 801.

Inzitari, B., 'La moneta', in *Trattato di diritto commerciale e di diritto pubblico dell'economia* diretta da F. Galgano, Vol. VI, Padova: Cedam, 1983.

Issing, O., Gaspar, V., Angeloni, I. and Tristani, O., *Monetary Policy in the Euro Area (Strategy and decision-making at the Central European Bank)*, Cambridge: Cambridge University Press, 2001.

Joerges, C., 'Vorüberlegungen zu einer Theorie des Internationalen Wirtschaftsrechts', *Rabels Zeitschrift für Auslandisches und Internationales Privatrecht*, 1979, Vol. 43, p. 6.

Kähler, L., 'Zur Entmythisierung der Geldschuld', *Archiv für die civilistische Praxis*, 2006, Vol. 206, p. 805.

Kahn, P., *La vente commerciale internationale*, Paris: Sirey, 1961.

Kauko, K., 'Interlinking securities settlement systems: a strategic commitment?', *ECB Working Paper Series*, 2005, n. 427, European Central Bank.

Kazarian, E., 'Integration of the securities market infrastructure in the European Union: policy and regulatory issues', *IMF Working Paper*, 2006, n. 241, IMF.

Knapp, G.F., *Staatliche Theorie des Geldes*, München, Leipzig: Duncker & Humblot, 1905.

Köngden, J., 'Privatisierung des Rechts. Private Governance zwischen Deregulierung und Rekonstitutionalisierung', *Archiv für die civilistische Praxis*, 2006, Vol. 206, p. 477.

Kronman, A.T., 'Contract law and the state of nature', *Journal of Law, Economics, and Organization*, 1985, Vol. 1, p. 5.

Lando, O., 'The *lex mercatoria* in international commercial arbitration', *International and Comparative Law Quarterly*, 1985, Vol. 34, p. 747.

Lando, O. and Beale H. (eds), *Principles of European Contract Law. Parts I and II combined and revised*, The Hague, London, Boston: Kluwer Law International, 2000.

Lemma, V., ' "soft law" e regolazione finanziaria', *La Nuova giurisprudenza civile commentata*, 2006, Pt. II, p. 600.

Libchaber, R., *Recherches sur la monnaie en droit privé*, Paris: Librairie générale de droit et jurisprudence, 1992.

Libonati, B., *Titoli di credito e strumenti finanziari*, Milano: Giuffrè, 1999.

Linciano, N., Siciliano, G. and Trovatore, G., 'The clearing and settlement industry. Structure, competition and regulatory issues', *Consob- Quaderni di finanza*, 2005, n. 58.

Löber, K.M., 'The developing EU legal framework for clearing and settlement of financial instruments', *ECB Legal Working Paper Series*, 2006, n. 1, ECB.

Macario, F., 'I contratti di garanzia finanziaria nella direttiva 2002/47/CE', *I contratti*, 2003, n. 1, p. 85.

Mann, F.A., 'England rejects "delocalised" contracts and arbitration', *International and Comparative Law Quarterly*, 1984, Vol. 33, p. 193.

Mann, F.A., 'The proper conflict of laws', *International and Comparative Law Quarterly*, 1987, Vol. 36, p. 437.

Mann, F.A., *The Legal Aspect of Money: with special reference to comparative private and public international law*, 5th edn, Oxford: Clarendon Press, 1992.

Marella, F., 'La nuova lex mercatoria. Principi Unidroit ed usi dei contratti del commercio internazionale', in *Trattato di diritto commerciale e di diritto pubblico dell'economia* diretto da F. Galgano, Vol. XXX, Padova: Cedam, 2003.

Maydell, B., von, *Geldschuld und Geldwert*, München: Beck, 1974.

Mayes, D.G. and Wood, G.E. (eds), *The Structure of Financial Regulation*, London, New York: Routledge, 2007.

Mazzocco, G.N., *Gli strumenti finanziari di mercato aperto*, 2nd edn, Torino: Giappichelli, 2005.

Merusi, F., 'Profili giuridici dell'equipollenza monetaria dei sistemi di pagamento', *Banca, borsa, titoli di credito*, 2006, I, p. 113.

Mises, L., von, *Theorie des Geldes und der Umlaufsmittel*, München and Leipzig: Duncker & Humblot, 1924.

Molle, G. and Desiderio, L., *Manuale di diritto bancario e dell'intermediazione finanziaria*, Milano: Giuffrè, 2005.

Moliterni, F., 'I sistemi di pagamento dalla direttiva 98/26/CE a TARGET (Sistema Trans-europeo automatizzato di trasferimento espresso con regolamento lordo in tempo reale)', *Diritto del commercio internazionale*, 2000, p. 703.

Moliterni, F., *Autoregolamentazione e sorveglianza nei sistemi di pagamento*, Bari: Cacucci editore, 2001.

Moloney, N., *EC Securities Regulation*, Oxford: Oxford University Press, 2002.

Moloney, N., 'Innovation and risk in EC financial market regulation: new instruments of financial market intervention and the Committee of European Securities Regulators', *European Law Review*, 2007, Vol. 32, p. 627.

Moravcsik, A., 'Preferences and power in the European Community: a liberal intergovernmentalist approach', *Journal of Common Market Studies*, 1993, Vol. 31, p. 473.

Moser, T. and Schips, B., *EMU, Financial Markets and the World Economy*, Boston, Dordrecht, London: Kluwer Academic, 2001.

Nappi, F., *Studi sulla compensazione: esercizi di una europafreundliche auslegung*, Torino: Giappichelli, 2004.

Nelson, N.R., 'Settlement obligations and bank insolvency', *Business Lawyer*, 1990, Vol. 45, p. 1473.

Norton, J.J. and Andenas, M. (eds), *International Monetary and Financial Law Upon Entering the New Millenium. A Tribute to Sir Joseph and Ruth Gold*, The British Institute of International and Comparative Law, London, 2002.

Nussbaum, A., *Das Geld in Theorie und Praxis des Deutschen und Ausländischen Rechts*, Tübingen: Mohr, 1925.

Nussbaum, A., 'Comparative and international aspects of American gold clause abrogation', *Yale Law Journal*, 1934–35, Vol. 44, p. 54.

Nussbaum, A., *Money in the Law National and International: a comparative study in the borderline of law and economics: a completely revised edition of 'Money in the law'*, Brooklyn: Foundation Press, 1950.

Olivieri, G., *Compensazione e circolazione della moneta nei sistemi di pagamento*, Milano: Giuffrè, 2002.

Olivercrona, K., *The Problem of the Monetary Unit*, Stockholm: Almqvist & Wiksell, 1957.

Ortino, M., 'The role and functioning of mutual recognition in the European market of financial services', *International and Comparative Law Quarterly*, 2007, Vol. 56, p. 309.

Osman, F., *Les principes généraux de la lex mercatoria: contribution à l'étude d'un ordre juridique anational*, Paris: Librairie générale de droit et de jurisprudence, 1992.

Pagano, M., 'Trading volume and asset liquidity', *The Quarterly Journal of Economics*, 1989, Vol. 104, p. 255.

Park, W.W., 'Arbitration in banking and finance', *Essays in International, Financial and Economic Law*, 1997, n. 10, The London Institute of International Banking, Finance and Development Law Ltd.

Peleggi, R., 'La compensazione nei principi Unidroit dei contratti commerciali internazionali e nei principi di diritto europeo dei contratti: un primo confronto', *Diritto del commercio internazionale*, 2002, p. 927.

Petschnigg, R., 'The Institutional Framework for Financial Market Policy in the USA seen from an EU Perspective', *ECB Occasional Paper Series*, 2005, n. 35.

Pierre-François, G.L., *La notion de dette de valeur en droit civil. Essai d'une théorie*, Paris: Librairie générale de droit et de jurisprudence, 1975.

Potok, R. (ed.), *Cross Border Collateral: Legal risk and the conflict of laws*, London: Butterworths, 2002.

Proctor, C., *Mann on the Legal Aspect of Money*, 6th edn, Oxford: Oxford University Press, 2005.

Proctor, C., *The Euro and the Financial Markets. The legal impact of EMU*, Bristol: Jordan, 1999.

Quadri, E., *Le obbligazioni pecuniaie*, in *Trattato di diritto privato* diretto da Rescigno, Vol. IX, 2nd edn, Torino: UTET, 1999.

Rogers, J.S., 'Policy perspectives on revised U.C.C. article 8', *UCLA Law Review*, 1996, Vol. 43, p. 1431.

Rogers, J.S., 'Conflict of laws for transactions in securities held with intermediaries', *Boston College Law School Legal Studies Research Paper Series*, 2005, n. 80.

Rose, A., 'Explaining exchange rate volatility: an empirical analysis of 'The Holy Trinity' of monetary independence, fixed exchange rates, and capital mobility', *Journal of International Money and Finance*, 1996, Vol. 15, p. 925.

Schlesinger, R.B. and Gundisch, H.J., 'Allgemeine Rechtsgrundsätze als Sachnormen in Schiedsgerichtsverfahren', *Rabels Zeitschrift für Auslandisches und Internationales Privatrecht*, 1964, Vol. 28, p. 4.

Schmidt-Trenz, H.J., *Außenhandel un Territorialität des Rechts-Grundlegung einer neuen Institutionenökonmik des Außenhandels*, Baden Baden: Nomos, 1990.

Schmiedel, H. and Schönenberger, A., 'Integration of securities market infrastructures in the euro area', *ECB Occasional Papers*, 2005, n. 33.

Schmidtchen, D., 'Territorialität des Rechts, Internationales Privatrecht und die privatautonome Regelung internationaler Sachverhalte', *Rabels Zeitschrift für ausländisches und internationales Privatrecht*, Vol. 59, 1995, p. 56.

Schmitthoff, C.M., *The Sources of the Law of International Trade, with Special Reference to East–West Trade,* London: Stevens & Sons, 1964.

Schmitthoff, C.M., 'Das neue Recht des Welthandels', *Rabels Zeitschrift für ausländisches und internationales Privatrecht*, Vol. 28, 1964, p. 47.

Scott, H.S., *International Finance: Law and Regulation*, London: Sweet & Maxwell, 2004.

Segré, C., 'Emissioni obbligazionarie estere sui mercati europei', *Moneta e Credito*, 1964, Vol. 27, p. 3.

Seligman, J. and Loss, L., *Fundamentals of Securities Regulation*, 4th edn, Gaithersburg, MD: Aspen Law & Business, 2001.

Sicchiero, G. (ed.), *Contratti bancari e revocatorie fallimentari*, Padova: Cedam, 2002.

Simitis, S., 'Bemerkungen zur Rechtlichen Sonderstellen des Geldes', *Archiv für die Civilistische Praxis*, 1960, Vol. 159, p. 406.

Slot, P.J., 'Harmonisation', *European Law Review*, 1996, Vol. 21, p. 378.

Søndergaard Birkmose, H., 'Regulatory competition and the European harmonisation process', *European Business Law Review*, 2006, Vol. 17, p. 1075.

Tapking, J., 'Pricing of settlement link services and mergers of central securities depositories', *ECB Working Paper Series*, 2007, n. 710.

Tiebout, C.M., 'A pure theory of local expenditures', *Journal of Political Economy*, 1956, Vol. 64, p. 416.

Trachtman, J.P., 'Recent initiatives in international financial regulation and goals of competitiveness, effectiveness, consistency and cooperation', *Northwestern Journal of International Law & Business*, 1991, Vol. 12, p. 241.

Treves, T., 'Les clauses monetaires dans les emissions d'euro-obligations', *Rivista di diritto internazionale privato e processuale*, 1971, p. 775.

Vagts, D.F., 'Securities regulation – an introduction', in *International Encyclopedia of Comparative Law*, Vol. XIII, *Business and Private Organizations*, Chapter 10, Tübingen: Mohr Siebeck; Dordrecht, Boston, Lancaster: Martinus Nijhoff Publishers, 2000.

Van Houtte, H., *The Law of Cross-border Securities Transactions*, London: Sweet & Maxwell, 1999.

Vardi, N., 'Reflections on trends and evolutions in the law of monetary obligations in European private law', *European Business Law Review*, 2007, Vol. 18, p. 443.

Verdun A. (ed.), *The Euro. European integration theory and Economic and Monetary Union*, Lanham, Boulder, New York, Oxford: Rowman & Littlefield Publishers, 2002.

Vereecken, M., 'Reducing systemic risk in payment and securities settlement systems', *Journal of Financial Regulation and Compliance*, 1998, Vol. 6, p. 107.

Wellens, K.C. and Borchardt, G.M., 'Soft law in European Community law', *European Law Review*, 1989, Vol. 14, p. 267.

Williston, S., *A Treatise on the Law of Contracts*, 4th edn, by R.A. Lord, Danvers, Mass: Thomson West; Rochester, NY: Lawyers Cooperative, 1990.

Zimmermann, R., *Comparative Foundations of a European Law of Set-Off and Prescription*, Cambridge: Cambridge University Press, 2002.

Index |

Printed and bound by CPI Group (UK) Ltd, Croydon, CR0 4YY
01/05/2025
01858402-0001